# SAINT CAESARIUS OF ARLES

## SERMONS

Volume III
(187-238)

*Translated by*
SISTER MARY MAGDELEINE MUELLER, O.S.F.
*Cardinal Stritch College*
*Milwaukee, Wisconsin*

THE CATHOLIC UNIVERSITY OF AMERICA PRESS
in association with
CONSORTIUM PRESS
Washington, D. C.

NIHIL OBSTAT:

### JOSEPH B. COLLINS, S.S., S.T.D.
*Censor Librorum*


IMPRIMATUR:

### ✠PATRICK CARDINAL A. O'BOYLE, D.D.
*Archbishop of Washington*


*January 6, 1972*

Library of Congress Cataloging in Publication Data

Caesarius, Saint, Bp. of Arles, 470?-543.
  Sermons.

  (The Fathers of the church, a new translation, v. 31, 47, 66)
  Vol. 2 has imprint: Washington, Catholic University of America Press;
v. 3 adds: in association with Consortium Press.
  Bibliography: v. 1, p. xxvi-xxvii.
  1. Sermons, Latin—Translations into English.
  2. Sermons, English—Translations from Latin.
I. Series.
BR60.F3C3     281.4     56-3628
ISBN 0-8132-0066-0

# CONTENTS

*Page*

Introduction ........................................ 1

Sermons†

187 A Homily to be Delivered Ten or Fifteen Days
Before the Birthday of Our Lord ............ 7

188 A Homily to be Delivered Before the Lord's
Birthday ................................. 11

*189 On the Coming of Our Lord................ 15

*190 On the Birth of Our Lord.................. 21

*191 On the Circumcision of Our Lord........... 25

192 On the Calends of January ................. 26

193 A Sermon of the Holy Bishop, Sedatus, on the
Calends of January ....................... 30

194 A Sermon of Bishop Faustinus on the Epiphany
of Our Lord; or for Tomorrow's Mass on the
Birthday of the Martyr, St. Lucian........... 35

*195 On the Epiphany of Our Lord Jesus Christ.. 38

196 On the Beginning of Lent .................. 41

*197 A Homily of St. Faustus on the Lenten Fast... 44

198 A Homily of St. Faustus on the Sunday Before
the Beginning of Lent ..................... 48

† For the meaning of the asterisk see Introduction, p. 2.

| Sermon | | Page |
|---|---|---|
| 199 | On the Discourse in Which it is Said: "Share your Bread with the Hungry"; Also that Almsgiving is Better than Fasting, that Strangers Should Be Received in some Corner of the House, and on Clothing Which has been Eaten Away | 53 |
| 200 | A Homily to the Catechumens | 58 |
| 201 | A Reproof for the People to be Read at the Recitation of the Creed | 63 |
| 202 | On the Lord's Supper | 65 |
| *203 | A Homily on the Pasch | 69 |
| *204 | On the Lord's Pasch | 71 |
| *205 | A Homily of St. Augustine on the Pasch | 75 |
| *206 | An Admonition of St. Augustine, That not only with the Tongue Should God be Praised, but by our Life and Deeds; In Addition, That What Follows in Deed will be the Same as What is Thought Within the Heart; Also on the Punishments of Purgatory and on the Abyss of Hell | 78 |
| 207 | On the Rogation Days | 82 |
| 208 | On the Rogation Days | 87 |
| 209 | Concerning the Rogation Days | 89 |
| *210 | On the Lord's Ascension | 93 |
| *211 | On Pentecost | 98 |
| *212 | On the Mystery of the Holy Trinity, and the Divine Nature of the Holy Spirit | 102 |
| *213 | On the Divine Nature of the Holy Spirit (II) | 106 |

214  A Sermon at the Anniversary of the Burial of St. Honoratus ............................ 111

215  On the Anniversary of St. Felix.............. 113

*216  A Homily of St. Augustine on the Nativity of St. John the Baptist...................... 117

*217  On the Nativity of St. John the Baptist...... 120

*218  On the Martyrdom of Blessed John the Baptist 124

*219  On the Feast of St. Stephen................ 127

*220  For the Feast of St. Stephen................ 132

*221  A Homily of the Bishop, St. Augustine, on the Feast of the Apostles James and John; He also Shows Here What is Going to Happen to Three Friends, and How the Speck is Nourished into a Plank  .................................... 134

*222  On the Feast of the Holy Innocents......... 139

223  On a Feast of Holy Martyrs................ 144

224  On Feasts of Holy Martyrs: That the Soul Should be Adorned with Good Works Just as the Body is Adorned with Expensive Clothing 148

225  On Feasts of Holy Martyrs................. 151

*226  A Sermon of St. Augustine on the Martyrs and on Grace  ................................. 156

227  On the Feast of a Church.................. 164

228  On a Church, or on the Consecration of an Altar  ................................... 168

229  On the Feast of a Church.................. 173

| Sermon | | Page |
|---|---|---|
| 230 | On the Consecration of a Bishop........... | 179 |
| *231 | A Sermon of St. Augustine on his Birthday... | 184 |
| *232 | A Homily of the Bishop, St. Augustine, on His Birthday ................................. | 189 |
| 233 | To the Holy Monks, Beloved Brothers in Christ, Who are Located at the Monastery in Blanzac ................................. | 192 |
| 234 | Another Sermon of St. Caesarius to Monks.... | 199 |
| 235 | To Monks ................................. | 204 |
| 236 | A Sermon to Monks ..................... | 209 |
| 237 | A Sermon to God's Servants or Handmaids on Giving a Good Example .................. | 214 |
| 238 | A Sermon to be Read to Monks During the Days of Lent ............................. | 220 |
| | Additional Sermon: A Sermon of St. Augustine on the Gospel Text Which Says: "Ask and It Shall be Given to You" ................... | 225 |
| Appendix ........................................ | | 229 |
| Indices | | |
| General Index .................................. | | 237 |
| Index of Holy Scripture ......................... | | 279 |

# INTRODUCTION

This third volume of the sermons of St. Caesarius completes the translation of the homiletic works of the Bishop of Arles.[1] Volume I (31 of the series *The Fathers of the Church*) comprised the first 80 sermons, the so-called Admonitions; Volume II (FOTC 47) presented the scriptural discourses, of which 81-143 are based upon the Old Testament and 144-86 upon the New; the present Volume III embraces the last three of the categories of sermons determined by Dom Morin: 187-213 the seasonal sermons, 214-32 the sermons on the saints, and 233-38 those addressed to monks. In the interest of completeness, a sermon whose text was unknown to Dom Morin and was published only in 1953 has been added after Sermon 238. This final volume also contains a general index to all three volumes and an index of Holy Scripture.

The pastoral character of the work of Caesarius is again evident throughout the sermons, and the universal applicability of the subject matter is remarkable. Obviously human nature today is essentially the same as human nature in the day of

---

1 See the Introduction to Vol. I for a treatment of the author's life and times, along with a Select Bibliography. More frequent reference has been made in this volume than in its predecessors to Msgr. Henry G. J. Beck's study, *The Pastoral Care of Souls in South-East France During the Sixth Century* (Analecta Gregoriana 51; Rome 1950). In another, more recent work, Caesarius is viewed as political philosopher: William M. Daly, "Caesarius of Arles, A Precursor of Medieval Christendom," *Traditio* 26 (1970) 1-28.

In this volume the following bibliographical abbreviations are used:

Beck, *Pastoral Care* See above.
CCL *Corpus christianorum: Series latina* (Turnhout 1953-)
Dekkers, *Clavis* E. Dekkers, *Clavis patrum latinorum* (second edition, Sacris erudiri 3; Steenbrugge 1961)
PL J.-P. Migne, *Patrologiae cursus completus: Series latina* (Paris 1844-64)

Caesarius, and the bishop, in forthrightly denouncing the evils
of his day and exhorting his listeners to the practice of positive
virtue, speaks also to us. The homilies directed to monks
contain a special note of humility on the part of the speaker,
for the bishop constantly stresses his feelings of inadequacy
in preaching to religious, who are committed to a life of
evangelical perfection.[2] However, Caesarius has evidently been
invited to preach to the monks by their superior, and so he
complies with the request, even if his sense of unworthiness
renders him reluctant to do so.

In these sermons of Volume III, as in the earlier ones,
Caesarius is found drawing heavily upon his predecessors,[3]
especially St. Augustine; he arranges his borrowings, however,
in his own way and generally supplies an original introduction
and conclusion. The fact of such indebtedness is indicated
in the same way as in the two preceding volumes.[4] An
asterisk stands before the serial number both when the sermon
appears in small type in Morin's edition and when it is marked

---

2 As casting further light on Caesarius' relation with religious, much can
be learned from his Rule for nuns. An annotated English translation
of this has been given by Sister Caritas McCarthy, S.H.C.J., in her
Catholic University of America doctoral dissertation published as
*The Rule for Nuns of St. Caesarius of Arles* (C. U. A. Studies in
Medieval History, N. S., 16; Washington, D. C. 1960).

3 [The steady progress of the *Corpus Christianorum: Series latina* facili-
tates the continued study of these borrowings. In the present instance
attention should be drawn to A. Mutzenbecher's new edition of the
sermons of Maximus of Turin (CCL 23; Turnhout 1962) and the
extraordinarily (but necessarily) elaborate edition by Fr. Glorie of
*Eusebius "Gallicanus": Collectio homiliarum* (CCL 101, 101A, 101B:
Turnhout 1970-1971). These badly needed critical texts will make
possible a control—and doubtless require some revision—of Morin's
findings. This is especially the case with the Eusebian collection. For
Morin, this assemblage of sermons (possibly in a form fuller than
that in which it is now known) predated Caesarius, who (it would
appear) drew upon it. Glorie, at least provisionally, sees the collection
as being later than Caesarius and as having been formed from as-
semblages of sermons and homilies brought together by Caesarius, for
his own use and that of his clergy. See Glorie's schema in CCL 101
p. ix.—ED.]

4 See vol. I p. xxv, 27 n. 1; vol. II p. xiii.

there by a dagger.[5] In the present volume an initial footnote to every sermon in question summarizes Morin's findings as there given in his own individual introductions and in his footnotes. Such notes were for the most part not provided in Volumes I and II; an appendix now supplies this omission.

In general, the translation of *The New American Bible* has been used for the scriptural quotations in this volume. When, however, the text of Caesarius demands it, the translation is drawn from other sources (occasionally the fact is stated) or, quite frequently, composed afresh, at least in part.

\*      \*      \*      \*      \*

[This volume was in page proof when a copy of the first volume of the *Sermons* as edited, translated, and annotated by Marie-José Delage (Sources chrétiennes 175; Paris 1971) became available. This book comprises an extended introduction (*ca.* 200 pp.) and the text and translation of Sermons 1-20. It is regrettable that the present translator could make no use of it.

New or revised sermons, in addition to the one translated below pp. 225-28, may be found in *R* (*evue*) *B* (*énédictine*) 66 (1956) 20-38 (Lambot); *ibid.* 67 (1957) 1-9 (Etaix) ; *Revue des études augustiniennes* 11 (1965) 9-13 (Etaix); RB 75 (1965) 201-11 (Etaix); cf. the article of J.-P. Bouhot, *ibid.* 80 (1970) 202-12. The two sermons published under the name of Caesarius by A. Höfer, *ibid.* 74 (1964) 44-53, are not authentic since they use texts of Gregory the Great.—For the content of this paragraph we are indebted to the kindness of R.P. Dom P.-P. Verbraken, O.S.B. (Maredsous).—Ed.]

---

5 Six sermons belong to the former category (190, 191, 195, 203, 210, 211), seventeen to the latter (189, 197, 204-06, 212, 213, 216-22, 226, 231, 232).

# SAINT CAESARIUS
# OF ARLES

# SERMONS

(Volume III)

*Sermon 187*

A HOMILY TO BE DELIVERED TEN OR FIFTEEN DAYS BEFORE
THE BIRTHDAY OF OUR LORD

THROUGH THE DIVINE MERCY, beloved brethren, the day on which we long to celebrate with joy the birthday of our Lord and Savior is almost at hand. Therefore I pray and advise that with God's help we labor as much as we can, so that on that day we may be able to approach the altar of the Lord with a pure and upright conscience, a clean heart, and a chaste body. Then we may merit to receive His Body and Blood, not to our judgment, but as a remedy for our souls. Truly our life depends upon the Body of Christ, as the Lord Himself said: "If you do not eat the flesh of the Son of Man and drink his blood, you have no life in you."[1] Therefore a man should change his life, if he wants to receive life, for if he does not change his life, he will receive it to his own judgment. Then he is corrupted by it more than he is healed; he is killed rather than given life. For thus the Apostle spoke: "He who eats and drinks without recognizing the body and blood of the Lord, eats and drinks a judgment on himself."[2]

(2) Although it is fitting for us to be adorned and distinguished by good works at all times, still on the day of the Lord's birth in particular, our good deeds, as He Himself said in the Gospel,[3] ought to shine before men. Consider, I

1 John 6.54 (53).
2 1 Cor. 11.29.
3 Cf. Matt. 5.16.

7

beseech you, brethren, a powerful or noble man who wishes
to celebrate either his own birthday or that of his son. With
what great effort he looks for anything disgraceful in his house
many days before. He arranges for it to be cleaned, for anything improper or unsuitable to be thrown away, and whatever is useful or necessary he commands to be displayed. If
the house is dirty, it is even whitewashed, the floors are
cleaned with brooms, strewn with different kinds of flowers,
and adorned; whatever affords delight to the mind and pleasure to the body is provided with every solicitude. What is
the purpose of all these preparations, dearest brethren, except
to celebrate with joy the birthday of a man who some day
will die? Now if you make such great preparations on the
occasion of your birthday or on that of your son, what great
and what kind of preparations should you make when you
are about to begin celebrating the birthday of our Lord? If
you make such preparations for one who is destined to die,
what kind of preparations should you make for one who is
eternal? Therefore labor as much as you can so that God
may not find in your soul whatever you do not want to find
in your home.

(3) If an earthly king or the head of a family invited you
to his birthday celebration, with what kind of garments would
you endeavor to adorn yourself when you approached? Surely
with new and shining ones, costly ones whose age or cheapness
or ugliness could not offend the eyes of the one who invited
you. Therefore with Christ's help strive as much as you can
with a like zeal, so that your soul may with an easy conscience
approach the solemn feast of the eternal king, that is, the
birthday of our Lord and Savior, if it is adorned with the
decoration of various virtues. Let it be adorned with the
jewels of simplicity and the flowers of temperance, gleaming
chastity, shining charity, and joyful almsgiving. For if Christ
the Lord recognizes that you are celebrating His birthday
with such dispositions, He Himself will deign to come and

not only visit your soul, but also rest and continually dwell in it. As it is written: "I will dwell with them and walk among them";[4] and again: "Here I stand, knocking at the door; if anyone rises up and opens the door, I will enter his house and have supper with him, and he with me."[5] How happy is the soul which, with God's help, has striven to direct his life in such a way that he may merit to receive Christ as his guest and indwelling person. On the contrary how unhappy and lamentable with a whole fountain of tears is the conscience which has defiled itself with evil deeds. It has so covered itself with the blackness of avarice, burned itself with the fire of wrath, polluted itself with continuous dissipation, and ruined itself with the tyranny of pride that Christ does not begin to rest in it, but the devil is starting to prevail! If the remedy of repentance does not quickly come to the aid of such a soul, he is abandoned by the light and occupied by darkness. He is rid of sweetness and filled with bitterness; he is invaded by death and rejected by life. However, a man of this kind should not fail to trust in the Lord's goodness. He should not be overcome by deadly despair but should rather have recourse to repentance at once. While the wounds of his sins are still new and warm, he should apply salutary medicines to himself. Our Physician is omnipotent, and He is so accustomed to heal our wounds that He does not allow even the trace of a scar to remain.

(4) Now just as you ought to refrain at all times from adultery and most wretched concubinage, beloved brethren, so, as often as you arrange to celebrate the birthday of our Lord or other feasts, you ought to keep away from your own wives for many days before it. Above all avoid drunkenness, resist anger as a most cruel wild beast, and reject hatred from your heart like a deadly poison. Let the love in your hearts be so great that it may reach not only your friends but also

---

4 2 Cor. 6.16.
5 Apoc. 3.20.

your very enemies. Then you may with assurance say in the
Lord's Prayer: "Forgive us the wrong we have done as we
forgive those who wrong us."[6] If a man knows that he has
hatred within himself for even one man, I do not know
whether he can approach the Lord's altar with assurance,
especially since blessed John the Evangelist exclaims in a
frightening manner when he says: "Anyone who hates his
brother is a murderer."[7] Now it is for you to judge whether
a murderer ought to presume to receive the Eucharist before
he repents. St. John also adds still more, when he exclaims
and says: "The man who hates his brother is in darkness;
he walks in shadows, not knowing where he is going, since
the dark has blinded his eyes."[8] Again he says: "The man
who does not love his brother is among the living dead";[9]
and still further: "If anyone says that his love is fixed on
God, yet hates his brother, he is a liar. One who has no love
for the brother he has seen, how can he love the God he has
not seen?"[10] Therefore if a man keeps hatred or anger in his
heart and is neither frightened nor aroused by such thunder,
he must be believed to be, not sleeping, but dead.

(5) As we continually think about these truths, dearest
brethren, those who are good should with the grace of God
strive to persevere in good works, because not he who has
begun, but "the man who holds out to the end is the one
who will see salvation."[11] Those who know that they are slow
in giving alms, prompt to anger, and swift in yielding to
dissipation, with the Lord's help should hasten to uproot
themselves from evil in order that they may merit to do what
is good. Then when the day of judgment comes, they will not
be punished with wicked sinners but will deserve to arrive
at eternal rewards along with the just and merciful: with the

6 Matt. 6.12.
7 1 John 3.15.
8 1 John 2.11.
9 1 John 3.14.
10 1 John 4.20.
11 Matt. 10.22; 24.13.

help of our Lord Jesus Christ, to whom is honor and glory for ever and ever. Amen.

*Sermon 188*

A Homily to be Delivered Before the Lord's Birthday

Beloved brethren, as we are about to begin with sincerest devotion a holy and desirable, glorious and excellent feast, that is, the Nativity of our Lord and Savior, with His help we ought to prepare ourselves with all our strength. Let us carefully examine all the recesses of our soul, lest perchance there be some hidden sin within us to confound and gnaw at our conscience and to offend the eyes of the divine majesty. Although Christ our Lord arose from the dead after His passion and ascended into heaven, nevertheless, as we believe, He considers and carefully notices how each one of His servants strives to prepare and dispose himself to celebrate His birthday without avarice, anger, pride, or dissipation. In proportion to the way He sees each one adorned with good works, in that measure He will dispense to him the grace of His mercy. If He sees a man clothed with the light of charity, adorned with the pearls of justice or mercy, chaste, humble, merciful, kind and prudent, through the ministry of His priests He will dispense His Body and Blood to such a man, not to his judgment, but as a remedy. But if He sees anyone adulterous, drunk, avaricious and proud, I am afraid that He may say to him what He Himself said in the Gospel: "My friend, how is it you came in here not having a wedding garment?"[1] Then—may God forbid it!—what follows may happen: "Bind him hand and foot and throw him out into

1 Matt. 22.12.

the night to wail and grind his teeth."[2] Behold what kind of sentence will be received on judgment day by the man who has approached the Lord's festival without the remedy of repentance and defiled with the filth of vices.

(2) On the Lord's birthday, beloved brethren, Christ was united with His spouse, the Church, as in spiritual nuptials. Then "truth sprang out of the earth," then "justice looked down from heaven,"[3] and then "the groom" came forth "from his bridal chamber,"[4] that is, the Word of God came forth from the womb of a virgin. He came forth with His spouse; that is, He assumed human flesh. Now since we have been invited to those sacred nuptials and are destined to attend the banquet of the Father, the Son, and the Holy Spirit, see with what kind of garments we should be provided. Therefore with God's help let us cleanse both our hearts and our bodies, as far as we can. Then that heavenly inviter will detect nothing disgraceful in us, nothing loathsome, nothing ignoble, nothing unworthy of His eyes. For this reason, beloved brethren, we ought to heed these truths with great trepidation and not as if in passing. For we have been invited to nuptials where we ourselves will be the bride, if we lead a good life. Let us think and consider to what kind of nuptials, to what kind of spouse, and to what kind of banquet we have been invited. Truly we have been invited to a table where no food of men is found but the bread of angels is served. Therefore let us see to it that we do not appear there wrapped in the old garments of vices within our soul, where we ought to be adorned with the pearls of good works. When chastity makes the good shine in whiteness in the sight of God, then dissipation will make the wicked appear clothed in dirty garments.

(3) As often as the birthday of our Lord or other feasts approach, as I have frequently advised, for many days before them do not only refrain from wretched intercourse with

---

2 Matt. 22.13.          3 Ps. 84 (85).12.          4 Ps. 18 (19).6.

concubines, but even keep away from your own wives and withdraw yourself from all anger. Redeem your past sins by almsgiving and repentance, and harbor hatred for no man in your heart. Let justice begin to spend in mercy on the poor what vanity was wont to squander through gluttony, and let love store up in heaven what dissipation or gluttony formerly wasted in the world.

(4) Although it is expedient that we always give alms, however on the holy festivals especially we ought to give more abundantly in proportion to our means. Above all let us summon the poor more frequently to a banquet, for it is not right that on a holy festival some of the Christian people who belong to the one Lord should become intoxicated, while others are tormented with the risk of dying from hunger. Both we and all Christian people are servants of one Lord, have been redeemed at one price, have entered this world on equal terms, and are destined to go forth from it by a similar departure; moreover, if we lead a good life, we will come to one and the same blessedness. Now why should not the poor man take food with you, since he is going to receive the kingdom with you? Why should not the poor receive at least your old tunic, since he is destined to receive the robe of immortality with you? Why should not the poor deserve your bread, since he has merited to receive the sacrament of baptism with you? Why should he be unworthy of receiving at least scraps of your food, since he is going to come to the banquet of the angels with you? Listen, brethren, and pay attention, not to my precept, but to the command of our common Lord. Thus He speaks in the Gospel: "Whenever you give a lunch or dinner, do not invite your wealthy neighbors who might invite you in return and thus repay you. No, invite beggars and the lame. You should be pleased that they cannot repay you, for you will be repaid in the resurrection of the just."[5]

5 Cf. Luke 14.12-14.

(5) Now someone says: Should I not, then, invite my friends and relatives to a banquet? Relatives and neighbors should be asked, but rather rarely. Moreover not too sumptuous and luxurious a feast should be prepared for them, but one that is so moderate and frugal and proper that there will be something left to refresh the poor and to spend for the needy. Then when the day of judgment comes, we may not hear with the wicked who now despise the poor: "Out of my sight, you condemned, into everlasting fire,"[6] but together with the just and merciful we may merit to hear: "Come. You have my Father's blessing! Inherit the kingdom, for I was hungry and you gave me food, I was thirsty and you gave me drink."[7] At the same time that desirable word will also be directed to us: "Well done! You are an industrious and reliable servant. Since you were dependable in a small matter I will put you in charge of larger affairs. Come, share your master's joy!"[8]

(6) In order that these truths which we have mentioned may be kept more closely in the thoughts of your charity, we repeat briefly what was said. This is what we have advised, brethren. Since the Lord's birthday is approaching, let us with Christ's help prepare ourselves for the nuptials and heavenly banquet by being clear of all dissipation and adorned with good works. Let us give alms to the poor and repel anger or hatred from our hearts like the devil's poison. Faithfully observe chastity even with your own wives, summon the poor to your small meals more frequently, attend vigils more promptly, pray or chant the psalms standing in church. Do not utter idle or worldly thoughts with your lips, and rebuke those who have freely spoken them; observe peace with all men, and recall to harmony those who you know are at variance. If with the help of Christ you are willing to fulfill these things faithfully, you will be able to approach the Lord's

---

6 Matt. 25.41.
7 Matt. 25.34, 35.
8 Matt. 25.21, 23.

altar in this life with an easy conscience and in the future
life will happily arrive at eternal bliss: with the help of
Him who lives and reigns for ever and ever. Amen.

* Sermon 189

### On the Coming of Our Lord[1]

I beseech you, dearest brethren, to strive zealously to love
with your whole hearts that charity which is known to be
the mother of all virtues, and humility in which the basis of
the Christian religion is proved to exist. Moreover steadfastly
hold them with all the power of your souls, and with the
Lord's help happily preserve them. Know truly that the man
who has willed to guard those two virtues, namely, humility
and charity, will be able to approach the Lord's birthday with
assurance. Therefore let us strive to devote ourselves to the
Lord in such a way that we can gather together, in these few
days, what may suffice us for the entire year. For we believe
that the Lord Himself spoke about those days of His coming
through the prophet: "On the days of your festivities you
shall mortify yourself."[2] Why did he say this? Because fasts,
vigils, and pious mortifications torment humbled bodies but
cleanse defiled hearts; they draw vigor from the limbs but
give it to consciences. Sins of desire are redeemed by the
weariness of bodies, and the delights of dissipation or the
flesh are punished through the exercises of a hard cross. Thus
the significance of future death is anticipated by present mortification. While the author of sin is humbled, the sin is con-

---

1 Dom Morin notes that while sections 1-3 are made up of pieces drawn
  from Augustine and "Eusebius Gallicanus" (see Introduction, p. 2 n. 3),
  the rest of the sermon offers in thought and expression much that is
  clearly Caesarian.
2 Cf. Lev. 16.29.

sumed; and while the torment of voluntary severity is inflicted on the body, the affront of a fearful judgment is assuaged. A little distress dissolves enormous sins which eternal fire would scarcely have destroyed. For if we ourselves impose a penalty for our own sins, if we condemn dissipation through bodily penance, we will make God propitious to us. If you acknowledge your sin, God forgives it, for how could it happen that God would deign to forgive sin which man disdains to acknowledge in himself?

(2) Now as we discuss the cause of our salvation, let us do within ourselves what doctors concerned with us habitually do. If something troublesome or annoying is felt in the outer skin of the body, a salve of rather soothing medicine is applied; but if a wound is hidden inside in the bones or is buried in the depths of the intestines, the hidden force demands a sharper, more violent medicine to overcome the spreading sore by burning or cutting and by pain to cause the pain to be conquered. A similar plan must be followed in the sickness of souls. If, perchance, sins are slight, for example, if a man has sinned in speech or some censurable desire, by sight or in his heart, the blemishes of words and thoughts must be cared for by daily prayer and must be wiped away by private cleansing. But if anyone who questions within his own consciousness has committed some mortal sin—if he has destroyed and betrayed his honesty by false testimony, profaned the revered name of truth by the rashness of perjury, stained the snowy tunic of baptism and the beautiful silk of virginity with the filth of polluting shame, killed the new man in himself by the crime of murder, handed himself as a captive to the devil by observing auguries under the influence of soothsayers, seers, and magicians—these and sins of this kind cannot be atoned for entirely by the usual moderate or secret satisfaction. Serious sins require more grave, sharper, and public cures. Thus one who has brought himself to ruin through the ruination of many others will likewise redeem

himself through the edification of many. Man himself even deceives himself if, although he feels disease burning within the marrow of his bones, he spreads a soothing ointment over the surface of his body.

(3) These mortal sins require an immense amount of wailing, lamenting and shedding of tears and must be wiped away by a vast amount of bitterness. "I roar with anguish of heart,"[3] and "every night I flood my bed with weeping; I drench my couch with my tears";[4] moreover: "I eat ashes like bread and mingle my drink with tears."[5] Let no one despise penance or scorn this humiliation; it was King David who said these words, it was a very great king who performed those deeds. Therefore it is proper to cry out loud as over a dead person, and to weep copious tears over a soul destroyed by sins. Just as a bereaved mother is accustomed to wail with a broken heart over the loss of her only son, so is it fitting to be grieved over our only soul, but with a hope of restoration. Concerning this one and only soul the prophetic word says: "Rescue my soul from the sword, my only one from the grip of the dog."[6] Why did it say "my only soul"? Either because it must be esteemed as unique or because it alone will have to render an account before the heavenly tribunal when all consolations have been removed. Therefore, I say, the entire weight of grief must be poured out with wailing and groaning over this one soul which was slain by the sword of sins, if by chance it may still be awakened, revived through the warmth of faith by the remedy of tears. Contrition must be kindled, and prayers strengthened by a remembrance of the future judgment, supported by works of mercy. The thought of the prophet Daniel should be heard, but heard by the ear of obedience, as he says: "O king, take my advice; atone for your sins by good deeds."[7] By this means the ears of

---

3 Ps. 37 (38).9.　　　4 Ps. 6.7.　　　5 Ps. 101 (102).10.

6 Ps. 21 (22).21. Because of the meaning given to *unicam* in the text, I have retained the translation "my only one" instead of "my loneliness" given in the *New American Bible*.

7 Dan. 4.24.

God can be penetrated on behalf of a sinner, because he does not lie who said: "God bestows his favor on the lowly";[8] and: "Love covers a multitude of sins."[9]

(4) In order that we may, with Christ's help, avoid entirely all the sins which the devil is accustomed to inflict on us, I beseech you, and I advise you with paternal solicitude to flee avarice, which "is the root of all evil."[10] Likewise flee the sewer of drunkenness and the slough of adultery as the devil himself. These three pitfalls, that is, avarice, drunkenness, and adultery, will seize careless souls, unless swift and fruitful repentance comes to assist them. If sudden death seizes them, they have to be put to the flames in the place where the devil must be consumed in fire. Now although I warn about this matter very frequently and also attest to it, nevertheless I hear that there still are certain unhappy souls to be lamented with a whole fountain of tears. Even though they are married, these men neither fear nor are ashamed to commit adultery. Although almost the entire populace is fully aware of this sin, nevertheless, because we cannot approve of it, we by no means remove them from communion with the Church. But if there were some who, for love of God and the welfare of these others, continually rebuked them, and if they refused to correct themselves, the former brought their sins to our lowly attention out of true love. Those others, then, for one or two years could and should be suspended, as a due penalty, from the communion, conversation, and communal living of Christians until they correct themselves. But those who know of this condition in truth, and neither strive to rebuke it themselves nor bring it to our attention, without any doubt will be participants in the sins of those others. I beseech you, brethren, that those who are married and those who are not neither indulge in drunkenness nor commit adultery. Although those who have no

---

8 James 4.6.
9 1 Peter 4.8.
10 1 Tim. 6.10.

wives when they could and should marry do not want to perform what is permissible, yet they are not ashamed to do what is not allowed. For this reason I call you to witness, and in the presence of God and His angels I declare both to married men and to the single, also, at the same time, to wives, that no one may presume to commit adultery. As I already said, whoever commits it will not escape eternal punishment, unless firm and fruitful repentance has helped him. But adulterers and the dissolute are going to suffer this, because they do not fear what is written: "God will judge fornicators and adulterers";[11] and further: "Every other sin a man commits is outside his body, but the fornicator sins against his own body."[12] Moreover: "All adulterers are like a blazing oven in their hearts";[13] and: "The man who is joined to a prostitute becomes one body with her";[14] and still further: "The price of a loose woman is scarcely a loaf of bread; but if she is married, she is a trap for your life."[15] Notice, brethren, how great sin is, that on account of the space of one hour, in which an unhappy soul is joined to a prostitute, he renders himself alien to eternal life and makes himself liable to punishment by eternal fire. Even if that unfortunate delight of pleasure should stretch out over the space of a hundred years, it would not be right, and the unhappy soul would suffer eternal punishments in return for the pleasure of a hundred years. Therefore fear with all your heart, brethren, and see how great is the sin which any adulterer commits: he receives from the devil the briefest pleasure of concupiscence, and he hands his soul over to the devil in death. Behold the kind of reward or exchange the unfortunate dissolute and lukewarm Christian gives back to Christ; his soul, which Christ redeemed with His precious Blood, he sells to the devil for a momentary pleasure.

11 Heb. 13.4.
12 1 Cor. 6.18.
13 Cf. Osee 7.4.
14 1 Cor. 6.16.
15 Prov. 6.26.

(5) This act drunkards also do not fear, nor are ashamed to commit. In their delight at passing wine for the smallest space of time across their palate and through their insatiable throats, for the sake of brief pleasure they store up everlasting punishment for themselves. Moreover they do not fear what is written: "No drunkards will inherit God's kingdom";[16] and further: "Wine and women make the wise fall away and bring reproach on the intelligent."[17] Furthermore: "Look not on the wine when it is yellow, when its color sparkles in the glass; it goes down smoothly, but in the end it bites like a snake or like a poisonous adder or serpent."[18] Understand this, brethren, that every drunkard who has made drinking a habit will have leprosy within, in his soul, because the soul of the drunkard is known to be such as the flesh of the leper is seen to be. Therefore one who wishes to free himself from the sin of drunkenness, where not only his soul is killed, but even his body is weakened, should drink merely as much as suffices. If he is unwilling to observe this rule, he will be hateful to God and an object of reproach to men. Now because it is proper for me to say it and necessary for you to hear it, I declare it and at the same time beseech you with the affection of a great love. If a man willingly listens to me and wants to observe it, as a result of the mercy of God I believe that the good Lord will deign not only to grant pardon, but even to repay with a crown. But if a man scorns it, he will receive the punishment which he deserves either in this world or in the next. May the good Lord deign to free us from this: who lives and reigns.

---

16 1 Cor. 6.10.
17 Sir. 19.2.
18 Prov. 23.31, 32.

## * *Sermon 190*

## ON THE BIRTH OF OUR LORD[1]

On this day, dearest brethren, Christ was born unto us. Let us prepare for Him in our hearts a dwelling full of patient merits; let us prepare a crib, a cradle brilliant with the flowers of a good life and the perpetual sweetness of its fragrance. Let us receive the tiny little Lord in our hearts; may He grow and make progress there, nourished by faith, may He ascend to youth there on the steps of life, and may He exercise the powers which are mentioned in the Gospel. Within us the Lord has a blind man to whom He can give light, a lame man whose step He can restore and bring to the path of truth without stumbling. In this room He finds a dead man, a corpse stretched out; He even finds a foul cadaver which the kindly one who raises from the dead may bring back from the tomb of sin. What He did in those who were dead He does in the living. He raises a man to life in the room of his heart, just as He did the daughter of the head of the synagogue, provided that the man repents of his sins of deadly thoughts. Because a man is already dead if he has decided to sin with an evil intention, He raises him to life in the room, if, before he commits the deed which he thought about, with secret compunction he has recourse to repentance for the crime that he had conceived. He also raises to life the corpse of a youth laid out for burial and, when he is revived, restores him to his weeping mother, that is, to the grieving Church. This happens when a man has committed

---

1 Caesarius drew this sermon, thinks Morin, from a now unknown early source, but not without clothing it, especially in sections 3 and 4, with forms of expression characteristic of himself. Since Morin published, scholars have attributed the sermon to Sedatus, Bishop of Nîmes around 500 (cf. Sermon 193 n. 1). See Dekkers, *Clavis* No. 1005.

a crime before he is buried, that is, before he is overcome by habit, provided that the man returns to repentance by belated compunction after condemning his offenses. But why do I speak about corpses which are hidden or buried? Our Lord and Savior despises neither those who are buried nor those who stink from rottenness. He even arouses those whom He has recalled to a better life by repentance, even though because of long habit they were rotting from the dreadful ugliness of their vices, as if they were in a tomb. He restores to a better life bodies which have been overwhelmed with the weight of sins as in a tomb, and He orders the corpse which was bound to be released from its bands, that is, from its deadly ties. This is done provided that the sinner feels the weight by which he is pressed down and recognizes his corruption and foul smell.

(2) For this reason, brethren, if the hidden concupiscence of any sin rebukes a man, he should hasten to be aroused in his room, that is, before he does what he conceived in thought. If there is a man whose death general lamentation has clearly revealed to the public, that is, who has committed whatever sin he intended, he should hurry and return to the restorer of life before he is overwhelmed by the weight of the tomb and before he begins to stink from rottenness. However he should not despair, even though the long-standing weight of sins has buried him in his foul-smelling condition as in fetid death. By those other resurrections which were accomplished for our hope, the Lord promises that He will restore life to all who desire to rise again. The goodness of our Lord is no less wonderful in the mystery than in the deed, for He has seen to it that the remedies for those who are willing to be cured are greater than the dangers, and that the remedies for restoring health are stronger than the wounds. Our Lord did not want to bring death to the human race through His birth. He became man so that man whom He had created might not perish; He suffered cruel torments in order that He might

free the unworthy from deserving punishments. He hung on
the tree of death in order to expiate the fault which was
derived from the tree through disobedience; for this He
died and descended into hell, in order to rescue from it the
dead who were kept in hell under the bond of sin. Overcoming death He came back bearing living spoils, that is, He
restored to the living the life of those who were dead. He was
not content to have man recover through His resurrection
only what he had lost by disobedience when he was deceived
by the poisonous inspiration of the serpent. For it was not
right that God our Redeemer should give to those who have
been redeemed by His death only what the hatred of the
hostile deceiver had cunningly destroyed. The latter expelled
man from his true country, the former brought him back;
the one took away paradise, while the other restored heaven.
Just as the devil overcame his captives by death, which was
himself, so our Lord, who is life, gave to the redeemed eternal
life and a share in His heavenly kingdom. Then we may
taunt the devil and boast in the Lord as we say what was
spoken through the prophet: "O death, where is your victory?
O death, where is your sting?"[2]

(3) The extent of the divine mercy has taken me quite
far away from the present feast. However it is connected in
such a way that the nativity could not be preached without
the passion, nor could the passion without the glory of the
nativity. Christ was born in order that He might suffer, He
suffered in order that He might die, He died in order that
He might descend into hell, He descended there in order that
He might free the dead. Although as God He was incapable
of suffering, by uniting the substance of a man with His
divinity He humbled Himself in such a way that, although
God, He was born as a man and as man He arose again to
God by triumphing over death. For this reason, dearest
brethren, the way came to those who were wandering, the

---

2 1 Cor. 15.55.

judge came to the guilty, the physician came to those who were sick, life came to the dead. Why? Because without the way the pilgrim could not return to his true country, without a judge the guilty could not be forgiven, and without life the dead could not be revived. Therefore we have a way of return on the road, mercy in our judge, a remedy in sickness, and deliverance in death. The way by which we can arise came down to us, the judge came to chastise death and to free man, the physician came to remove infirmities and to grant endless health to the sick, life came to descend into hell, in order that it might free the dead from it by killing death. O Lord, with what joy and exultation shall we describe the benefits of such great goodness? What more is there that we who are sick might ask than what You have offered of Your own accord to those who did not deserve it? And yet we poor sinners also beseech You to love in us what You bore for us. If only we might love our own life in the same way that You deign to love Your death in us.

(4) Therefore, dearest brethren, let us love our price and let us make ourselves worthy of it by good deeds and right actions, since we have merited to be redeemed and even freed by the death of our Lord. For this reason, too, let us keep our life pure and undefiled for our Lord and Redeemer as it was entrusted to us. As we joyfully celebrate the feast of His nativity, with His help may we endeavor to live in such a way that such great and immense benefits of our God may not bring us judgment but may lead to our profit: because He Himself is worthy of it, who lives and reigns with the Father.

## * Sermon 191

### ON THE CIRCUMCISION OF OUR LORD

Our Savior, dearest brethren, was born of the Father as true God before all ages, and at the end of ages the same Son of God was Himself born as true man. For the redemption of the human race He wished to experience the condition of human weakness, He wanted to fulfill all of the precepts of the Law, and on the eighth day, which we commemorate today, He willed to be circumcised in His body. This was not to cleanse His flesh, but to free us from all wickedness and to extend everything that was accomplished by Him to our profit. But someone will say: Why was Christ circumcised, or even presented in the temple according to the Law? We will reply to him that "He came, not to abolish the law, but to fulfill it,"[1] in order not to be different from the fathers of whose race He was begotten. Thus the Jews may not excuse themselves and say: You are unlike our fathers, and therefore we are unwilling to believe in you.

(2) What is the circumcision of Christ, dearest brethren, except our chastity, whereby God is delighted in us? For it behooves us to be circumcised, not in body, but in spirit; that is, every vice should be cut out of us so that we may be "holy and blameless in his sight,"[2] subduing desires of the flesh, "growing in the knowledge of God and multiplying good works of every sort."[3] Let us carefully reflect on the day of our death, because no more useful remedies can be found for all the wounds of sins than for each one diligently to pay attention to that hour on which he is going to depart from this life. For how can any serious sin be committed by a

---

1 Matt. 5.17.
2 Eph. 1.4.
3 Col. 1.10.

man if at every moment he thinks that he is being summoned
from this life? Thus the Scriptures truly say: "Remember that
death does not tarry,"[4] and again: "Remember your last days,
and cease from sin."[5]

(3) As we reflect on these truths with great fear and solicitude, dearest brethren, let us most earnestly hasten to the
remedies of repentance and the medicine of almsgiving. Then
we may happily come before the tribunal of Christ to be
crowned, not damned: with the excellent help of our Lord
Jesus Christ, to whom is honor and glory for ever and ever.
Amen.

*Sermon 192*

## ON THE CALENDS OF JANUARY

The day of those calends which are called the Calends of
January, beloved brethren, derived its name from a dissolute
and wicked man, Janus. This Janus formerly was the chief
leader of the pagans. Ignorant and rustic men feared him
as if he were a king, and they began to worship him as a
god; while they were afraid of his kingly power, they conferred unlawful honor upon him. Men at that time, truly
foolish and ignorant of God, esteemed as gods those whom
they perceived to be more exalted among men. Thus it happened that worship of the one true God was carried over to
the many names of deities or rather of demons. For this
reason they named the day of today's calends after the name
of Janus, as was already said, so that they assigned the end
of one year and the beginning of another to the man upon
whom they wished to confer divine honors. Now because to
them the Calends of January were said to complete one year

---

4 Sir. 14.12.
5 Sir. 28.6; and cf. *ibid*. 7.36.

and begin another, they placed this Janus, as it were, both at the beginning and at the end, for he was believed to end one year and begin another. From this stems the fact that ancient worshipers of idols themselves fashioned two faces for Janus, one facing the front and the other the rear: one to look at the past year, and the other to see the coming one. Moreover by thus ascribing two faces to him, foolish men have made him a monster, even while they want to make him a god; what is unnatural even in animals they have willed to be a marked characteristic of their god. And so, in the clearest manifestation of their error and in judgment upon it, while wishing, in their empty devotion to images, that he seem a god, they have openly revealed him a demon.

(2) From this arises the fact that in these days pagan men have perverted the order of all things and cloak themselves with detestable ugliness, so that those who worship make themselves like the one who is adored. For in these days miserable men and, what is worse, even some who are baptized, assume false forms and unnatural appearances,[1] and certain features in them are especially worthy of laughter or rather of sorrow. For what wise man can believe that men are found to be of sound mind, if they are willing to make themselves a small stag or to be changed into the condition of wild beasts? Some are clothed in the skins of sheep, and others take the heads of wild beasts, rejoicing and exulting if they have transformed themselves into the appearance of animals in such a way that they do not seem to be men. From this they declare and show that they have not only the appearance of beasts but also their feelings. For although they want to express in themselves a likeness to different kinds of animals, still it is certain that the heart of sheep is within them rather than only their likeness. Moreover, how shameful and how disgraceful it is when those who were born as men are clothed in the tunics of women. By a most

---

1 See Sermon 193 n. 2.

unseemly change they make their manly strength womanish by means of girlish fashions, not blushing to put the arms of a soldier into the tunics of women. They show bearded faces, but want to appear like women. Those who change into the dress of women fittingly no longer possess manly strength, for it must be believed to be happening by God's just judgment that they should lose the strength of a soldier when they deform themselves with the appearance of women.

(3) Now since our kind God has deigned to inspire you out of love for the faith to remove this wretched habit entirely from this city, I beseech you, dearest brethren, let it not be sufficient for you that with God's help you yourselves do not commit this evil. Whenever you see this happen elsewhere, rebuke, correct, and reprove it, by your salutary counsel recalling foolish men from this miserable wickedness. And in order that you may consecrate yourselves completely to the divine mercy, reject also, as the devil's poison, those other observances which very many of the Christian people—and this is worse!—do not blush to follow. There are some who observe omens on the Calends of January in such a way that they do not give fire or any kind of favor from their household to one who asks it, but they both accept diabolical gifts from others and themselves give them to others. On the very eve of this feast there also are some simple men who set their little tables full of many things which are necessary to eat, and they want to keep them arranged this way throughout the night, believing that in this way the Calends of January can benefit them, so that throughout the year their banquets will continue with such plenty. Now because, as it is written, "a little yeast can affect the entire dough,"[2] these deeds and others similar to them, which it would take too long to mention but which the ignorant believe are either small sins or no sins at all, you should command to be removed from your households. Moreover, command them to observe these

---

2 Gal. 5.9.

calends in the same way as they are wont to regard those of
other months. If anyone wills to observe any practice from the
custom of pagans on these days, it must be feared that the
name of Christian will not be able to help them.

(4) Therefore when our holy ancient fathers observed that
the majority of the human race were obeying gluttony or
dissipation on these days and were possessed with a mania
for drunkenness and wicked dances, they passed a decree for
the whole world. Throughout all the churches a public fast
was imposed, so that those miserable men might realize that
they had committed such a great evil that it was necessary
for all the churches to fast on account of their sins. For this
reason, dearest brethren, let us fast on these days, and with a
true and perfect charity let us grieve over the foolishness of
miserable men, so that they may understand their wickedness
as they see a public fast being observed for them. For we
should not despair that through your prayer and abstinence
God may correct them, for with ineffable goodness He promised this through His Apostle when he said: "The person
who brings a sinner back from his way will save his soul from
death and cancel a multitude of sins."³ Anyone who shows a
kindly feeling to the foolish men who indulge in wanton
amusement on these calends should not doubt that he is a
participant in their sins. The man who faithfully thinks about
the salvation of his soul ought to grieve or weep over them
rather than to open his soul to miserable laughter with them
or over them. It is not right, brethren, for you who have been
wont to exclaim daily to the good God, "My eyes are ever
toward the Lord,"⁴ and again: "To you I lift up my eyes,"⁵
—it is not right for your eyes, which are continually sanctified
by watchful looking to God in church, to be defiled by seeing
the wickedness of foolish men. You ought rather to disdain
and despise the works of the devil, so that the charity of

---

3 James 5.20.
4 Ps. 24 (25).15.
5 Ps. 122 (123).1.

Christ may remain spotless in you. Therefore cry out with the prophet and say: "Turn away my eyes from seeing what is vain."[6] Moreover fear what the Apostle says: "You cannot drink the cup of the Lord and also the cup of demons; you cannot partake of the table of the Lord and likewise the table of demons."[7] However I believe that in God's mercy their foolishness is to be corrected by your chastisement. Then double rewards will be repaid by the Lord, not only for yourselves, but also for the correction of those who will profit by your example: with the help of our Lord Jesus Christ, to whom is glory and honor for ever and ever. Amen.

*Sermon 193*

A SERMON OF THE HOLY BISHOP, SEDATUS,[1] ON THE CALENDS OF JANUARY

Every sin, dearest brethren, the devil introduces through either pride or false notions: false ideas through ignorance, and pride through contempt. These two are the sources of all sins. False notions are, as it were, a slighter sin, as is the appetite for pleasures, excessive gluttony, wanton jokes, shameful pleasure, the ostentation of the theater, a slanderous tongue, thoughtless and confused boldness. Other false ideas are the useless observance of omens, the worship of the days of old superstition, and inquiry into the future. But these things cross over to pride when they remain without amendment even though recognized. For thus it happens that,

---

6  Ps. 118 (119).37.
7  1 Cor. 10.21.

---

1  Sedatus was bishop of Nîmes around the year 500. In Morin's judgment, only the sermon's first section, which he finds different in style from the rest, is drawn from him.

through the full indulgence of drunkenness and the shameful songs at games because of foolish joy, the demons are invited as if to their own sacrifices when the days of the calends or the vanity of other superstitions is observed. It is truly a delightful sacrifice for them when we either say or do something whereby decency, a friend of justice, departs sullied by wicked deeds. For what is so absurd as by shameful dress to change the sex of a man into the form of a woman? What is so foolish as to disfigure one's face, to assume an appearance which even the demons themselves greatly fear?[2] What is so mad as with shameless pleasure to sing the praises of vices along with disorderly gestures and immodest songs; to be clothed in the manner of wild beasts and to become like a deer or a stag, so that a man who was made to the image and likeness of God becomes a sacrifice to the demons? By these means that contriver of evil introduces himself, in order that he may gain control over minds which have been gradually captivated by the similarity of these spectacles. Therefore, as was said above, when these things have gained strength, pride, which is opposed to God, succeeds; through a neglect of duty and contempt for the fear of God, it first introduces disputes even against Sacred Scripture. Then raging with ambition, swelling with vainglory, longing for what is unseemly, despising what is proper, in the spirit of pride it proceeds to the shipwreck of good morals like the unrestrained wind of a storm. As a result of this, envy, the root of all evils, which is distressed at the advantage of another as though it were evil to itself, even now with a hidden fire consumes the souls of the living by an inextinguishable flame like the fire of hell in the world to come, and it chokes them with biting cares. Now what can be more miserable than a man who is made unhappy by the good fortune of another? or where can he find a remedy, when he is miserable, not only over his own misfortunes, but even over the good of

2 On these carry-overs of pagan practice, see Beck, *Pastoral Care* 281-82, where contemporary corrective legislation is cited.

another? Because of this, anger, which is always opposed to counsel, devises a pit for him to fall into and spreads snares by which he may be captured.

(2) Now since God has deigned to give you a virtuous and prudent life, dearest brethren, by constant reproof transfer the holy life which you received through a divine gift to your neighbors and your servants. Do not permit them to utter shameful words or dissolute songs, because every sin redounds to the man who refuses to stop sinners even when he can. Therefore if on the Calends of January anyone shows a kindly disposition toward the wretched men who have a mania for sacrilegious rites, rather than jest, he should realize that he has given himself over, not to men, but to the demons. For this reason if you do not want to share in their sins, you should not permit a small stag, even one that is a year old, or any other kind of omens to come before your homes. Rather rebuke and correct and, if you can, even punish with severity, so that when God repays you may be able to receive a twofold reward as the result of your own salvation and the amendment of others. I beseech you, beloved brethren. Since we trust in your fidelity and the uprightness of your life through the goodness of God, let it not be enough for you that you yourselves are good. As we already suggested above, strive that through your advice you may also correct the carelessness of others, so that you may receive eternal rewards, not only as a result of your own holy life, but also from the amendment of others. Therefore admonish your household not to observe the wicked customs of the miserable pagans.

(3) What is worse, there are some men whom harmful religious observance subverts in such a way that on the day of the Calends, if perchance it is needed by neighbors or travelers, they omit to give of their fire. Besides, many are wont to offer new year's gifts themselves and to accept them from others. Above all, brethren, in order to confound the carnal and wicked pleasure of the pagans, let us all fast with

the Lord's help, except those who are unable to abstain
because of infirmity. Let us further pray to God as much as
we can on behalf of those wretched men who observe these
Calends out of gluttony or wicked custom. Now while we
shudder at the things which they do, above all we pray for
them; then through the Lord's gift we may rejoice doubly
because of our kindness and as a result of their amendment.
By the goodness of God, beloved brethren, you listen so
devoutly and willingly for the salvation of your soul that
we strive to suggest with boldness and charity the things
which we know are necessary for your salvation; we endeavor
to show you what you ought to do and what you should
avoid. This, then, I beseech you, brethren, that under God's
inspiration you yourselves despise the ancient custom of the
pagans out of love for religious observance. Moreover if you
see others observing anything of this kind, reprove them with
charity and patience.

(4) Some, indeed, fall into the evil of carefully noting on
what day they are departing on a journey, paying honor to
the sun or the moon or Mars or Mercury or Jupiter or Venus
or Saturn. These unhappy souls do not know that if they do
not amend their lives by repentance they will have a share
in hell with those to whom they are seen to pay empty honor
in this world. Above all, brethren, flee from all these wicked
deeds, and avoid them as the deadly poisons of the devil.
Truly God created the sun and the moon for us and to be
beneficial to us; not in order that we might worship those
two heavenly bodies as gods, but so that we might give as
much thanks as we can to Him who gave them to us. For
Mercury was a wretched man, avaricious, cruel, wicked and
proud; Venus was a most shameless harlot. Moreover those
monstrous portents, that is, Mars and Mercury and Jupiter
and Venus and Saturn, are said to have been born at the
time when the sons of Israel were in Egypt. If they were born
then, surely these days which are called by their names already

existed at that time. Moreover they possessed their names according to what God had ordained, that is, the first day, the second, the third, the fourth, the fifth, and the sixth. But miserable and ignorant men who worshiped those exceedingly base and wicked men, as we said above, through fear rather than through love, in their sacrilegious worship of them consecrated all the days of the week to them one by one in name, as if to honor them. Because they venerated their wicked deeds in their hearts, they seemed to have their names frequently on their lips. But for our part, brethren, since we are known to have hope in the living and true God, not in dissolute and wicked men, let us think that no day should have the name of demons, and let us not observe on what day we ought to set out on a journey. Let us even disdain to utter with our lips those exceedingly despicable names, and let us never say the day of Mars, or the day of Mercury, or the day of Jupiter. Let us rather call them the first or second or third day, according to what is written.[3] Furthermore advise your households concerning these names, for then perfect health of soul will remain in you, if through your admonition spiritual medicine comes to those who have been wounded by many sins. Therefore not only rebuke, frequently and with severity, those who belong to you, but also continually admonish with charity those who are not of your household. Then the kind and merciful Lord will grant you eternal rewards, not only for your own salvation, but also because of the salvation of others: to whom is honor and glory for ever and ever. Amen.

---

3 Martin of Braga, in the sixth century, was to repeat this instruction, with striking results for the Portuguese language; see in this series Vol. 62, pp. 11, 76.

## Sermon 194

A SERMON OF BISHOP FAUSTINUS ON THE EPIPHANY OF OUR LORD; OR FOR TOMORROW'S MASS ON THE BIRTHDAY OF THE MARTYR, ST. LUCIAN[1]

The solemn feast which has proceeded from the Nativity of our Lord, dearest brethren, we have celebrated with the faith with which we hold God born of man; we venerate it with the same respect with which God was proclaimed in a man. There He is hidden in weakness; here He is revealed in strength. For today a star, which is destined to reveal Christ to those who seek Him, led the Magi, who were coming from the east, to the place of the Savior's birth. The sacred birth is seen beneath a lowly covering; He who shines in the stars is adored in swaddling clothes. His pure majesty is adored in swaddling clothes, that is, beneath the lowliness of human corruption; the greatness of the divine mercy is revealed at the beckoning of the mystery. In the fact that the Ethiopians —that is, the Gentiles—approached Christ first, the firstfruits of the Gentiles were consecrated. In the recognition of truth the Church of the Gentiles preceded the synagogue of the Jews, removing the blackness of sin and putting on the brightness of faith. For this reason the Church seeks our salvation in the crib; that is, the multitude of unbelievers which was fierce at first grows tame when it has been received within the stable of the Church. The Jews, indeed, boast that worship among them is divine, but ambassadors of the Gentiles are

---

1 The "Faustinus" from whom certain elements in this sermon may have been drawn is Faustus, fifth-century bishop of Riez (France, dé-partement Alpes et Haute Provence), of British or Breton origin and semi-Pelagian in his doctrine on grace.—St. Lucian is the renowned martyr of Nicomedia (feast January 7; Beck, *Pastoral Care* 312 at n. 96), whose cult at Arles is of very early date. The saint's "birthday" (*natale*) is the day of his death, his birth into everlasting life.

the first to see Christ. The sound eye of a Christian follows the light, but the corrupted vision of the Jews is suffused with the light itself, and when light is applied weak vision becomes still more darkened.

(2) In the meantime the blessed embassy wonders that it has been led to the holy cradle by a ray of light streaming from above; the farthest nation is the first to enjoy the common good. What a wonderful favor! He who embraces heaven and earth is held within the embrace of His mother; He who left the kingdom of His Father lies hidden in the bosom of His mother. Through a simple service the spiritual treasure is revealed: humanity is perceived, but divinity is adored. Those who offer gold, frankincense, and myrrh show more in mystery than they offer in knowledge. In the gift of gold royal dignity is indicated, in the smoke of the frankincense divine majesty, and in the appearance of myrrh humanity which is destined for burial. Thus the number of their offering bespeaks the Trinity, while their single devotion gives evidence of unity.

(3) Following this example, if we wish to reach Christ, let us endeavor to behold heaven with the ever watchful attention of our heart. May the star of justice direct the path of a perfect life for us. Let us offer the gold of fidelity, the spices of devotion, and the burnt-offering of chastity to Him who said: "No one shall appear before me empty-handed."[2] May we possess spiritual myrrh within us to temper our souls in such a way that it may keep them unharmed by the corruption of sin. Let us change our life, if we desire to reach our true country, that is, the heavenly one. Let there be this exchange between the two so that we may prepare for ourselves the substance of that future life by our use of this present one. Just as eternal life will be the reward of this life, let us labor in such a way that this one may be the price of that. Now the evangelist says that the Magi were

---

2 Exod. 23.15.

warned in sleep "not to return to Herod, but to go back to their own country by another route."[3] This was also spiritually commanded to us, that we should return to our true country by another way, that is, by another way of life.

(4) Perhaps someone will ask how it can be done. If a man desires to know this, he should listen to the prophet when he says: "Turn from evil, and do good; seek peace, and follow after it."[4] Now through this order there is a return to our true country on another path. Since we have fallen in the world through pride, it is necessary for us to return to paradise through humility; we came to the service of the devil through avarice, and so we must return to Christ our Lord by mercy; we experienced the exceedingly harsh yoke of the devil through passion and dissipation, and so we must hasten to take up the light yoke of Christ through charity and justice. If we have departed from the company of the angels by unhappily serving the devil along paths of infidelity and wickedness, let us strive to return to our eternal country on the way of goodness and fidelity.

(5) If through this order we are willing to leave deadly paths and cling to the way of eternal life, we can, by passing from the left side to the right, devoutly and happily imitate the journeys of the Magi. Does not a man seem now to be traveling on another way to his true country, as it were, if, when he was wont to take away the possessions of another, he now begins to spend his own wealth in mercy? Does not a man seem to you to walk on another path, if he was an adulterer and is now chaste, if he was a drunkard and is now temperate, if he habitually cursed and now blesses, if he was spiteful and is now kind? If by prayer together with good works and God's help we strive through this order to change the paths of our lives for the better, we will be able to arrive happily at eternal bliss: with the help of our Lord Jesus Christ, who lives and reigns for ever and ever. Amen.

---

3 Cf. Matt. 2.12.  4 Ps. 33 (34).15.

## * *Sermon 195*

### ON THE EPIPHANY OF OUR LORD JESUS CHRIST[1]

Epiphany is a Greek word, dearest brethren, and is interpreted as a manifestation. Therefore since He was manifested on this day, the redeemer of all nations made it a solemn feast for all people. Tradition has it that our Lord Jesus Christ, who was born twelve days earlier, was adored by the Magi on this day. The truth of the Gospel says that this was done, and the excellent authority of this feast proclaims everywhere on what day it happened. Now those Magi, as the firstfruits of the Gentiles, recognized Christ our Lord, and although they were not yet advised by His word, followed the star which appeared to them and which spoke visibly like a heavenly tongue instead of the word of an infant. Therefore it has seemed just that the Gentiles recognize with pleasure the day of salvation as their firstfruits, and dedicate it to Christ our Lord with thanksgiving and solemn devotion. The firstfruits of the Jews appeared unto faith in the revealed Christ among those shepherds who saw Him by coming from nearby fields on the very day when He was born. A multitude of angels informed those shepherds, but a star told the Magi. What was said to the shepherds was "Glory to God in high heaven,"[2] but in the Magi was the fulfillment: "The heavens declare the glory of God."[3] Truly, for both, the foundations of two walls sprang up from the opposite directions, as it were, of the Jews and the Gentiles, or circumcision and uncircumcision, extending to the corner-

---

1 Caesarius has here adapted St. Augustine's Sermon 203; Morin notes that the conclusion is undeniably Caesarian.
2 Luke 2.14.
3 Ps. 18 (19).2.

stone in order that He might be their "peace, making the two
of them one."[4]

(2) Now those shepherds gave praise because of the fact that
they saw Christ, but the Magi adored Him when they saw
Him. There was grace in the former, but humility was more
abundant in the latter. The Jews, indeed, possessed grace
first, but the Gentiles who came later received Christ our
Lord with greater humility. However, notice carefully what
the shepherds and the Magi did when they came to Christ:
the shepherds gave praise, and the Magi adored. Perhaps
those shepherds were lesser sinners, because they already knew
the law of God and for this reason rejoiced more eagerly
when they heard about salvation; but the Magi, that is, the
Gentiles, without any knowledge of God and burdened with
sins, were seeking pardon with bowed body and lowered
head. This is the humility which Sacred Scripture commends
in the Gentiles. Finally there was that centurion among the
Gentiles who, although he had already received the Lord
Jesus with all his heart, still said that he was unworthy to
have Him enter his house and that he believed his sick son
could be cured by the power of His word alone.[5] There also
was that Canaanite woman among the Gentiles, who cried out
to our Lord with humility. When our Lord had said that she
was a dog and unworthy to have the children's bread given
to her, in humility she did not refuse to be a dog but said:
"Please, Lord, even the dogs eat the leavings that fall from
their masters' tables."[6] Now this she said and asked for leavings like a dog, and for this reason she did not deserve to be
a dog, because she did not deny what she had been. See at
last what the Lord said to her: "Woman, you have great
faith!"[7] First she was called a dog, but afterwards a woman.
Truly, before the coming of Christ the Church was a dog,

---

4 Cf. Eph. 2.14.
5 Cf. Matt. 8.5-9.
6 Matt. 15.27.
7 Matt. 15.28.

which had been wont to lick the blood of sacrifices like a dog by serving idols, but afterwards it merited to receive the Blood of Christ. For this reason have we mentioned this, brethren, in order that we may show the humility of the Gentiles.

(3) Now the shepherds came from nearby to see Him, and the Magi from afar to adore. From the farthest ends of the earth the Gentiles were looking for Him whom the unhappy Jews despised although He was near at hand. The Jews disdained to seek Him, even though He was foretold to them and born before them; but like insensate stones and inscribed mile-markers they show the way to others while they themselves fail to walk it. However, as the Magi looked, because Christ the Lord was to be born in Bethlehem, in thirteen stages they met Him whom the Jews disdained to seek in three thousand. This is the humility of the Gentiles whereby the wild olive[8] deserved to be planted and, contrary to its nature, to produce the olive, because by grace it merited to change its nature. For although the whole world grew thick with the wild olive, since it has now become fruitful through the grafting of grace, it has shown that it became the olive of true charity. Therefore all nations come like the wild olive, "from the east and the west, from the north and the south,"[9] who "will find a place at the banquet in the kingdom of God with Abraham, Isaac, and Jacob."[10] Thus the whole world, even from its four parts, is called to faith by the grace of the Trinity. According to this reckoning, by the threefold calling of four, the number of the twelve Apostles is consecrated, as if prefiguring the salvation of the whole world unto the grace of the Trinity from the four parts of the world. For while the Trinity is preached in the east and in the west, in the north and in the south, as was said, the mystery of the Trinity is shown to all nations, and

---

8  Cf. Rom. 11.17.
9  Luke 13.29.
10  Matt. 8.11; Luke 13.29.

the number of the twelve Apostles is clearly indicated. This number was also expressed in that dish which was shown to Peter full of all kinds of animals, like all the nations.[11] Now that dish, which was suspended by the four corners and came down from heaven three times, was chosen so that four times three might make twelve. Perhaps the Magi, the firstfruits of the Gentiles, came to see and adore Christ just when twelve days were added after the birth of our Lord, in order that the very number of days might most clearly be shown to be related to the four parts of the world and the number of the Apostles. Finally when the Magi came after twelve days, they merited, not only to find their own salvation, but also to manifest the salvation of all nations. Therefore let us also celebrate the appointed day most devoutly, and let us adore the Lord Jesus dwelling in heaven, whom those firstfruits of ours adored as He lay in the inn. What we worship as fulfilled, they adored as still to come.

(4) In the meantime let these truths suffice for your charity. After the labor of your vigils I should not weary you by too lengthy a sermon. If any one desires to be solicitous for the salvation of his soul, he should come to church rather early tomorrow: with the help of our Lord, who together with the Father and the Holy Spirit lives and reigns for ever and ever.

*Sermon 196*

On the Beginning of Lent

Behold, dearest brethren, through the mercy of God the season of Lent is approaching. Therefore I beseech you, beloved, with God's help let us celebrate these days, salutary for bodies and healing for the soul, in so holy and spiritual

11 Cf. Acts 10.11-12.

a manner that the observance of a holy Lent may lead to progress for us and not judgment. For if we lead a careless life, involving ourselves in too many occupations, refusing to observe chastity, not applying ourselves to fasting and vigils and prayers, neither reading Sacred Scripture ourselves nor willingly listening to others read it, the very remedies are changed into wounds for us. As a result of this we shall have judgment, where we could have had a remedy.

(2) For this reason I exhort you, dearest brethren, to rise rather early for the vigils, and above all to come to terce, sext and nones. Let no one withdraw himself from the holy office unless either infirmity or public service or at least great necessity keeps him occupied. Let it not be enough for you that you hear the divine lessons in church, but read them yourselves at home or look for someone else to read them and willingly listen to them when they do. Remember the thought of our Lord, brethren, when He says: "If he were to gain the whole world and destroy himself in the process, what can a man offer in exchange for his very self?"[1] Above all keep in mind and always fear greatly what is written: "The burdens of the world have made them miserable."[2] Therefore busy yourself in your home in such a way that you do not neglect your soul. Finally, if you cannot do more, at least labor as much on behalf of your soul as you desire to labor for the sake of your body.

(3) For this reason, dearest brethren, "Have no love for the world, nor the things the world affords,"[3] because "the

---

1 Matt. 16.26.
2 This quotation, which is used not less than twelve times by Caesarius, was tracked to its probable source by B. Fischer, O.S.B., "Impedimenta mundi fecerunt eos miseros," *Vigiliae Christianae* 5 (1951) 84-87; viz., *Visio Pauli* 10 and 40 (ed. M. R. James, *Apocrypha anecdota* [Texts and Studies 2.3, Cambridge 1893]) p. 14 line 25, p. 33 line 15. The quotation in *Regula Magistri* 86.7 is nearly identical; cf. the note of A. de Vogüé, *La Règle du Maître* (Sources chrétiennes 106; Paris 1964) 351.
3 1 John 2.15.

world with its seductions is passing away."[4] What, then, remains in a man except what each one has stored up in the treasury of his conscience for the salvation of his soul by reading or prayer or the performance of good works? For miserable pleasure, still more wretched lust and dissipation, through a passing sweetness prepare eternal bitterness; but abstinence, vigils, prayer, and fasting lead to the delights of paradise through the briefest hardships. The truth does not lie when He says in the Gospel: "Strait and narrow is the road that leads to life, and how few there are who find it!"[5] Not for long is there rejoicing on the broad way, and not for long is there labor on the strait and narrow road. After brief sadness those who travel the latter receive eternal life, while those who travel the former, after short joy, suffer endless punishment.

(4) For this reason, dearest brethren, by fasting, reading, and prayer in these forty days we ought to store up for our souls provisions, as it were, for the whole year. Although through the mercy of God you frequently and devoutly hear the divine lessons throughout the entire year, still during these days we ought to rest from the winds and the sea of this world by taking refuge, as it were, in the haven of Lent, and in the quiet of silence to receive the divine lessons in the receptacle of our heart. Devoting ourselves to God out of love for eternal life, during these days let us with all solicitude strive to repair and compose in the little ship of our soul whatever throughout the year has been broken or destroyed or damaged or ruined by many storms, that is, by the waves of sins. And since it is necessary for us to endure the storms and tempests of this world while we are still in this frail body, as often as the enemy wills to lead us astray by means of the roughest storms or to deceive us by the most voluptuous pleasures, with God's help may he always find us prepared against him.

---

4 1 John 2.17.
5 Matt. 7.14.

(5) Therefore I beseech you again and again. During these holy days of Lent if you cannot cut off the occupations of this world, at least strive to curtail them in part. By fleeing from this world, through an expedient loss and a most glorious gain you may take away from earthly occupations a few hours in which you can devote yourselves to God. For this world either laughs at us or is laughed at by us; either we yield to it and are despised, or we despise it in order to obtain eternal rewards. Thus you either reject and despise the world, or you yield to it and are pursued or even trampled upon by it. But it is better for you to despise the world and by trampling upon it to make a step for yourself whereby you may ascend on high. If in accord with your usual practice you both willingly heed and strive faithfully to fulfill, dearest brethren, the truths which we are suggesting for the salvation of all by presuming upon your obedience, you will celebrate Easter with joy and will happily come to eternal life. May He Himself deign to grant this, who together with the Father and the Holy Spirit lives and reigns for ever and ever. Amen.

## * Sermon 197

### A HOMILY OF ST. FAUSTUS ON THE LENTEN FAST[1]

Behold, beloved brethren, the holy and spiritual days of Lent are already at hand, and during them losses of the body are transformed into gains for the soul. Now since, as the Apostle says, "the acceptable time and the day of salvation"[2] are coming let us prepare our souls as for a spiritual harvest.

---

1 The sermon, Morin tells us, is a typical example of Caesarius' adaptative technique, and it shows relation with a homily of "Eusebius Gallicanus" (see Introduction, p. 2 n. 3), who had drawn upon Faustus (for whom, see above on Sermon 194).

2 2 Cor. 6.2.

Let us strive to devote ourselves to the Lord in such a way that in these few days we may be able to accumulate stores enough to provide for our needs during the whole year. Concerning these days we believe that the Lord said through the prophet: "On the days of your solemn feasts you shall mortify yourselves."[3] Why did He say this? Because fasts and vigils and holy mortifications afflict bodies that are humbled but they purify hearts that have been defiled; they take strength away from limbs but add a bright sheen to consciences. Sins of pleasure are redeemed by bodily weariness while the physical delights of dissipation are punished by the distresses of a hard cross. Thus by present mortification the sentence of future death is suspended. While the author of a sin is being humbled, the fault is consumed, and while the pain of voluntary punishment is inflicted on the body, the displeasure of the terrible judge is appeased. Short labor makes up for huge sins which eternal fire was going to consume only with difficulty. If we ourselves impose self-discipline for our sins, if we condemn dissipation of the flesh through repentance, we will make God immediately merciful to us. If you confess your own sin, God forgives it; but how can it happen that God should deign to forgive a sin which man refuses to acknowledge in himself?

(2) Therefore as we consider the cause of our salvation, let us do within ourselves what doctors attending us usually do. If an injury or symptom is felt on the surface of the bodily skin, the healing power of a soothing medicine is applied. But if the wound is hidden in the bones or buried deep in the intestines, the hidden force demands a harsher and more violent medicine so that the huge ulcer may be overcome by cautery or by cutting and the pain may be conquered by pain. A similar method ought to be applied in the sickness of souls. If perchance sins are rather slight—for example, if a man has offended in word or by some blameworthy desire, with his

---

3 Cf. Lev. 16.29.

eyes or in his heart, the stains of thought should be cared for through daily prayer and cleansed by individual repentance. But if when a man examines his conscience within himself, he has committed some serious sin—if he broke his word and betrayed it by false testimony, defiled the sacred name of truth by the rashness of perjury, stained the snow-white tunic of baptism and the shining silk of virginity with the filth of defiling shame, killed the new man in himself by the crime of murder, delivered himself to the devil as a captive by observing omens through soothsayers and prophets and magicians—these and similar sins cannot be entirely expiated by the usual moderate and secret satisfaction. Serious causes require more grave and harsh and public cures. When a man has destroyed himself along with the ruin of many more, he should redeem himself in like manner by the edification of many. For when a man feels a disease burning within in the marrow of his bones, he deceives himself if he applies a soft ointment over the surface of his body.

(3) Therefore these serious sins need a fountain of tears together with much crying and groaning. With the prophet it should be exclaimed: "I roar with anguish of heart,"[4] and "Every night I flood my bed with weeping, I drench my couch with my tears";[5] and again: "for I eat ashes like bread, and mingle my drink with tears."[6] Let no one despise repentance, let no one disdain such humiliation, for it was King David who said this, and a very great king who performed those deeds. For this reason it is proper for us to cry out loud as over a dead person and to utter loud wailing over the soul that has died of sins. Just as a bereaved mother is wont to mourn with a broken heart over the loss of her only son, so it is fitting to be distressed, but with the hope of restoration, over our one soul. Concerning this one soul the prophetic word says: "Rescue my soul from the sword, my only one

---

4  Ps. 37 (38).9.
5  Ps. 6.7.
6  Ps. 101 (102).10.

from the grip of the dog."[7] Why did he say "only one"? Either because it alone is to be loved, or because before the tribunal of Christ it is going to render an account alone, when all assistance has been removed. For this reason, I repeat, it is necessary to pour forth a whole load of grief, together with crying and groaning, over this one soul which has been killed by the sword of sins. Perhaps then it may be revived by the remedy of tears and the warmth of faith. Compunction must be aroused, and in remembrance of the future judgment prayers must be strengthened. The thought of Daniel the prophet should be heard, but heard with the ear of obedience, for he says: "O king, take my advice, and atone for your sins by good deeds."[8] Moreover the example of that man in the Gospel should be heard as if it were truly written for our redemption: "I give half my belongings, Lord, to the poor."[9] We have listened to our Lord in the Gospel where He speaks with ineffable condescension and charity concerning them: "He who did it for one of my least brothers, did it for me."[10] These words with heavenly authority recommend to us the fruits of almsgiving.

(4) Now when we talk about almsgiving, perhaps straitened poverty may become frightened and say that it has nothing which it can give to the poor. No one will be able to excuse himself in this matter, when our Lord promised that He would give a reward for a cup of cold water and praised the widow who had put two coins into the treasury. Truly our God is not appeased by an abundance of giving but by the good will of the one who is bestowing the gift. Moreover I believe, brethren, that our Lord has permitted poor people to live in this world in order to prove the faith of the rich in the person of the poor, or in order that He may have compassion on the rich in their mercy to the poor. Thus the

---

7 Ps. 21 (22).21; also cf. Sermon 189 n. 6
8 Dan. 4.24.
9 Luke 19.8.
10 Cf. Matt. 25.40.

rich do not lack an occasion for good works and their own redemption, and another's want enriches the man who is kind and merciful, for anyone who is rather wealthy can acquire great gains from the needy. By a wonderful and excellent exchange, while a man bestows mercy on the poor through his generosity in time, he prepares for himself eternal treasures. Therefore let us regulate our actions, and out of love for eternal life let us devote whatever we can and as much as we are able to the exercise of good will and to pursuits of mercy and justice. Let us run while we have the light and before darkness embraces us.[11] In that world it will no longer be possible to look for amendment and redemption, as the divine word says: "For among the dead no one remembers you."[12] Just as no loss of merits will be feared there, so no remission of sins will be granted there any more, and no longer will an opportunity be afforded to perform good works.

(5) As we think about these matters prudently and devoutly, dearest brethren, let us hasten to have recourse to the remedies of repentance. Through chastity and humility, and by works of justice and mercy, let us prepare for ourselves eternal rewards in the sight of God: with the help of our Lord Jesus Christ, to whom is honor and might for ever and ever. Amen.

## Sermon 198

### A HOMILY OF ST. FAUSTUS ON THE SUNDAY BEFORE THE BEGINNING OF LENT[1]

Our Lord and Savior exhorts us through the prophet and advises us how we ought to come to Him after many negli-

---

11 Cf. John 12.35.                    12 Ps. 6.6.

1 The homily is titled "of St. Faustus" since Caesarius in composing it had before him a sermon of the Eusebian collection (see above on Sermon 197) that he believed was composed by Faustus.

gences, saying: "Come let us bow down in worship, let us kneel before the Lord who made us";[2] and again: "Return to me with your whole heart, with fasting, and weeping, and mourning."[3] If we notice carefully, dearest brethren, the holy days of Lent signify the life of the present world, just as Easter prefigures eternal bliss. Now just as we have a kind of sadness in Lent in order that we may rightly rejoice at Easter, so as long as we live in this world we ought to do penance in order that we may be able to receive pardon for our sins in the future and arrive at eternal joy. Each one ought to sigh over his own sins, shed tears, and give alms in such a way that with God's help he may always try to avoid the same faults as long as he lives. Just as there never has been, is not now, and never will be a soul without slight sins, so with the help and assistance of God we ought to be altogether without serious sins.

(2) Now in order that we may obtain this, if burdens of the world keep us occupied at other times, at least during the holy days of Lent let us reflect on the law of the Lord, as it is written, by day and by night.[4] Let us so fill our hearts with the sweetness of the divine law that we leave no place within us devoid of virtues so that vices could occupy it. Just as at the time of the harvest or vintage, brethren, enough is gathered so that the body may be fed, so during the days of Lent as at a time of spiritual harvest or vintage we ought to gather the means whereby our soul may live for ever. Whenever a careless person fails to gather anything at the time of vintage or the harvest, he will be distressed by hunger throughout the entire space of the year. In the same way if anyone at this season neglects to provide and gather spiritual wheat and heavenly wine in the storehouse of his soul by fasting, reading, and prayer, he will suffer forever the most severe thirst and cruel want. Know for sure, dearest brethren, that

2 Ps. 94 (95).6.
3 Joel 2.12.
4 Cf. Ps. 1.2.

the soul which is not fed continuously by the word of God is like a body which receives food only after many days. Just as the body becomes thin and dehydrated, almost like a shadow, through hunger and want, so the soul which is not fed on the food of God's word is found to be parched and useless, fit for no good work. Consider, brethren, if every year we fill the barn and wine cellar and storehouse in order that our body may have food for one year, how much do you think we ought to store up so that our soul may be nourished for ever?

(3) For this reason, brethren, at least during these few days let the 'burdens of the world' which, according to Scripture, 'make' many careless souls 'miserable'[5] disappear. Let carnal pleasure depart, as also the allurements of this world, which are full of poison. Let bodily joys be lessened, so that spiritual gains may be provided for the soul, because of what is written: "Woe to you who laugh now, for you shall weep in your grief";[6] and further: "Blest are the sorrowing, for they shall be consoled."[7] Let spiritual reading begin to occupy the time which frenzied addiction to the playing-table formerly took away from you; let discourses on Sacred Scripture take the place of useless stories, biting jokes, and poisonous slander. In the course of the hours when we were wont to be engaged in hunting to the loss of our soul, let the sick be visited, those who are put in prison sought out, travelers received, and the discordant recalled to harmony. If we do these things, brethren, we can provide medicines for ourselves out of the things with which we had inflicted wounds upon ourselves.

(4) Above all, on days of fast let us spend on the poor what we earlier were accustomed to eat at lunch. Then no one will endeavor to provide for himself sumptuous dinners and banquets of choice delicacies or seem to have changed rather than taken away an abundance of food from his body.

---

5  Cf. Sermon 196 n. 2.
6  Luke 6.25.
7  Matt. 5.5 (4).

It avails nothing to have extended a long fast throughout the day if afterwards the soul is ruined by delight in or excess of food. When the mind is satiated, it immediately becomes sluggish, and when the earth of our body is watered, it will sprout the thorns of unlawful pleasures. Therefore let our food be moderate, and the stomach never filled too much. Let us think more about food of the heart than of bodily nourishment, because within, in the inner man, we were made to the image of God, while in our body we were formed from the slime of the earth. Now see, brethren, whether it is right for the body which was made from the earth sometimes to take food twice a day, and for the soul in which there is an image of God scarcely to receive the word of God after several days. Yet, we ought to honor the image of God within us more than our body. For men who think only about the body are like wild animals or sheep, and those who do this have already crushed God's image within them. Therefore the flesh should be managed like a maidservant, and the soul should be preferred as the lawful mistress. If we do otherwise, not recognizing that we have been made to the image of God and thinking more about our body than about our soul, I am afraid that the Holy Spirit may be rebuking us when He says through the prophet: "Thus man, for all his splendor, does not abide; he resembles the beasts that perish."[8]

(5) Willingly listen to the divine lessons in church, as you usually do, and read them over again in your own homes. If anyone is so busy that he cannot take time for holy Scripture before lunch, he should not be ashamed to read over something of it at his own little meal. In this way just as the body is fed with food, so the soul is refreshed by the word of God; then the whole man, that is, both the exterior and the interior, may rise up satisfied from the holy and salutary feast. For if only the body is refreshed, but the soul is not fed on the word of God, the handmaid is satisfied but the mis-

---

8 Ps. 48 (49).13.

tress is tormented by hunger, and your holy selves know how wrong this is. For this reason, as I have already said, you ought to read and listen to the sacred lessons with such eagerness that you may be able to speak about them and teach them to others both in your own homes and elsewhere, wherever you are. As you, like clean animals, masticate the word of God by continuous reflection, you may be able both to procure useful flavor for yourselves, that is, their spiritual meaning, and with God's help give it to others. Then will be fulfilled in you what is written: "Your cup overflows!"[9] Moreover, you will fulfill what the blessed Apostle encourages and advises when he says: "The fact is that whether you eat or drink—whatever you do—you should do all for the glory of God."[10] If infirmity does not prevent it, fast daily. Hasten to the vigils with cheerful and fervent devotion because of what is written: "O God, my soul yearns for you in the night";[11] and again: "To you I pray, O Lord; at dawn you hear my voice";[12] and still further: "At midnight I rise to give thanks to your name, O Lord."[13] To this our Lord and Savior also exhorts and encourages us when He says in the Gospel: "Be on guard, and pray that you may not undergo the test."[14] May He Himself deign to grant this, to whom are honor and might together with the Father and the Holy Spirit, world without end. Amen.

---

9 Cf. Ps. 22 (23).5.
10 1 Cor. 10.31.
11 Cf. Isa. 26.9.
12 Ps. 5.4.
13 Ps. 118 (119).62.
14 Matt. 26.41.

*Sermon 199*


On the Discourse in which it is Said: "Share Your Bread with the Hungry";[1] Also that Almsgiving is Better than Fasting, that Strangers Should be Received in Some Corner of the House, and on Clothing Which has been Eaten Away


I beseech you, dearest brethren, that at this prescribed and very holy season of Lent no one should presume to eat before the principal meal except on Sundays, except of course the man whom ill health does not allow to fast. On other days there is healing or a reward in fasting, but during Lent it is a sin not to fast. At another season the man who fasts will receive forgiveness, but on those days the man who can fast but fails to do so will be afflicted with punishment. Moreover, the man who is not able to fast should rather secretly prepare for himself alone what he should have, or if there is another like him who is sick, he should prepare it with him in his own home; however, he should not invite to the meal those who are able to fast. If he does invite them, not only God but even men will realize that he is not unable to fast because of ill health but rather refuses to do so because of his appetite. It should suffice for him that he is not able to fast himself, and he should all the more take his food with groaning and sighing and grief of soul because of the fact that he was not able to abstain from food when other men were fasting. What need is there for a sick man to invite a well person to his meal, with the result that he increases his own sin as the result of the appetite of another? Because of the fact that he is not able to fast, he ought to give more generously to the poor in order that he may redeem through almsgiving the sins which he cannot heal by fasting.

1 Isa. 58.7.

(2) It is good to fast, brethren, but it is better to give alms. If anyone can do both, those are two good acts; but if he cannot, the almsgiving is better. If there is no possibility of fasting, almsgiving without fasting is enough for a man, but fasting without almsgiving does not suffice at all. Therefore if a man cannot fast, almsgiving without fasting is good; but if he can do so, fasting along with almsgiving is a double good work. Indeed, fasting without almsgiving is no good unless it happens that a man is so poor that he possesses nothing at all that he can give. For such a man good will is sufficient, if he has nothing to give, according to what is written: "Glory to God in high heaven, peace on earth to men of good will."[2]

(3) Who will there be who can excuse himself, when our Lord promises that He would give a reward even for a cup of cold water? Now why did He say cold water? Perhaps so no poor man could excuse himself because of lack of wood or say in truth that he had no vessel in which to heat the water. Finally, even through the blessed prophet, dearest brethren, the Lord exhorts and admonishes us to almsgiving in such a way that almost no one is so poor that he can excuse himself. For thus he speaks: " 'This is the fasting that I wish,' says the Lord: sharing your bread with the hungry."[3] He did not say that he should give it all, because perhaps that poor man had nothing else, but 'sharing it,' he says. This means that even if your poverty is so great that you have nothing but one loaf, nevertheless break off some of it and give it to the poor. 'Sheltering the oppressed and the homeless,'[4] he also says. If anyone is so poor that he has no food to give to the poor, at least he should prepare a little bed for the stranger in some corner of his house. What are we going to say to this, brethren? What excuse will we be able to offer if we have roomy, spacious homes but scarcely ever condescend

---

2 Luke 2.14. The Confraternity of Christian Doctrine translation has been used.
3 Isa. 58.6, 7.
4 Cf. Isa. 58.7.

to receive a stranger? We do not know, or rather do not believe, that Christ is received in all strangers, as He Himself
said: "I was a stranger, and you welcomed me,"[5] and "As
often as you did it for one of my least brothers, you did it
for me."[6]

(4) If it is troublesome and disagreeable for us to receive
Christ in the person of the poor in our land, I am afraid
that He will reciprocate in heaven and not receive us in His
blessedness. If we despise Him in the world, I fear that He in
turn will despise us in heaven, according to what He Himself said: "I was hungry and you gave me no food,"[7] "I was
away from home and you gave me no welcome,"[8] and "As
often as you neglected to do it to one of these least ones, you
neglected to do it to me."[9] Now what follows after this,
brethren? May God avert it from us, for He added afterwards:
"Out of my sight, you condemned, into that everlasting fire
prepared for the devil and his angels."[10] Now let us not listen
to these truths in a passing fashion or only with our bodily
ears, dearest brethren. Let us rather devoutly pay attention
and both by word and example teach others to cling to them
and fulfill them.

(5) After this, then, what did our Lord say through the
prophet? "Clothe the naked when you see him."[11] For my
part I judge no one in this sentence; let each one pay attention to his own conscience. However, I blame and rebuke
myself because several times it has accidentally happened that
through carelessness garments of mine, which the poor should
have received, were eaten by moths. Thus I am afraid that
my very clothing will be brought forward as evidence against
me on the day of judgment, according to what the Apostle
James frightfully exclaims when he says: "Come now, you

5 Matt. 25.35.
6 Matt. 25.40.
7 Matt. 25.42.
8 Matt. 25.43.
9 Matt. 25.45.
10 Matt. 25.41.                11 Isa. 58.7.

rich, weep and wail over your impending miseries. Your
wealth has rotted, your wardrobe has grown motheaten, your
gold and silver have corroded, and their corrosion shall be a
testimony against you; it will devour your flesh like a fire.
You have stored up treasure for yourselves on earth; you
have fattened yourselves for the day of slaughter."[12] Although,
as I said, all of these things which Christ threatened through
the Apostle should terrify us very much, dearest brethren, still
there should be no despair of the mercy of God. Both I and
other souls like myself who have been careless up to this point
can, with God's help, correct ourselves, provided that we are
willing to dispense more generously the alms which until
now we have given too sparingly. In addition we should beg
the Lord's mercy for our past sins with sorrow and groaning
and with the hope of forgiveness.

(6) Therefore as we suggested above, dearest brethren, let
an abundance of almsgiving make our fasts acceptable, for
fasting without almsgiving is like a lamp without oil. Just
as a lamp which is lit without oil can smoke but cannot give
light, so fasting without almsgiving pains the body, to be sure,
but does not illuminate the soul with the light of charity. As
for our present course of action, brethren, let us in the meantime fast in such a way that we lavish our lunches upon the
poor, so that we may not store up in our purses what we intended to eat, but rather in the stomachs of the poor. Truly
the hand of the poor is the treasury of Christ. Whatever He
receives He stores up in heaven so that it will not be lost on
earth, because the reward for a good work is hidden in heaven,
even though the food which the poor man receives is consumed. If we strive to lay out our luncheons along the lines
of a dinner, with choice delicacies and a multitude of courses,
not only are pleasures not taken from our body, but they are
even doubled. In this way nothing is gained for the soul, just
as nothing is taken from the body.

---

12 James 5.1, 2, 3, 5.

(7) I am recalling these truths, brethren, in fear rather than because I believe something evil about you. I know, indeed, that through the goodness of God very many of you frequently receive strangers and often give alms to the poor. For this reason what I am suggesting should effect this good, that the man who was accustomed to do so does it still more, while the one who did not do so at all or perhaps did it reluctantly adopts as a habit a course of action so good for himself and so pleasing to God. Now I believe that through the inspiration of God as the special feasts approach, you dear people always observe chastity even with your own wives several days before that. Nevertheless, although it is unnecessary, at the sight of your dear selves I even remind you of what I believe you are doing. If with God's help you observe chastity throughout Lent and even to the end of Eastertide, then at that sacred Paschal feast when you are clothed with the brightness of charity, purified by almsgiving, adorned by prayer, vigils, and fasts as with heavenly, spiritual pearls, at harmony not only with your friends but also with your enemies, when you approach the altar of the Lord with a secure and easy conscience, you will be able to receive His Body and Blood, not to your judgment, but as a remedy.

(8) When we speak about almsgiving, distressing poverty should not be troubled. The man who has done what he could has fulfilled all things, because a perfect will is regarded as the fulfillment of a deed. A man is able to do this, if he is willing to consider every poor man as he does himself, and if he gives to the poor in the same way as he would want to be treated himself if he were in such need. The man who does this has fulfilled the precepts of both the Old and the New Testaments, accomplishing what the Lord says in the Gospel: "Treat others the way you would have them treat you: this sums up the law and the prophets."[13] May the good Lord bring you to this law of true and perfect charity, under His

---

13 Matt. 7.12.

protection, with the help of our Lord Jesus Christ, to whom is honor and might for ever and ever. Amen.

*Sermon 200*

A HOMILY TO THE CATECHUMENS[1]

Today, dearest brethren, the sermon of our humble self is especially directed to the catechumens. Although our exhortation is addressed particularly to them, we believe it is applicable to all of the baptized faithful who show concern for the salvation of their souls. All can profit from this humble advice, even though we wish to admonish mainly those who now desire the sacrament of baptism. First of all, then, catechumens ['fellow askers'] should know why they are called by this name. They are so called because they are asking together, just as people who are seated together are nothing else than a group sitting together or like conversationalists who speak together or fellow-runners who run together. Thus catechumens cannot be recognized as anything except those who are asking together.[2] So now catechumens have learned why they bear this name, but they should also know what they are asking.

(2) What, then, do those who desire the sacrament of baptism ask? What else except that those who were vessels of

---

1 For the sake of convenience I have adopted the term "catechumens," though Caesarius' customary term for aspirants to baptism is *conpetentes,* i.e., those, as he himself explains, who "together" (*con-*) "seek" (*-pet-*) the gift of baptism. On the *conpetentes* and the rites of Christian initiation as provided for by Caesarius at Arles, see Beck, *Pastoral Care,* chap. V.

2 It is impossible adequately to translate this passage with its original force, because there are no English words corresponding to the Latin *conpetentes—simul petentes; consedentes—simul sedentes; conloquentes —simul loquentes; concurrentes—simul currentes.*

the devil may merit to become instruments of Christ, and
that when they have received forgiveness of all of their sins
they may devote themselves to good works and desire eternal
rewards? What, I repeat, should catechumens ask? Surely this,
that those who were the habitation of demons and the cave
of robbers may deserve to become the temple of God according to what the Apostle says: "The temple of God is holy,
and you are that temple."[3] Then those who before were the
abode of the devil may become the dwelling of the Holy
Spirit, as the Apostle says: "You must know that your body is
a temple of the Holy Spirit, who is within."[4] Therefore,
brethren, as you yourselves see, catechumens ask this, that the
devil may be banished and they may merit to become the
house of God. It is a good thing you are seeking, a great thing,
the highest bliss, eternal happiness. For this reason I admonish
you with God's help devoutly to prepare both your bodies
and your hearts, because what you are asking is very great. In
truth if God wanted to offer you individual silk garments, you
would not be able to accept them with filthy, dirty hands.
How much more so, then, when He deigns to give His own
self to you, should you not receive Him except in a heart
that has been cleansed by faith? If, according to the Lord's
precept, "people do not pour new wine into old wineskins,"[5]
how will any man be able to receive God Himself, if he has
been unwilling to cleanse himself entirely of his old way of
life? Several days before Easter offer your name in such a way
that what had been written in the book of death because of
the sin of the first man may be inscribed in the book of life
through the grace of God. Although you first fought under
the most cruel tyranny of the devil, by despising him you may
return to the service of Christ, your rightful king. Approach
the imposition of hands and the blessing with oil several days
earlier, so that the devil may always find you prepared against

3  1 Cor. 3.17.
4  1 Cor. 6.19.
5  Matt. 9.17.

him like the bravest athletes. Just as athletes who are wrestlers are anointed in such a way that they cannot be grasped by their opponent, so the Holy Spirit through His ministers deigns to anoint you in such a way that the devil may not be able to ensnare you. For everything that is outwardly done to you by men is perfected inwardly in your soul by the blessing of the Holy Spirit. To be sure, a man puts his hand on your head, but the blessing comes down from heaven. Believe it to be most certain, then, that whatever is done to you bodily by the tongues or hands of men is completed spiritually in you through the ministry of angels.

(3) And so I beg and admonish all of you catechumens, and at the same time I declare and say to you that with God's help during these days and even until Easter you should carefully examine your consciences, so that not even one of you keeps hatred in your heart against anyone. If a man who is to be baptized preserves anger or hatred in his heart, I do not know whether divine grace will profit him. Indeed he is about to say: "Forgive us the wrong we have done as we forgive those who wrong us."[6] Now if what he prays is going to take place in him, what remains except for divine justice to forgive him in the same way in which he himself has forgiven others, according to what the Lord Himself said: "Give, and it shall be given to you; pardon, and you shall be pardoned"?[7] Thus the man who has not forgiven, himself closes the door of divine mercy against himself by saying "Forgive us as we forgive."[8] First of all, then, catechumens should especially pay attention to this, not to retain hatred for any man. Secondly they should question their own consciences, and if, as often happens, they have injured anyone they should quickly ask pardon. Thirdly, if they have taken anything from another through theft or false testimony or some craftiness of false weights or deceitful measures, granted that they cannot follow

6 Matt. 6.12.
7 Luke 6.38, 37.
8 Matt. 6.12.

the example of Zachaeus and restore it fourfold, they should at least pay back the equivalent. I do not know with what boldness a man thinks he can receive the grace of divine mercy, if he fails to restore the goods of another which he took away wrongfully.

(4) It is further necessary for catechumens to pay attention to this if they know that through the devil's persuasion they have committed theft or murder or adultery, or if a woman catechumen has ever taken diabolical potions for purposes of abortion and has killed her children when they were either still in the womb or already born, for this is a very grave sin. For all of these actions they should ask God's mercy with groaning and sorrow, and then come to the sacrament of baptism when they have been cleansed through repentance. Above all, catechumens who are known to be married should listen to this: before baptism they should observe chastity, and for a considerable time after baptism they should refrain from carnal pleasure.

(5) Men should flee from poisonous envy, so that they may not seem to be imitators of the devil, concerning whom it is written: "By the envy of the devil, death entered the world, and they who are in his possession experience it."[9] Pride, too, through which the devil himself fell, they should strive to avoid, because Christ whom they wish to follow was "gentle and humble of heart";[10] and very much to be feared is what is written: "God resists the proud, but to the humble he shows kindness."[11] Moreover, they should not utter lies with their lips according to what is written: "You destroy all who speak falsehood";[12] and again: "A lying mouth slays the soul."[13] Not only from perjury, but even from oaths men should keep away because He does not lie who said: "A man who often swears heaps up obligations; the scourge will never be far

9 Wisd. 2.24, 25.
10 Matt. 11.29.
11 Cf. Prov. 3.34.
12 Ps. 5.7.
13 Wisd. 1.11.

from his house."[14] During these days they should drink little wine, and when the Paschal days come, with great care should guard against intoxication or drunkenness. This is to prevent what was cleansed and made bright through the sacrament of baptism from becoming darkened through intemperance if intoxication creeps in unawares. Therefore even if some men want to force them to drink, out of wicked friendship, they should shun it altogether and never inwardly agree to it; they should rather take only what is proper and useful in food or in drink. Since the womb of Mother Church, through Christ's inspiration, has conceived all catechumens, they should practice nothing unjust or dishonest, lest by their sinful actions they shake off the flesh of their mother and that holy mother cast them forth before their proper birth like an abortion. Instead, all catechumens should be kind, humble, mild, and temperate. Then when they come to the salutary sacrament of baptism in the right course of events, they may be changed from goats into lambs and transferred from the left side to the right. With those already on the right side, they will happily hear that desirable word: "Come. You have my Father's blessing! Inherit the kingdom prepared for you from the creation of the world."[15]

(6) If your charity listens carefully, as is your custom, you can realize that although our advice is directed to the catechumens, nevertheless it can be profitable to all of the baptized faithful. For this reason those of us who were reborn in Christ a long time ago should in all respects give the example of a holy life to those who are to be baptized. Thus if they want to imitate us, they will not be drawn to death on the broad, wide road but will merit to reach life on the strait and narrow path. Not only by examples, but even by words you ought to urge them on to every good work. Above all, those who desire to receive them with pious love as sons and daughters should not cease to admonish them, both before and after they are

14 Sir. 23.12 (11).
15 Matt. 25.34.

baptized, and to teach them about chastity, humility, temperance, and peace. They should realize that they are a surety for the catechumens, because they reply for them that they will renounce the devil, his pomps and his works. For this reason both those who receive and those who are received, that is, both fathers and sons, should strive to keep the agreement which they make with Christ in the sacrament of baptism and never long for any of the devil's pomps or the wanton pleasures of this world. If with God's help those who receive the sons have lived chastely and justly, and those who are received have been willing to imitate them, as we believe, they will equally arrive at eternal rewards. With the help of our Lord Jesus Christ, who with the Father and the Holy Spirit lives and reigns for ever and ever. Amen.

*Sermon 201*

A REPROOF FOR THE PEOPLE TO BE READ AT THE RECITATION
OF THE CREED

Behold, beloved brethren, through the goodness of God the days of forgiveness now are at hand; therefore as good and perfect sons of the Church prepare your souls with the help of God. Strive to labor as much as you can, in order that on the sacred festival of the Pasch your banquets may be so temperate and moderate that the holy and desirable festivity will not be turned into grief for us through the sin of intemperance. For if after holy fasting excess in food or drink creeps in imperceptibly, it will immediately germinate thorns of passion, as well as destroy and undermine by dissipation of the flesh the fruits of chastity which you happily acquired throughout the whole of Lent.

(2) Because I know that on account of your faith and devotion you intend to invite again to your feast some of the new converts, I admonish you, brethren, and I likewise warn you that no one of you should either encourage or urge them to drink more than is proper. Do not let them seem to defile, by intoxication or drunkenness, the robe of baptism which they have merited to receive through the gift of heavenly grace. You yourselves ought all the more to be sober and always to speak what is good and honorable at your feasts, and alternately to recite from the Scriptures something which pertains to the salvation of the soul. If those who have been clothed in white garments are willing to imitate you when you act in this way, they may merit to reach eternal bliss along with you. For just as the man who shows new converts the example of an evil life will have to render an account both for himself and for them on the day of judgment, so on the contrary, those who are willing to rouse them to good conduct by their words and to incite them by pious deeds will merit to receive a double reward in eternity when the Lord repays.

(3) Although I believe, dearest brethren, that through the goodness of God you faithfully preserve cleanness of heart and body at the Paschal feast, yet anticipating your charity and because of my love and paternal solicitude for you, I suggest again what I have frequently advised. With the Lord's help preserve even to the end of the Paschal feast the chastity which you maintained throughout Lent out of love for Him, as we believe. Thus if in the whole Paschal solemnity, with a clean heart and chaste body you reserve in your heart hatred against no man, you will be able to approach the altar of the Lord with a free mind, and with a peaceful conscience receive His Body and Blood, not to judgment but as a remedy for your soul. May He deign to grant this, who lives and reigns forever. Amen.

*Sermon 202*

## ON THE LORD'S SUPPER

Today, dearest brethren, we are going to hear the Evangelist say that "when the Lord had risen from the meal, he took off his cloak, tied a towel around himself, and began to wash his disciples' feet."[1] What shall we say about this occasion, most beloved? Or what excuse will we be able to offer, we who scorn to give to strangers the service which He deigned to offer to His servants? Possibly there are some powerful and noble men or delicate women who scorn to bend down to the footsteps of the saints who are sojourning in this world. Not only do they themselves refuse to wash the feet of strangers, but neither do they command any of their servants to do it for them. Perhaps Christian men or women blush to touch the feet of the saints in this world with their delicate hands, because the prerogative of birth does not allow it. Wicked nobility, which makes itself ignoble before God through pride! The noble and mighty blush to wash the feet of saints and strangers in this world, but if they do not amend their lives, they will have more to be ashamed of and to lament when they will have to be separated from companionship with them in the future life. Then they will be tormented without any remedy of repentance, when they shall see those whom they despised receive the kingdom because of their humility, while they on account of their pride have merited punishment. Let us fear, brethren, what the blessed Apostle Peter feared, when he heard the Lord say: "If I do not wash you, you will have no share in my heritage."[2] For if, perchance, we disdain to wash the feet of the saints, we will not merit to have a share with

1 Cf. John 13.4, 5.
2 John 13.8.

them. Let us rather bend down to the feet of saints or of strangers; because when we fulfill this service with holy humility, indeed we are not merely touching their feet with our hands, but we are cleansing the meanness and filth of our souls through faith and humility, and we are cleansing not only the smallest, but even the most serious of our sins.

(2) Rejoice, therefore, dearly beloved, and be glad in the Lord who has consecrated for us on this day the mystery of health-giving comfort. What led the Lord to commit to us His body and blood? What, indeed, but His humility? For if He were not humble, He would not be eaten or drunk. Reflect on the sublimity of Him: "In the beginning was the Word; the Word was in God's presence, and the Word was God."[3] Behold the nature of the eternal food! Angels partake of it, the powers on high partake of it, the heavenly spirits partake of it, they eat and are filled; and still what satisfies and fills them with joy remains whole and entire. But what man is able to ascend to that food? Because man could not ascend to partake of that bread, for this reason the bread itself deigned to descend to man, and this indeed was done with ineffable compassion. Because it was fitting that the food of angels should give nourishment and come down even to His little ones. This the wisdom of God did, thus He fed us with heavenly bread by assuming flesh, for "the Word became flesh and made his dwelling among us."[4] Consider, then, His humility, for "the bread of the angels was eaten by men";[5] that is, the eternal Word, by which the angels are fed and which is equal to the Father, became the nourishment of man.

(3) Therefore, dearest brethren, because our Lord has taught us patience, has freed us from punishment, and has redeemed us from death, let us always trust in the Lord and let us presume nothing against His will and without His

3 John 1.1.
4 John 1.14.
5 Ps. 77 (78).25.

assistance. For you know what blessed Peter rashly promised Christ: "Though all may have their faith in you shaken," he said, "mine will never be shaken."[6] The Lord, who knew the weakness of human nature, also knew that virtue lies, not in the promise, but in fulfillment of the promise, and He said, "I give you my word, before the cock crows tonight you will deny me three times."[7] Blessed Peter answered him, "Even though I have to die with you, I will never disown you."[8] Consider, brethren, the response of this disciple, and understand that what he said sprang from love. Now because what he willed was promised only through the eagerness of his love, without the added help of the Lord, what depended on divine help could not stand by relying only on man. Indeed he was strong in the act of the will, but not in courage, just as the Lord Himself said, "The spirit is willing but nature is weak";[9] and also: "Apart from me you can do nothing."[10] He promised even unto death and then denied Christ in time of fear. He would have made a wonderful confession of faith, if he would have possessed courage in fulfilling it.

(4) Because of all of this, most beloved brethren, I warn and admonish you that everyone should revert to the only qualified witness, his own conscience. If there he discovers any wounds of sins, let him have recourse to the healing power of tears; let him be sorry for what he did; let him begin to attend most vigilantly to his past actions, to avoid present sins, to anticipate future ones, and to banish every evil with the assistance of God; because as long as a man is ignorant of how long he can live in this world, he cannot escape if repentance does not precede him. Before all else, most beloved brethren, reflect, with dutiful faith and with

---

6 Matt. 26.33.
7 Matt. 26.34.
8 Matt. 26.35.
9 Matt. 26.41.
10 John 15.5.

all the devotion of your soul, on what pertains particularly
to the faithful, that you are about to approach the altar of
your Lord and God. Observe all the hidden places of your
heart, lest by chance there be some sins there which have not
yet been cared for by almsgiving and fasting. Moreover, fear
the words of the Apostle: "Whoever eats the body and drinks
the blood of the Lord unworthily sins against the body and
blood of the Lord. A man should examine himself first; only
then should he eat of the bread and drink of the cup."[11] Let
no one of you harbor in his heart hatred against any man, so
that you will be able to say fearlessly: "Forgive us the wrong
we have done as we forgive those who wrong us."[12] Before
all else, guard your chastity, restrain your appetite, shun
drunkenness, and give alms to the poor according to your
means.

(5) And I ask this above all, dearest brethren, that tomorrow you may perfect in the passion of the Lord that joy
which you have given us thus far because of your devotedness.
For it is not he who begins, but he "who holds out till the
end will escape death."[13] Therefore you ought to act in such
a way that you do not destroy through a single day's negli-
gence what you have acquired throughout the entire forty
days of Lent. For if someone were zealous to fast, to pray, or
to chant the psalms all during Lent, and at the time of the
Lord's passion, that is, at the Passover, were to withdraw
from church, it would be the same as if someone were to be
anxious to cultivate his land at great effort and not deserve
to receive the harvest. Therefore I beseech you that no one
withdraw himself from church, unless by chance either bodily
infirmity or great and important duties keep him busy. For
a man will be able to occasion real joy at the Paschal solemnity
if he refuses to withdraw from the church's services at the
Lord's passion. I have confidence that anyone who willingly

11  1 Cor. 11.27, 28.
12  Matt. 6.12.
13  Matt. 10.22; 24.13.

listens to me in this suggestion will be repaid by God both in this world and in the next with glorious rewards. May He deign to grant this, who with the Father and the Holy Spirit lives and reigns world without end. Amen.

* *Sermon 203*

A HOMILY ON THE PASCH[1]

Rejoice, dearest brethren, because the price of our redemption has been paid. We cost a considerable amount, since He who redeemed us became the purchase price. Christ our Lord and Savior was born in such a way as to teach us, He died as He did to heal us, and He arose again in order to reward us. The cross brought death to Christ but salvation to the Christian. The Savior appeared showing all the marks of His divinity, for a star followed Him after His birth, glory after His burial. An angel, who had announced that He was to be born, watches His exit from life. Hell relinquishes its victor, and heaven receives Him in triumph. By His birth He removed error, and by dying He trampled death under foot. He called back from hell man whom He had created; on His cross hung both our ransom-price and our heaven. The creature which formerly had been covered with darkness because of sin returned to the light with the Lord, for from the light you deserved to receive light, which you had lost when Christ closed His eyes. Let heaven cast out the darkness which our Savior refused even to hell. The elements which had mourned should rejoice at this, that Christ lost nothing of His majesty when He freed man whom He had created.

(2) The perfidious Jews, however, sealed the stone of the

---

1 Pieced together, Morin tells us, from passages in sermons of the Eusebian collection, but the conclusion is typically Caesarian.

tomb so that Christ might not have a way to get out. But if
the world does not receive Him, how can a tomb keep him?
How can He who rules everywhere be held within a tomb?
It might be difficult to rise from the dead, if He had not
raised other men to life before He arose again. How could
He fail to leave the grave, when He came forth from an
undefiled womb through chaste virginity? He deceived the
guards, left the tomb, and appeared to the disciples although
the doors were not open. He left the former even though He
was shut in, and He entered the latter in spite of being shut
out. Even in death He revealed the hidden secret of His
boundless majesty. He who was crucified returned from hell
and is in triumph. Thomas, put your hand into the side
of your Savior; touch the wounds which our sins caused,
examine where the blood flowed from in order that it might
give us a cup of healing medicine. Look at our purchase-price,
Thomas, carefully notice the marks of the nails, and in those
very wounds recognize the medicine which is a treasury of
the human race. If He had not been fastened to this wood,
the sin of that wood would by no means be removed. That is
why He willed to be pierced Himself, so that sin might strike
us no longer; He delivered up the innocent in order that
He might free the guilty. Who could worthily describe such
great goodness? An innocent person is struck down, in order
that one who is more guilty may be set free; the son is killed,
in order that the servant may be ransomed. He performs the
service of a kind and very brave king, while He shows the
scars which He received for the salvation of His people.

(3) Look at the empty tomb, Pharisees, and learn the wickedness of your crime. We recognize the nails which you fastened, and we adore Him whom you killed. See whom you
have offended. At His resurrection the Lord could have
closed the places where the nails were fastened, but they
were kept open for this purpose, so that those who had
committed this sacrilege might see them and be confounded.

O Pharisees, we see that you are wicked and provident; death was administered to one man in order that it might be taken away from everyone. However, when Christ our Lord accepted death, He did not feel its destroying effects, just as virginity did not lose its integrity when He was born. Hurry, disciples, and since you have received authority, spread abroad through all nations. Let those who are born of the flesh be reborn in spirit; let the water of baptism wash clean whatever sin has defiled. Let all nations be baptized in the name of the Father and of the Son and of the Holy Spirit, in order to fulfill what was written: "No one can enter into God's kingdom without being begotten of water and Spirit."[2]

(4) We ourselves, beloved, who have been made worthy to be freed from the prison of hell and from the darkness of eternal night without any preceding merits of our own, should strive to live so moderately, chastely and devoutly that we may keep our baptismal robe spotless and free from any stain of sin. Then we may happily come to the dwelling of the eternal bridegroom and to that heavenly nuptial feast, shining with charity and adorned with the pearls of good works: with the help of Him who lives and reigns with the Father and the Holy Spirit for ever and ever. Amen.

## * Sermon 204

### On the Lord's Pasch[1]

The Pasch of Christ, dearest brethren, is the kingdom of heaven, the salvation of the world, the destruction of the

---

2 John 3.5.

---

1 In his discussion of the origin and relations of this sermon, Morin finds that the true style of Caesarius begins with section 4, the earlier sections having been drawn from Maximus of Turin.

damned, the glory of those in heaven, the life of believers, the resurrection of the dead, a testimony of divine mercy, the price of human redemption and the grief of death, which it has destroyed. This feast of God, which was consecrated in mystery and is recognized in a sacrament, announces through angels the power of the Lord's resurrection, manifests it through the apostles, and increases through the just hearts of believers. Therefore, dearly beloved, "this is the day the Lord has made,"[2] a day more illustrious for all, more joyful for everyone. On it, as you have heard, the Lord arose, raised from the dead the bodies of the blessed, and acquired for Himself a new people, by the spirit of regeneration. As you yourselves see, on this day He filled the minds of each one with joy and exultation and adorned the face of the earth with the beauty of seasons and a variety of creatures. Truly this day of the Lord's resurrection is a foretelling of the eternal resurrection. For the resurrection of Christ is life for the dead, pardon for sinners, and glory for the saints. Indeed it elevates men from the depths by the effect of virtue, lifts them up from earthly things, establishes them on high, perfects the just, strengthens the doubtful, and damns the unbelieving. To this end the Lord arose today, in order that He might show us an example of our future resurrection. Therefore the people of God, by rising today through life-giving baptism, brighten our Church in the manner of the resurrection with the splendor of snow-white beauty.

(2) We should give thanks to our God, for while we celebrate the solemnity of the holy Pasch, we already see the beauty of future resurrection. For as the human race is destined to arise after death at the end of the world, so they now rise in baptism. Then the people of God must be raised up after the sleep of death, but now they are raised up after faithlessness; then they must be freed from their condition of mortality, but now they are freed from the blindness of ig-

---

2 Ps. 117 (118).24.

norance; then they are to be reborn to eternity, but now they are reborn to salvation. Now all of those who, although formerly baptized in Christ, are not able to put on a white garment, should at least not abandon their spotless way of life. A soul that is quite pure often is hidden under a dark appearance, nor does it make much difference if a man does not have a white garment. Such was that robber in the Gospel who, when he was crucified with the Savior, is said to have exclaimed: "Jesus, remember me when you enter upon your reign."[3] Observe, therefore, dearly beloved, and see what faith obtains, what holy devotion merits. The robber on the cross demands the kingdom of the Savior, and while he suffers a like penalty he is brought to eternal rewards. Therefore imitate his devotion, imitate his love. The kingdom of Christ, which the robber demands at his death, do you desire by a good life. Paradise is opened because of his faith, and strength is shown to our hope of eternal rewards. Let us be happy, then, and exult on this day when, by rising, the Lord brought peace and salvation. If our hearts are at peace through Him and in Him, we may celebrate with joy the Paschal feast and may happily come to eternal rewards.

(3) Through the goodness of Christ I have such confidence in your charity and most faithful devotion, dearest brethren, that I freely and with every assurance presume to suggest and mention to your charity all the things which I know are necessary for your salvation. For this reason, too, I beg and admonish you. As often as the Paschal feast comes, if any men or women spiritually receive sons from the sacred fount, they should realize that they are bondsmen for them in the sight of God, and therefore should bestow on them the solicitude of true love. They should admonish, reprove, and rebuke them, in order that they may cling to justice, guard chastity, preserve virginity until marriage, refrain from curses or false oaths, and not utter evil or wanton songs with their lips.

---

3 Luke 23.42.

They should further not be proud or envious, not retain anger or hatred in their hearts, not consult fortune tellers, never hang amulets or devilish signs on themselves or their household. Let them avoid magicians as ministers of the devil, hold to the Catholic faith, eagerly and often attend church services, condemn verbosity, and listen to the divine lessons with attentive ears. Let them receive strangers and, in accord with what was done for themselves in baptism, wash the feet of their guests; they should also both keep peace themselves and strive to recall the discordant to harmony, and they should pay to priests and to their parents the honor and love of true charity. If, then, you endeavor to admonish your sons and daughters about all these truths and similar things, then you will happily come to eternal bliss along with them.

(4) Let no one deceive himself, dearest brethren; "none of us lives as his own master and none of us dies as his own master."[4] As I have frequently suggested, however many people anyone has edified by the example of a holy life, with that many and on behalf of that many he will receive a reward of happy recompense. On the other hand to however many he has given the example of a wicked life, even if they do not follow him, still he knows that he is going to render an evil account for all of them. For this reason, as I have already suggested above, with the Lord's help we ought to show our new converts the example of a good life, as far as we can. Thus we will merit, not to receive punishment because of their subversion, but rather to obtain the forgiveness of sins for edifying them. With the help of our Lord Jesus Christ, who lives and reigns for ever and ever. Amen.

---

4 Rom. 14.7.

## * Sermon 205

### A Homily of St. Augustine on the Pasch[1]

Although the singing of the Alleluia is delightful for us both to utter and to hear at every season, dearest brethren, we have become accustomed to listen to it more particularly and with greater pleasure on these days. For Alleluia is interpreted as "Praise God." To be sure, that is a short word, but it is great praise. Now because, whenever we sing Alleluia we are known to praise God, we ought to consider and faithfully to see that what resounds in the mouth is kept in the heart. This should be done lest perchance when Alleluia, that is praise of God, is spoken with the mouth, shameful or wicked thoughts be kept in the heart, or lest while our tongue praises God, evil thoughts destroy our soul. Therefore let us praise God, dearest brethren, in word and in our hearts, by our lives and by our tongues, in words and in deeds. For thus God wants Alleluia to be said to Him, so that there is no discord in the one who praises Him. May our tongue first agree with our life, our mouth with our conscience, our speech with our habits, lest perhaps our good words bear testimony against our evil life.

(2) The days which are now passing, dearest brethren, are allotted to the sacrament of infants. Those who were called catechumens before are now called infants. They used to be called catechumens, when they were striking against their mother's womb in order that they might be born by asking it;[2] they are called infants because, although they had been born earlier in the world, they were just reborn in Christ. In them is a new life which should already be perfected in us. For this reason those of you who are already believers should

---

1 Morin notes derivations from Augustine, effected, however, in the fashion characteristic of Caesarius.
2 Cf. Sermon 200 n. 1.

not give these infants examples whereby they will perish but those from which they can profit. Those who were just born notice how you live who were born some time ago. This is also done by children, who are seen to be born of their carnal parents according to Adam. First they are very small children, but afterwards, when they have begun to notice the habits of their elders, they pay attention to what they should imitate; the younger follows where the older one leads. Now we should pray to God that the older walk ahead by means of a good way of life, lest perhaps, if the younger follows the older on an evil path, both the one and the other perish.

(3) Therefore, dearest brethren, who have already been reborn in Christ for a long time, and who are their parents through a life of rebirth, I encourage and exhort you to live so justly, chastely, and moderately that not only will you not be lost with those who imitate you, but that rather you may happily reach eternal joys. Someone just reborn in Christ sees a believer who has already been baptized for a long time nevertheless given to drunkenness. I am afraid that he says in his heart: Why can I not act the same way? is not this man a believer? does he not communicate at the altar? and he drinks so much that he frequently appears intoxicated. He sees another man speaking wanton words and singing disgraceful love songs. If he desires to listen willingly or to imitate him, he will perish along with him, if suitable regret for his sin does not come to his aid. For this reason, dearest brethren, men who deceive those who are good by the example of their wicked deeds will have to render an evil account to God both for themselves and for those other men.

(4) But now let us address those who were just baptized. I admonish and exhort you whom the grace of Christ has changed from chaff into grain. I beseech you and warn you, "not to receive the grace of God in vain."[3] Always strive to be grain, but, as much as you can, avoid and flee from the

---

3 2 Cor. 6.1.

chaff, which is carried about by the wind. Do not follow the wicked, for if you will to imitate them you will perish along with them. Stay on the threshing-floor by the weight of your charity, so the blast of pride does not toss you out like chaff. For this reason I beseech you, brethren, as sons, as the new seeds of our mother, the Church, and through the grace which you have received I adjure you to think continually of Christ whose members you have merited to be. Follow Christ who has called you, who sought you when you were lost. Do not follow the paths of the wicked in whom the name of "the faithful" goes astray, and in whom the sacraments of Christ suffer harm. The question is not what they are called, but whether they correspond to their title. Now I am addressing and warning the man who lives carelessly. If you have been born, where is your new life? If you are a believer, where is your faith? I hear a name, but I recognize the reality. You, my sons, you a new planting, choose for yourselves the ones whom you should imitate—those who fear God, who enter His church with fear, who listen carefully to His word, who retain it in their memory, and who fulfill it in deed. Choose such men for your imitation. No one should say within his heart: And where will I be able to find such people? Every like thing is attracted to another like one. If you have lived in a wicked manner, you unite to yourself none but the wicked. Begin to live well; do you see how many companions surround you, in how large a group of friends you rejoice? Finally, do you not find anything to imitate? Then be such that someone else may imitate you. For if you are willing to consider these truths carefully, brethren, you will strive to show the example of a good life to all men, and you will happily receive eternal rewards both for yourself and for the others. With the help of our Lord Jesus Christ, who lives and reigns with the Father and the Holy Spirit for ever and ever. Amen.

*Sermon 206*

AN ADMONITION OF ST. AUGUSTINE, THAT NOT ONLY WITH THE
TONGUE SHOULD GOD BE PRAISED, BUT BY OUR LIFE AND DEEDS;
IN ADDITION, THAT WHAT FOLLOWS IN DEED WILL BE THE
SAME AS WHAT IS THOUGHT WITHIN THE HEART; ALSO ON THE
PUNISHMENTS OF PURGATORY AND ON THE ABYSS OF HELL[1]

The resurrection and glorification of our Lord Jesus Christ,
dearest brethren, shows us the kind of life we are going to
receive when He comes to restore what is just to the upright,
evil to the wicked, and good things to the just. To be sure,
all wicked men can now sing Alleluia with us. However, if
they persevere in their evil life, they will be able to sing the
hymn of our future life with their lips, but they cannot obtain
that life which then will exist in Him in truth, although now
it is only signified. This will be the case because they have
refused to reflect before it comes and have been unwilling to
cling to what was destined to come. For this reason, dearest
brethren, we are now exhorting you to praise God, and this is
what we all tell ourselves when we say Alleluia: Praise God.
You tell another, he tells it to you, for when all exhort one
another, they all do what they are urging. But praise God
with your whole self; that is, not only your tongue and voice
should praise God, but also your senses, your life and your
deeds. Indeed we praise Him now when we are gathered in
church, but when each one goes his own way, as it were, he
ceases to praise God. If a man does not cease to live well, he
is always praising God. You cease to praise God at the time
when you turn away from justice and from whatever is pleasing to Him. If you never desist from a good life, even though
your tongue is silent, your life shouts aloud, and the ears of
God look to your heart. Just as our ears are attuned to our

---

1 Morin notes that the whole first section is drawn from Augustine's
  *Enarratio* on Ps. 148, and that "Eusebian" elements also may be noted.

words, so the ears of God are attuned to our thoughts. It is
impossible for the man who has good thoughts to have wicked
deeds, for actions proceed from thought. No one can do anything or move his body toward any action, if the command of
thought has not come first. In the same way, whatever a ruler
commands or whatever you see happening throughout the
provinces issues from within a palace, although it is directed
throughout the Roman empire. How much activity takes
place at the single command of the ruler who is seated inside!
He only moves his lips when he speaks, and still the whole
province is moved when what he says is carried out. Thus, too,
there is within each one of us a ruler seated in our heart. If a
good man orders good actions, good things happen; if an evil
man orders evil actions, evil results. When Christ is seated
there, what can He order except what is good? When the devil
is in possession, what can he command except evil? Moreover,
God has placed it in your choice for whom you will prepare
a place, whether for God or for the devil. When preparations
have been made, the one who takes possession will give the
commands. For this reason, brethren, do not listen only to the
sound; when you praise God, do so with all of your being.
Let your voice sing, but also your life and your deeds. If there
still are groaning, tribulation, and temptation, hope that all
of these things are passing and that the day will come when
we shall give praise without any defect.

(2) In the meantime, until that day comes, when we shall
merit to be joined with the angels and to praise God without
any weariness and without end, let us strive to devote ourselves to good works as much as we can so that we may be able
to reach that ineffable joy. As we daily examine our consciences, if we know that there is something on the garment of
our soul either torn by neglect, sullied by dissipation, consumed by wrath, cut apart by envy, or darkened by avarice,
with God's help let us hasten to heal what was wounded while
it is still within our power to do so. Let us quickly restore what

was lost and recall to the brightness of justice what had become darkened, so that if, perchance, we come before the tribunal of the eternal judge destitute of good works and covered with the filthy garments of vice, that terrible sentence may not be directed to us: "Out of my sight, you condemned, into that everlasting fire prepared for the devil and his angels!"[2] Therefore let us endeavor to produce fruits of justice as much as we can, fearing what the Lord said: "Every tree that is not fruitful will be cut down and thrown into the fire."[3] This sentence clearly shows that not only the fact of having done evil, but even the neglect of good will be deserving of condemnation. For this reason let us with attentive hearts continually think about what we have said, so that we will not repent too late, when we are in sight of the eternal fire which will examine our hearts, our interior, and our very thoughts. Then each one who is to be punished will ardently wish that he had never coveted the wife of another, that he had never defiled the garment of his own body or the silk garment of baptism, that he had never neglected the advice and admonitions of priests! For if it is very dangerous for priests not to rebuke the sins of others, how much more dangerous will it be to have refused to correct one's own sins, and not only not to have corrected them but even to have defended them and to have added to them by this self-defense?

(3) And so the inextinguishable fire after death will have to make amends for whatever a healing repentance and a salutary conversion have refused to repair here on earth. The burning pit of hell will be open, and there will be a way down to it but no rising from it. There souls without the garment of faith and dead through mortal sin will be buried forever. They will have to be cast into the outer darkness, where God will not visit; because they have unhappily been shut out into the outer darkness, they will have to be shut in even more unhappily. Concerning this pit the prophet prays and says:

---

2  Matt. 25.41.
3  Matt. 3.10.

"Let not the abyss swallow me up, nor the pit close its mouth over me."[4] Now this is why he said "nor the pit close its mouth over me," because when it has received wretched sinners without the remedy of repentance, it will be closed from above and opened downwards. There will be a wide path into the abyss, but no breath or free respiration will be left when the doors press down from above. As they take leave of the creatures of nature, they will be pushed down there, and since they refused to know God they will henceforth not be recognized by Him; those who are about to die to life are destined to live to endless death. Happy the men who now make good use of their opportunities. Because they are either content with what is necessary for their bodies or generous with their possessions, chaste themselves, and not cruel to others, they free themselves from the fiery night of this deep pit. This punishment awaits those who have lost their baptismal innocence and have not had it restored by repentance. They will be lost forever, and to them it is said: "But the chaff he will burn in unquenchable fire."[5] However concerning those who have done what is deserving of temporal punishment, the Apostle says: "If a man's work burns, he will suffer loss; he himself will be saved, but only as through fire."[6] This is the fiery river about which the prophet's word says: "A surging stream of fire flowed out before him."[7] They will cross through this fiery river and the shallow water that is dreadful because of burning masses of flame. The delay in crossing will be in proportion to the amount of sin; the discipline of fire will in true proportion inflict as much punishment upon a man as his guilt demands, and wise pain will rage in proportion to what foolish sinfulness committed. Somewhere the divine word compares the soul of the sinner to a bronze pot, when it says, "Set the pot empty on the coals till its bronze

4 Ps. 68 (69).16.
5 Matt. 3.12.
6 1 Cor. 3.15.
7 Cf. Dan. 7.10.

glows red and its tin melts."[8] There idle words and unkind
or mean thoughts, there a multitude of slight sins which had
defiled the purity of glorious human nature will disappear;
there the tin or lead of various sins which had crept in to
obscure the divine image will be destroyed. Here, all of these
things might have been removed from the soul, in a quick
transaction, through almsgiving and tears of repentance.
Thus He who gave Himself for man's sake and fastened the
laws of death when He was bound by nails will demand from
man an accounting. Since this is true, dearly beloved, let us
understand that men will not be able to avoid the intolerable
punishments and eternal fire, unless they have first extinguished within themselves the fire of carnal desire and manifold passions. For this reason, dearest brethren, let us turn
ourselves to better actions while the remedies are still in our
power. Let us hasten, while we still possess the light of life,
and let us not neglect the fleeting time of salvation. By dying
to sin let us destroy death here, and by the merits of our life
here let us acquire life.

*Sermon 207*

## On the Rogation Days[1]

Behold, dearly beloved, holy, spiritual days are approaching, days which are medicine for our souls, and so whoever
wants to heal the wounds of his sins should not despise the
salutary potion. The man who does not feel that he is sick

---

8 Cf. Ezech. 24.11. Where most texts show a word meaning 'filth' or the
like, our text shows *stagnum;* this word, Morin states, is written for
*stannum,* which means either an alloy of silver and lead or tin.

1 Beck, *Pastoral Care* 104-06, deals with Rogationtide as observed in
sixth-century Arles.

does not need a physician. But who is there, dearly beloved, who rejoices that he can defend himself in the arena of this world in such a way that he can receive no wound from the devil? Or who has always been able to stand so armed against many thousands of demons by day and by night, that he has never been struck by the cunning of the devil? Who could enumerate—not to say imagine—the deceits and snares of the ancient enemy concerning whom it is written: "He has a thousand names, a thousand means of doing harm"?[2] For this reason, dearest brethren, just as he always tries to wound us from every side, so with God's help each one of us should be prepared with all our strength against his plots. Because he strives to weaken us not only through difficult circumstances but also through agreeable ones, and we often receive wounds inflicted by him that are not only unpleasant but—what is worse—even unfortunately pleasant, we should always keep spiritual medicines ready. Therefore let us listen to the advice of the blessed Apostle, and protect ourselves against the snares of the devil with spiritual weapons. "Hold faith up before you as your shield," he says, "with justice as your breastplate, the helmet of salvation and the sword of the spirit, the word of God."[3] For what evil will a man be able to suffer from the devil, if he has provided himself with such weapons? The devil rises up with faithlessness, do you arise with faith; he fights with pride, do you do so with humility; he displays wantonness, but you should preserve chastity; he seizes upon wickedness, so you hold fast to justice; he brings anger, but you strive after patience; he instigates covetousness, but do you exercise mercy; he shows gluttony, do you practice temperance; he shows wickedness, but you should exhibit goodness. Likewise in other matters we should always strive to extend opposing weapons against the wickedness of the devil; then his snares will be able to deceive us either never or only with difficulty. Therefore in order that with

2 Vergil, *Aeneid* 7.337.
3 Eph. 6.16, 14, 17.

God's help we may be able to fulfill these actions and to conquer that most cunning enemy, with grace assisting us to discern him, we should continually provide for ourselves the
arms of fasting, vigils, and prayers.

(3) Now although these things are proved to be necessary
at all times, especially on these three days which the Church
regularly solemnizes throughout the world, no one should
withdraw himself from the holy assembly. No one should
leave the Church, which is the school of the heavenly physician, or desert the spiritual camp because he is involved in
earthly activities. For you know, dearest brethren, that if a
man who fights for an earthly king withdraws from battle
just as he is about to enter the contest, because he is con-
strained by fear, not only does he fail to receive the glory and
the rewards prepared for him, but he even does not escape
danger in the present life. For this reason the man who leaves
Christ's Church on these three days doubtless should be considered like the one who deserts the army of an earthly king.
So if a man deserts the people of God on these days without
some illness or a definite engagement, he should realize that
he is going to receive from that heavenly king not reward but
reproach, not glory but dishonor. Indeed, just as if he were a
fugitive or a deserter from the heavenly camp, such a man
will suffer eternal confusion and a punishment worthy of his
merits. However, dearest brethren, far be it from us to suspect
such things of you. Rather than think something bad about
you, I fearfully presume to suggest this. Trusting more in your
devotion, I believe that like very wise bees you faithfully
hasten to the beehive of Christ, in order that you may be
able to receive the sweetness of spiritual honey from the
divine lessons. Then with the prophet you may say: "How
sweet to my palate are your promises, O Lord; sweeter than
honey from the honeycomb to my mouth!"[4]

---

4 Ps. 118 (119).103.

(3) Because throughout the year, dearest brethren, the wounds of our sins deceive us, so on these three days let us faithfully hasten to church. With a contrite heart and humbled body let us beseech the mercy of God, so that by these three days of healing devotion we may restore all the wounds of our sins to their former health, as if a spiritual antidote had been received. Not only on these days but at all times avoid the gaming-table, which, as a nursery of sins, is contrary to the salvation of one's soul. Therefore no one should purposely endeavor to provide occupations for himself or to busy himself with idle gossip, lest he inflict wounds on himself from the very source from which he might have prepared a remedy. On these three days no one should let himself be bled or accept a potion, unless perchance a very critical illness makes this necessary. Except for the sick who must take a little meat, let us prepare for ourselves small meals as we do in Lent. By reading, singing the psalms, and praying, let us seek a spiritual banquet for our souls rather than bodily pleasures. If we are entirely devoted to God and humbly implore His mercy, through the mercy of God we may deserve to be healed of all of our infirmities, rescued from all of our sins, set free from the very frequent flooding of waters. We ought to believe for certain, dearest brethren, that if our sins cease, the divine mercy will immediately remove the punishments which were due to us. Thus He Himself has deigned to promise through the prophet when he said: "Return to me, and I will return to you,"[5] and again: "If you groan and return to me, then you shall be saved."[6] Therefore let us turn to a better life while the remedies are still in our power. By our good deeds let us summon to mercy the kind and merciful Lord whom we provoked by our sins. According to His usual practice, He will then deign to keep adversities from us and in His clemency to grant us good fortune.

---

5 Zach. 1.3.
6 Cf. Isa. 30.15.

(4) Again and again I beseech you, as I have already said.
People who hasten with solid devotion to the beehive of the
Church as to the exceedingly sweet honeycomb of Christ, like
very wise bees prepare within themselves from the variegated
flowers of Sacred Scripture little cells from which they may
take holy, heavenly honey. However, those who come late or
leave too soon and are not satisfied to wait until the divine
mysteries are finished should not be considered part of the
swarm of Christ. Such men do not gather spiritual honey by
means of their good conduct, but through their pride and
contempt they both confound themselves and pervert others
by the wicked example of their life. Therefore, dearest brethren, men who truly love God, come to church without delay,
and leave late should persevere in their good work. As they
reject idle or worldly stories like the poison of the devil, they
should rather endeavor to sing psalms and to pray; despising
the bitterness of this world, they should seek in church the
source from which they may receive the sweetness of Christ.
Men who are careless not only come to church late but also
depart before the divine mysteries are finished, and even in
church they are busy with idle gossip, do not sing the psalms
themselves, and do not permit others to sing them or to pray.
People of this kind should quickly amend their lives, so that
they may not procure death for themselves in the very place
where they could have found life. I am advising what is within
my authority; the man who despises the herald should fear
the judge. The iron instruments of a physician are hard, but
they make men well; the pleasures of this world are delightful, but they deceive in a wicked fashion. For this reason
listen to me when I beg you, brethren, hear me giving you
advice with fatherly devotion, so that in this world God may
grant you bodily health, fruitful abundance, and the forgiveness of your sins, and in the future life enable you to
reach the happy attainment of eternal rewards. Let the divine
goodness so regulate our actions and deign to direct our

souls, that when the time of retribution comes, I who am admonishing you with love may merit to obtain pardon, and your dear selves may reach the crown because of your loving obedience. With the help of our Lord Jesus Christ.

## Sermon 208

### ON THE ROGATION DAYS

We ought to know and understand, dearest brethren, that we are solemnizing days of humility and repentance. For this reason we should not become dissipated through excessive laughter or in careless and unbecoming mirth, fearing what the Lord said in the Gospel: "Woe to you who laugh, for you shall weep in your grief";[1] and elsewhere it is written: "The end of joy may be sorrow."[2] It should not seem harsh to some people that we seem to invite you to sadness and mourning rather than to joy and gladness. For if you listen carefully, brethren, our Lord exhorts and admonishes this in all of the Scriptures, that we should be solicitous in this world in order that we may be free from anxiety in the world to come. As the psalmist says, "Those that sow in tears shall reap rejoicing,"[3] and in the Gospel we read, "Blest are the sorrowing; they shall be consoled."[4] Since "strait and narrow is the road that leads to life, wide and clear the road that leads to death,"[5] it is better for us to reach eternal bliss after a few difficulties than to go down into the depths of hell after brief joy. That is why we ought to work with all of our strength, so that we may be able to avoid the punishment of the rich man who was clothed in purple, and to attain the blessedness of the

1 Luke 6.25.
2 Prov. 14.13.
3 Ps. 125 (126).5.
4 Matt. 5.5 (4).
5 Cf. Matt. 7.14, 13.

poor man, Lazarus. For in what way did pride help that rich man? Here that excessively wealthy man was fed on his delicacies for a short time, and now he feeds the endless flames of hell with the marrow of his bones. For this reason it is better for us to invite you to salutary grief for a short time, and afterwards merit to reach eternal joy together with you, than to suffer eternal bitterness with you afterwards, if we have been willing to bring you temporary false pleasure.

(2) Now at all times, dearest brethren, you ought to seek God's mercy with repentant body and remorseful heart, and devoutly to beg Him for the forgiveness of sins. However, we ought to implore the mercy of God with loud crying and groaning, continuous prayers, and more abundant almsgiving, because an exceedingly burdensome dryness which is due to our sins is threatening us. May He grant us the blessing of heavenly waters and deign to restore peace, to give us the forgiveness of our sins, to bestow good things on us because of His kindness. On these days, especially, let us try to put an end to idle gossip and strive to pray and sing the psalms as much as our strength permits. If we desire to receive the peace of the season, let us not dissimulate the observance of peace with our neighbors. For if you want the devil, your enemy, to be overcome in truth, let your neighbor promptly be reconciled with you. Let your anger rage against no man, and the divine indignation will immediately desist from you, according to that promise of our Lord and Savior: "If you forgive the faults of others, your heavenly Father will forgive you yours."[6]

(3) No one should purposely look for tasks whereby he can withdraw himself from the assembly in church. Doubtless a man loves the wounds of his sins if on these three days he does not seek spiritual medicine for himself by fasting, prayer, and the singing of psalms. Sins abound, and the acts of neglect which we have heaped up in the space of a whole year

6 Matt. 6.14.

are exceedingly many. For this reason, then, at least on these
three days let us strive to do what tends to the cleansing and
splendor of our souls. Do not withdraw yourself from the
assembly in church, because we are not exhausted by such a
long space of time that we are not able to stand it. Just as
the man who does not withdraw himself from the assembly
in church these six hours is known to provide a great remedy
for his soul, so on the contrary, men who refuse to be present
through passion or because of some other less necessary occu-
pation, produce cruel wounds in themselves when they could
have had salutary medicine. Such men burden themselves with
what might have relieved them. But I believe that in the
mercy of God He will deign to inspire you in such a way that
you do not pursue sinfulness through neglect, but rather
through repentance are able to reach the remedy of forgiveness by fasting, prayer, singing the psalms, and almsgiving.
With the help of our Lord Jesus Christ, to whom is honor and
glory for ever and ever. Amen.

*Sermon 209*

## CONCERNING THE ROGATION DAYS

With exceedingly salutary advice, dearly beloved, and with
kind, paternal affection the Lord exhorts us when He says
through the prophet: "Delay not your conversion to the Lord,
put it not off from day to day."[1] "You know not what any
day may bring forth."[2] "Between morning and evening the
weather changes."[3] Elsewhere we are also advised with a
salutary precept: "Let us walk while we still have the light,

---

1 Sir. 5.8.
2 Prov. 27.1.
3 Sir. 18.26.

before darkness comes over us."[4] Now some careless person may say: When I reach old age, then I shall have recourse to the healing of repentance. The wretched man does not know that if a man has been accustomed to commit sins with a promise of repentance, never or only with difficulty will he merit to obtain the fruit of repentance. Since "no one makes a fool of the Lord,"[5] he deceives himself if, having led a wicked life for a long time, he arises to seek life when he is already half-dead. He should listen to the prophet say: "If the sinner turns away from his sins,"—if he turns away, he says, not if he only talks about it—"he shall live because of the virtue he has practiced."[6] Surely you have noticed that healing medicine of this kind must be asked with the lips, but it must be brought to completion by deeds. That gift of repentance which is received at the end of one's life should be believed to be profitable if it is accepted with a sublime intention, much crying and groaning, and is further enhanced by more abundant almsgiving. However, there must be as much piety on the part of sinners in healing the wounds as the intention of the mind was quick and active in doing evil.

(2) Again someone says: Even if I do not fulfill the commandments of God by my actions, the sacrament of baptism sets me free; faith and knowledge of the undivided Trinity are sufficient for me. In matters of God, dearly beloved, not only the reason of a believer is required, but the faith of one who wills it. Therefore faith that is devoid of merits is useless and empty, as the Apostle says: "What good is it to profess faith without practicing it? Faith alone has no power to save one, has it?"[7] He continues and says: "The faith that does nothing in practice is thoroughly useless."[8] I beseech you, dearest brethren, let no one deceive himself. Listen to a thought which is not human but divine; hear the Lord Him-

---

4 Cf. John 12.35.
5 Gal. 6.7.
6 Ezech. 18.21, 22.
7 James 2.14.
8 James 2.17.

self say: "He who obeys the commandments he has from me is the man who loves me."[9] He not only said "He who has my commandments," but also added "and obeys them." It is not at all helpful if God's precept is kept in the mind but is not observed in one's life. It is of no avail if we profess that we are Christians with our lips but do not fulfill it in deed, for the Lord said: "Anyone who loves me will be true to my command."[10] And again He said to the Apostles: "You are my friends if you do what I command you."[11]

(3) Since, as it is written, "the kingdom of God does not consist in talk but in power,"[12] let us not deceive ourselves with a false security, believing, as it were, that faith alone without good works can deliver us against the day of judgment. Let us with great fear and trembling rather consider that terrible word of our Lord in the Gospel, where it is said: "Every tree that does not bear good fruit will be cut down and thrown into the fire."[13] Pay careful attention to this, brethren, because He did not say "that bears bad fruit," but "that does not bear good fruit will be cut down and thrown into the fire." As a result of this, let us consider what expectation Christians who lead a wicked life will have, when those who do not live good lives will be thrown into the fire. Finally, when the sheep are separated from the goats on judgment day, the Lord is not going to say to them "Out of my sight into everlasting fire"[14] because you did not believe, but because you failed to perform good deeds. "I was hungry and you gave me no food."[15] Those who are on the right are not crowned only for their faith, but also for their good deeds; nor are those on the left condemned only for their lack of faith, but for their barrenness in good works. That threshing

---

9 John 14.21.
10 John 14.23.
11 John 15.14.
12 1 Cor. 4.20.
13 Matt. 3.10. The Confraternity of Christian Doctrine version of this text has been used.
14 Matt. 25.41.
15 Matt. 25.42.

floor which the Lord in the Gospel promised that He would fan, is known to contain neither heretics nor pagans but only Catholic Christians. For thus the Lord spoke: "And he will clear the threshing floor."[16] What is the threshing floor except the Catholic Church? Now because there are many in it who receive the sacrament of baptism but do not observe the precepts of Christ, it is said concerning them: "But the chaff he will burn in unquenchable fire."[17] For this reason I beseech you, brethren. While it is possible and while with God's help it lies in our power, the man who feels that he is chaff because of his wicked life should strive to change himself into wheat through good deeds, so that he may merit to be transferred from the left to the right side. Just as the man who today is wheat quickly becomes changed into chaff if he is careless, so the man who is chaff is changed into wheat this very day if he is willing to be converted in truth. Since not he who has begun but "whoever holds out to the end" in these things "will escape death,"[18] let us turn to good deeds in such a way that with God's help we may continue to persevere in them to the very end of our life.

(4) Now days which are healing for the soul, that is, the Rogation Days, are approaching. On these days the wounds of sins which human frailty is wont to incur the rest of the time, with God's help should be restored to their former health by means of prayers, vigils, fasting, and almsgiving. That is why I beseech and admonish you, brethren, and at the same time I warn you. On these three days, from the fourth to the sixth day of the week,[19] no one should withdraw himself from the assembly in church, unless perhaps some bodily infirmity does not permit him to come to church. It ought to be enough for us, brethren, that throughout the space of the entire year we

---

16 Matt. 3.12.
17 *Ibid.*
18 Matt. 10.22; 24.13.
19 That is—to use the names that Caesarius would have Christians avoid (Sermon 193.4)—Wednesday through Friday. On the days on which sixth-century Arles held the Rogations, see Beck, *Pastoral Care* 104-06.

are busy with some bodily advantage or need; at least on these three days let us reflect more carefully on the salvation of our soul. Let each one arrange for a small meal to be prepared for himself as in Lent, and in order that the very fast may be helpful for his soul, he should give what he intended to eat to strangers or to the poor. The man who willingly listens to me and willingly fulfills what I am humbly suggesting will quickly rejoice over the good condition of his soul. But the man who acts otherwise will be doubly guilty, because he has both despised his father who was humbly admonishing him and has not sought a remedy for his soul. We trust in God's mercy, however, that He will deign to inspire your hearts in such a way that you will be able to receive a reward because of your humble obedience. Therefore, dearly beloved, let us live in such a way that the days of healing may benefit us as a healing remedy, not as wounds. May He Himself help and assist us, who lives and reigns for ever and ever. Amen.

## * Sermon 210

### ON THE LORD'S ASCENSION[1]

Our Savior, dearly beloved, has ascended into heaven; therefore let us not be disturbed on earth. Let our spirit be there, and peace will be here. Meanwhile let us ascend with Christ in heart, and when His promised day comes, we shall also follow in body. Nevertheless, we ought to know that pride or avarice or dissipation did not ascend with Christ. No vice of ours ascended with our physician. And for this reason, if we desire to ascend and follow the physician, let us strive here to lay aside our vices and sins. For all of our iniquities sur-

---

1 Largely based, Morin notes, on Augustine's Sermon 261, but the adaptation clearly shows the hand of Caesarius.

round us as if with fetters, and they strive to bind us in the network of our sins. Therefore with God's help, according to what the psalmist says: "Let us break their fetters."[2] Then we will be able to say to the Lord with assurance: "You have loosed my bonds, to you will I offer sacrifice of thanksgiving."[3] The resurrection of the Lord is our hope; His ascension is our glory.

(2) Today we are keeping the solemn festival of the Ascension. If, therefore, we celebrate the Lord's ascension in a manner that is right, holy, faithful, devout, and pious, we must ascend with Him and lift up our hearts. Now as we ascend, let us not be lifted up with pride or presume upon our merits as if they were our own. For we ought indeed to lift up our hearts, but to the Lord alone. A heart lifted up but not to the Lord is called pride; a heart lifted up to the Lord is called a refuge. See, brethren, the great miracle. God is on high. You exalt yourself, and He flees from you; you humble yourself, and He descends to you. Why is this? Because "the Lord is exalted, yet the lowly he sees, and the proud he knows from afar."[4] He recognizes what is lowly from close at hand in order that He may raise it up; what is high, that is, what is proud, He knows from afar in order that He may bring it down. Christ truly arose from the dead in order to give us hope, because the man who dies rises again. He gave us assurance, so that we might not despair in dying and think our whole life ended in death. We were troubled about our very soul, but by rising from the dead He also gave us confidence in the resurrection of the body.

(3) Believe, then, that you may be purified. You must believe first, so that afterwards you may merit to see God through faith. Truly you wish to see God; you seek a good thing, a great thing. I exhort you to will it. Do you want to see God? Listen to Him: "Blest are the clean of heart for

2 Ps. 2.3.
3 Ps. 115 (116).16, 17.
4 Ps. 137 (138).6.

they shall see God.''[5] First of all think about purifying
your heart. Have this as your task, call yourself away to it,
apply yourself to this task, cleanse your heart. What you
wish to see is clean, but I am afraid that the place where
you wish to see it is unclean. If the earth fell into your line
of vision and you wanted me to show you the sun, you would
first look for someone to clear your line of vision. So great is
the mass of earthly desires, so great is the uncleanness of the
sins in your heart, and still you wish to see God! If avarice or
dissipation is there, examine and judge whether you can—
whether you merit to—see God in the midst of this filth on
your conscience. You are gathering together what you cannot
take with you from this life. You do not know that along with
avarice you are collecting the profits of a multitude of sins,
that you are dragging mud into your heart. And the psalmist
exclaims to you: "Sons of men, how long will you be dull of
heart?"[6] How comes it about, then, that you will be able to
see God?

(4) You say to me: Show me your God. I tell you: Pay a
little attention to your heart. Show me your God, you repeat.
Again I answer: Pay attention to your heart for a little while.
Remove whatever you see there that is displeasing to God.
God wants to come to you. Listen to Him say: "I and my
Father will come to him and make our dwelling place with
him."[7] Behold what God is promising. If I, as frail a man as
I am, promised to come to your home, doubtless you would
clean it, you would throw out the superfluities, you would
prepare what was necessary. God wishes to come to your
heart, and are you reluctant to cleanse your house for Him?
All vices are inimical to God, and so with His help remove
them if you wish to receive Him. For God does not like to live
with sordid, impure, and insatiable avarice, whose commands
unfaithful men wish to serve and at the same time want to

5 Matt. 5.8.
6 Ps. 4.3.
7 John 14.23.

see God. What man does what God has commanded? And
what man can be found at all who does not do what avarice
commanded? God commanded you to clothe the naked:[8] you
trembled. Avarice commanded you to plunder clothing: you
became mad. If you had done what God commanded, you
would possess God Himself. You did what avarice commanded: what do you have? Perhaps you answer and say:
I have whatever I took away from another. Therefore by
taking it away you have something with you, but you destroyed
yourself through your injustice. You do not know that a man
who does not possess himself has nothing. I do have, he says.
Where, I ask you? Surely either in my room or in a little bag
or in a box. I do not wish to say anything further. Wherever
you have it, still you do not have it with you now. You think
you have it in a box, and perhaps it has perished, and maybe
you do not know it. When you return, you do not find what
you have lost. I am searching your heart, I am asking what
you have there. Behold, you filled your box and strangled your
conscience by robbery or by collecting money from loans, or
at least by deceit through false weights and fraudulent measures, or through business transactions. Rather imitate blessed
Job, who was rich in relation to God and poor in body. See
that he is rich, and learn to be filled in the same way. "The
Lord gave and the Lord has taken away," he said; "blessed be
the name of the Lord!"[9] Certainly he had lost everything and
had remained naked. For what reason, then, did he utter those
jewels of praise of the Lord? Why, unless because he had
remained rich in heart?

(5) Therefore cleanse your heart. Do so as much as you
can; effect this, so that Christ may purify the place where He
abides. Ask and beseech it; humble yourselves. Listen to the
Scriptures say: "God resists the proud."[10] Be humble, in order

---

8 Cf. Isa. 58.7.
9 Job 1.21.
10 James 4.6.; 1 Peter 5.5.

that God may rest in you, as He Himself said: "This is the
one whom I approve, the lowly and peaceable man."[11] God
wishes to dwell in you. In order that you may not be unable
to receive Him because you are full, if you are filled elsewhere, let your heart be freed of superfluities so that it may
be filled with what is necessary. Vices should be expelled, in
order that there may be room for virtues. To say briefly what
is useful and quite necessary, let carnal desires be rejected and
charity invited. As long as we do not expel evil, we cannot be
filled with the good, because jars filled with slime cannot
take and hold precious ointment. Just as a thorny field does
not nourish the seeds that are sown in it but suffocates them,
unless the industriousness of the farmer first clears it, so the
soul that is full of worldly desires and cares is not able to
receive the divine word or to take and receive its God. Now
since you do not accept "In the beginning was the Word;
the Word was in God's presence, and the Word was God,"[12]
receive the fact that "the Word became flesh and made his
dwelling among us."[13] Why do you still not accept "In the
beginning was the Word"? Because "the light shines on in
darkness, a darkness that did not overcome it."[14] What is the
darkness, except wicked desires? Pride, avarice, ambition, dissipation, envy—all of these are the darkness. For this reason
the man who does not know God is not able to see Him
either, because the eyes of his heart are burdened with many
vices and sins. To be sure, the light shines in darkness, but
the darkness is not able to comprehend it at all. God is very
near to you, but He became man; what was far from you is
close to you by having become man. God is where you are;
man is where you are going. The very same Christ is both
our way and our true country; considered as man He is the

---

11 Cf. Isa. 66.2.
12 John 1.1.
13 John 1.14.
14 John 1.5.

way, considered as God He is our true country. If you run
faithfully, you advance through Him and you reach Him. In
order to be the way for you, He assumed what He was not yet
did not lose what He was. Let us, then, implore His mercy,
so that He may grant us upright faith and an understanding
pleasing to Him for the exercise of good works. To Him is
honor.

* Sermon 211

ON PENTECOST[1]

Today, dearest brethren, everything that has been read to
us comes together along with the solemn feast. The psalm
says: "Give me back the joy of your salvation, and with a
perfect spirit sustain me."[2] Moreover, the Gospel says: "The
Spirit of truth comes,"[3] while a passage in the Acts of the
Apostles tells us: "All were filled with the Holy Spirit."[4] Now
everything has been fulfilled and made perfect. The psalm
asked the coming of the Holy Spirit, the Gospel promised that
He would come, and the passage in the Acts related that He
had already come. Therefore in the texts nothing is lacking
to the order of the divine happenings, because there is a plea
in the prophet, a promise in the Gospel, and fulfillment in
the Acts. Concerning the same Holy Spirit, the blessed Apostle
Paul also gives witness when he says: "To one is given wisdom in discourse, to another the power to express knowledge,
another receives faith through the same Spirit. But it is one

---

1 The word *Quinquagesimo* in the title manifestly refers to the fifty-day
  period between Easter and Pentecost and not to "Quinquagesima," the
  pre-Lenten Sunday that fell approximately fifty days before Easter.
2 Ps. 50 (51).14.
3 John 16.13.
4 Acts 2.4.

and the same Spirit who produces all these gifts, distributing them to each as he wills."[5]

(2) Perhaps at this point someone says: If the Spirit divides His gifts only to those He wishes, the man who does not receive a gift is beyond blame, because the division of graces does not depend upon the will of the recipient but upon the decision of the dispenser. This is true, dearly beloved, but only in such a way that we understand it concerning special powers and not about life. We cannot all obtain special powers, even if we wanted them, but with God's help we can all receive life if we ask it, according to what is written: "For the one who asks, receives; the one who seeks, finds."[6] So the division of sublime and unusual graces belongs to the will and dispensation of the Holy Spirit, while the living of a good life depends upon the faith and effort of man: "For the one who asks, receives; the one who seeks, finds." A man should ask and seek this much with his whole heart, for doubtless He who commanded you to seek will assist you to be able to find. Does the divine word lie? "Knock," it says, "and it will be opened to you."[7] Now why did He command us to knock, unless because He wants to open to those who do knock? This kind of injustice does not occur even among men, that a man who is unwilling to yield wants to be asked. Only the man who has no will to give assistance refuses the request of a man who asks. There is no man who wants to be asked unless he has first decided within himself that he will give help. For this reason God, who wants to be generous to everyone, wants to be asked by all men, since He says: "Ask, and you will receive; seek, and you will find."[8]

(3) Perhaps someone may still say: If everyone who asks receives, then even if we ask for special powers, we will receive them. For why should we not ask for special gifts, if we can

5 1 Cor. 12.8, 9, 11.
6 Matt. 7.8.
7 Matt. 7.7.
8 *Ibid.*

receive everything we ask? This is not the case, dearly beloved. It is an indication of pride and beyond the human condition to ask for the grace of special powers. The appeal of man ought to be humble, not conceited, asking salvation alone, not vanity. Since no man is able to be without sin, what impudence is it for a man to seek special powers when he is still unable to be completely assured about his own pardon? For this reason it is enough for a man to merit the Lord's mercy. The man who is able to obtain forgiveness ought to believe that he has obtained from God the grace of the greatest gift. If a man asks for something with presumption, he deserves to receive less by reason of the fact that he has presumed to demand what is too lofty. It comes to this, that if the man who seeks the grace of special powers does not offend God through the presumption of his prayers, he may still run that risk because of his vanity. For it is not expedient for everyone to possess the gift of exercising special powers. There are some people who are more safe when they are situated in a lowly position than when they are puffed up boasting of their holiness; they are the ones for whom sublime gifts are themselves a source of danger. If the man who is placed in a lofty position does not know how to stand firmly, he falls all the more heavily because of the very fact that he has risen higher. For this reason the blessed Apostle says: "There are different gifts";[9] and "It is one and the same Spirit who produces all these gifts, distributing them to each as he wills."[10] Well does he say "as he wills," because nothing is better for a man than what He wills. The will of the Holy Spirit knows very well how to dispense His gifts, and nothing is more useful for a man than to have as much of His gifts as the Holy Spirit has decided He ought to confer upon him.

(4) Doubtless if anyone desires to obtain the grace of special powers, he has virtues which he may ask for without harm.

---

9 1 Cor. 12.4.
10 1 Cor. 12.11.

He should seek chastity, seize hold of moderation, cling to self-discipline, and love charity; for with God's grace we all can and should possess these virtues. We should not believe that special powers are present only in driving out demons or healing the sick and restoring good health. Every good action is a special gift. If you perform good deeds every day, if you live piously and justly, you daily accomplish holy acts of virtue. Is a man unable to cure the bodily disease of his neighbor? He should cure the sickness of his own soul. It is not asked of a man that he provide the gift of good health which has not been granted by the divine will; he can attain nothing greater than to merit to reach the state of well-being for his own soul.

(5) After the effort of the vigils, it is not necessary for you to be wearied still more by a longer sermon. Whoever is spiritually minded and desires to hear a fuller sermon on the divinity of the Holy Spirit may come to church early in the morning tomorrow, eagerly and devoutly. Anyone who neglects to come will very clearly show that he is not spiritually minded. However, we believe that in God's mercy the grace of the Holy Spirit will prevail with you more than the business of this world: with the help of our Lord Jesus Christ, to whom is glory for ever and ever. Amen.

## * Sermon 212

### ON THE MYSTERY OF THE HOLY TRINITY, AND THE DIVINE NATURE OF THE HOLY SPIRIT[1]

When there is a sermon about God, dearest brethren, the concern of inquiry is useful just as the intention to contradict is harmful. In the latter case the meaning is obscured by stubbornness, while understanding is nourished in the former by questioning. In the one, opposing faithlessness delights in being corrupted, but in the other, obedient humility merits to be instructed. Do you, dearest brethren, prepare the holy receptacle of your heart for the divine water which is flowing in, and receive in peace and quiet what we want to suggest about the mystery of the Holy Trinity and the divinity of the Holy Spirit. We want to confirm the evidence of Sacred Scripture where the Holy Spirit can clearly be recognized as equal to the Father and to the Son in all powers.

(2) We read in the Old Testament that "in the beginning God created the heavens and the earth,"[2] and "a mighty wind swept over the waters."[3] In God understand the Father, in the beginning accept the Son, and recognize the Holy Spirit as spread over the waters. The excellence of the one in authority swept over the waters, prefiguring even then, I believe, the gifts of baptism. In creating man, too, the threefold repetition of the divine nature shows that there is need of not one but three persons. For thus we read: "Then God said: Let us make man in our image, after our likeness."[4] Notice that the sentence is simple in its intention but manifold in its

---

1 Like the following sermon, clearly a free Caesarian adaptation of Faustian originals; so Morin.
2 Gen. 1.1.
3 Gen. 1.2.
4 Gen. 1.26.

reply. "Then God said: 'Let us make man.' " What is this except the substance of unity speaking, and the power of the Trinity in operation? See how the name of God is mentioned three times in the creation of man, for we have it in Genesis: "Then God said: 'Let us make man' "; again: "God created man";[5] and a third time: "God blessed him."[6] God said, God created, God blessed; the Father said, the Son created, the Holy Spirit blessed. The one divine nature is repeated three times because of the three persons. Understand clearly here, too, the mystery of their unity. See how the image and likeness of God is given to each and every man by all three, and still it is recognized as only one. "God said: 'Let us make.' " Listen carefully how one speaks but not only one creates. He does not say 'to our images' and likenesses, nor, to be sure, 'to my image and likeness.' He establishes their unity by the singular number, their trinity by the plural possessive. For this reason, in the fact that He says "Let us make man to *our* image" the number of persons is declared, but where He says "to our *image and likeness*" the undivided godhead is brought together into one substance.

(3) When God had appeared to Abraham at the door of his tent and in a wonderful manner three persons presented themselves before his eyes, in those three men Abraham, conscious of their majesty, adored one in the three. In the psalms, too, the Trinity is clearly designated in their persons: "Cast me not out from your presence," it says, "and your holy spirit take not from me."[7] See how when the prophet prays to the Father, he dreads no less the displeasure of the Holy Spirit than that of the Son and of the Father in saying: "Cast me not out from your presence." Just as the Son is the image of the Father, so He is also regarded as the face of the Father. For this reason we read: "Philip, whoever has seen me has

---

5 Gen. 1.27.
6 Gen. 1.28.
7 Ps. 50 (51).13.

seen the Father";[8] and likewise: "Where can I go from your spirit? from your presence where can I flee?"[9] Notice the mystery of the Trinity in that perfect confession of faith. The prophet speaks to the Father, professes that the Son is the face of the Father, and proclaims that the Holy Spirit is diffused throughout everything. Concerning the Son, the Lord also says to Moses: "My face shall go before thee."[10] This name, that is, face, has reference to unity of substance and eternity of majesty. Isaias, too, includes one Holy Spirit in the glory of the Trinity when he says: "I saw the Lord seated on a high throne; seraphim were stationed above and cried one to the other: "Holy, holy, holy is the Lord of hosts!"[11] And in a following passage he says: "I heard the voice of the Lord saying: 'Go and say to this people: Listen carefully, but you shall not understand! Look intently, but you shall see nothing!'"[12]

(4) Let us at least believe Paul, most distinguished herald of the truth, that the Holy Spirit was that Lord of hosts whom Isaias saw and who spoke through Isaias. Since in a triple response he causes "Holy, holy, holy," to burst forth, let us see whether this honor does not relate to the whole Trinity. When Isaias says "I have seen the Lord of hosts,"[13] he is known to preach the Father to the Jews. John the Evangelist is considered to assert the Son openly when he speaks in this fashion: "The reason they could not believe in Jesus was that, as Isaias says: 'He has blinded their eyes.' Isaias uttered these words because he had seen Jesus' glory, and it was of him he spoke."[14] Isaias, too, said the same thing: "I heard the voice of the Lord saying: 'Go and say to this people: Listen carefully, but you shall not understand! Look intently, but you

---

8 John 14.9.
9 Ps. 138 (139).7.
10 Exod. 33.14. The Douay version has been used.
11 Isa. 6.1, 2, 3.
12 Cf. Isa. 6.8, 9.
13 Isa. 6.5.
14 John 12.39, 40, 41.

shall see nothing!' " This Lord, as we have said, the Apostle
Paul confirms to be the Holy Spirit. For this reason you see
that this word—Holy, holy, holy—proclaims the entire
Trinity. Just as there is no difference or distinction in these
words, so there can be no difference in the essence of the
Trinity.

(5) Now you say: The Holy Spirit is clearly shown to be
less in that He is called the finger of God. This is not true.
When you hear concerning the Holy Spirit, "If it is by the
Spirit of God" or "by the finger of God that I expel demons,"[15]
you know that there is no lessening of glory shown but unity
of substance, not a difference in honor but harmony of operation. Then what? In the meantime, because the Holy Spirit
is called a finger, is He for this reason believed to be less
than the Father and the Son? Flee the error of this belief.
See whether in this designation of the finger he does not on
several occasions include the Father and the Son. We recall
that there was mention of not one finger only when we read:
"When I behold your heavens, the work of your fingers."[16]
When you say that in the fingers this is only expressed with
regard to the Son and the Holy Spirit under some kind of
dual nature, lest you try to assert this about two persons,
Isaias in another place mentions the whole Trinity in the
number of fingers when he says: "Who hath poised with three
fingers the bulk of the earth?"[17] What is more obvious or
more clear with regard to the unity of the Trinity? Here in
the three fingers did he not balance the equality of one godhead in some mysterious scale? For this reason, as it has been
said, do not doubt the equality of their power, since you have
already been taught about the connection of their operation.
Therefore by saying "Who hath poised with three fingers the
bulk of the earth?" he simply wanted to speak of the shared

---

15 Matt. 12.28; Luke 11.20.
16 Ps. 8.4.
17 Isa. 40.12. The Douay translation has been used here also.

operation of the godhead and the unity of substance which is proved to be one and the same in the three fingers.

(6) Although the Holy Spirit always inflames your heart to hear the word of God, so that your pious desires can hardly be satisfied, still caution must be observed. Preaching the word of God should be moderated in such a way that it is continually desired by you and always increased. For this reason what has already been said should be enough for your charity, and we believe that something of this sermon should be kept in reserve for you. If you assemble again early tomorrow morning, as you usually do, you will hear what was reserved on purpose, without any weariness and after the completion of morning prayers. With the help of our Lord Jesus Christ, to whom is honor for ever and ever. Amen.

*\* Sermon 213*

### On the Divine Nature of the Holy Spirit (II)[1]

If you approve, in peace and quiet you can now fitly and conveniently hear what was kept for your charity yesterday, concerning the divine nature of the Holy Spirit. When we show that the person of the Holy Spirit is proper to Him and confess that the Father is unbegotten, we realize that the Son is the only begotten one. But someone of you asks me whether the Holy Spirit should be confessed as unbegotten, begotten, or something else. Sacred Scripture speaks about the godhead and divinity of the Holy Spirit, but does not say whether He should be called begotten or unbegotten. See what confusion a lack of faith creates. You do not want to know what God did not want to be unknown, and you want to know what He did not decree should be asked. He did not say 'begotten,'

---

1 See Sermon 212, n. 1.

lest you believe Him the Son; He did not say 'unbegotten,' so
you would not think Him the Father. In order to distinguish
His essence, He declared that He proceeded from the Father,
as we read: "The Paraclete comes from the Father."[2] Since
this is true, realize that the Holy Spirit possesses His own
person. The difference in title shows that there is a third
person in addition to the two. The unity of their majesty
indicates that the third person does not proceed from God in
order or rank, for the one who proceeds from the interior of
God is proved to be the substance of God, not His creature.
Do not inquire into how He is God, since it has been shown
that He is God. In this matter the means lies hidden, but the
truth is evident. Why do you ask how a person is the com-
panion or equal of a king, if it is agreed that he possesses
kingly honor and birth? Inquiry about a title is pursued needlessly when there is no doubt about the superior nature of a
being. Because the Holy Spirit proceeds from both persons,
it is said: "If anyone does not have the Spirit of Christ, he
does not belong to Christ";[3] and in another place: "He
breathed on them and said: 'Receive the Holy Spirit.' "[4]

(2) You ask whether He was begotten or not. Sacred Scripture has said nothing about this, and it is wrong to violate
the divine silence. Since God did not think that this should
be indicated in His writings, He did not want you to question or to know this through idle curiosity. Does the glory
or the substance of the Holy Spirit consist in this, whether
He is shown to be unbegotten or begotten? The fact that it
is not read that He was unbegotten does not take anything
away from the Son, nor does the fact that He is not considered
begotten detract from the Father. In talk of this kind there
is the distinct nature of a title but not a difference in reality.
Begotten or unbegotten belongs to a difference in person,
not in nature.

2 John 15.26.
3 Rom. 8.9.
4 John 20.22.

(3) When our Lord and Savior was about to go to heaven, He spoke thus to His Apostles concerning the Holy Spirit: "When the Paraclete comes, the Spirit of truth who comes from the Father—and whom I myself will send—he will bear witness on my behalf";[5] and again: "He will instruct you in everything."[6] What does this mean, dearly beloved, that our Savior said He was going to send the Holy Spirit to teach the disciples? Had He not taught His Apostles? or was the teaching of Christ to be considered only half-complete? No, beyond any question. But because your faith lies in the Father and the Son and the Holy Spirit, by sending the Holy Spirit our Savior wanted to show this. Thus the will of God the Father established His Church, the passion of the Son redeemed it, and the teaching of the Holy Spirit confirmed it. How can this be known more surely? How, except because God the Father sent His Son for our redemption, the Son saved us through His passion, and the Holy Spirit inspired faith in us? Thus the salvation of the Church is the work of the whole divine Trinity. The goodness of the Father did not want the human race to perish, the Son freed us from death, and the Holy Spirit brings us to the kingdom of heaven.

(4) Now believe in the Holy Spirit in such a way that you do not think that He is the Father or the Son, but rather the Spirit of the Father and the Son. This entire Trinity is one God; there is no difference in it, no separation. For if the spirit which is in man is a greater portion of man himself, how can the Spirit of God be considered less? For this reason the Holy Spirit is neither the Father nor the Son but the Spirit of the Father and the Son. That the Holy Spirit is the Spirit of the Father, our Lord and Savior said: "The spirit comes from the Father."[7] That the same Holy Spirit is also the Spirit of the Son, the Apostle teaches when he says: "If anyone does not have the Spirit of Christ, he does not belong

---

5 John 15.26.
6 John 14.26.
7 John 15.26.

to Christ."[8] Therefore in the Gospel our Lord said to His disciples after His resurrection: "Go and baptize all the nations in the name of the Father, and of the Son, and of the Holy Spirit."[9] "In the name," he says, not "in the names." And so the Father is God, the Son is God, the Holy Spirit is God; there are not three gods, but one God. The person divides three aspects, but their divine nature joins them together. The Trinity, the divine nature, does not know how to be greater or lesser, because one who is God cannot be other than perfect. For this reason if a man does not believe in the name of the Holy Spirit, it does him no good to confess the Father and the Son. The Holy Spirit must be believed with one and the same faith, worshiped with equal trembling. When you have said "the Father, the Son, and the Holy Spirit," you have explained the persons; when you have said "God," you showed their substance. We say "the Father, and the Son, and the Holy Spirit" so that you will not think you should believe there is only one person. We likewise say "one God" so you will not think that there are three natures. In these three persons there can be a number, but there can be no rank. Even if the Trinity allows a distinction, their equality knows no rank. For in the Trinity there is not something lesser or greater. If there is said to be something less in God, His divine nature is accused of being imperfect. Moreover, whoever says that the Holy Spirit is less than the Father or the Son in His divine nature not only injures the one whom he considers lesser, but also the one whom he thinks greater. Since the equality and majesty of the entire Trinity is one, whatever insult is uttered against the person of one is equally felt by the whole Trinity.

(5) Dearest brethren, we who have merited to be "a temple of the Holy Spirit,"[10] with His help should prepare a habitation for the Holy Spirit to which He will delight to come, and

---

8 Rom. 8.9.
9 Matt. 28.19.
10 1 Cor. 6.19.

in which it will give him pleasure to dwell. Let the brightness of a pure heart attract Him, let the chaste blush which is like dark red roses invite Him, let undefiled virginity which resembles white lilies in fragrance and color attract Him. Let gentle charity, generous kindness, sublime humility, cheerful compassion, and pure childlike faith receive Him. May the eternal inhabitant and everlasting benefactor find nothing of the meanness of the old man there, nothing of his lapses and weaknesses. Let the dissipation of exceedingly disgraceful passion disappear, also the conscience that is pale with remorse, dread fear, tottering drunkenness, and wantonness that is more ugly than everything dreadful. When all of these failings are lacking in us, then the brightness of purity will go ahead and open the way to virtue, and enclose the Holy Spirit in the habitation prepared as a dwelling for Him. We have mentioned this, dearest brethren, so that with God's help we may labor with all our strength as much as we can. Let not avarice be displeasing in us, lack of faith weaken us, or wicked passion defile us. May we rather merit to become the dwelling of God, when we have been completely cleansed and purified, and may the Holy Spirit, who is read to have come down upon the Apostles today, always deign to live in us. To Him is honor and glory, together with the Father and the Son for ever and ever. Amen.

## Sermon 214

### A SERMON AT THE ANNIVERSARY OF THE BURIAL OF
### ST. HONORATUS[1]

To enlighten the human race, beloved brethren, our Lord lit many spiritual lamps in this world. Since worship and heavenly doctrine shine through holy men, one who has wished to see the light of truth is never totally enveloped in the darkness of error. What, however, are these lamps, which our Lord permitted to dispel and illuminate the fog of faithlessness? First the patriarchs, then the prophets, afterwards the apostles, and finally the bishops of all the churches. Among these, divine compassion gave this city sublime Honoratus, of blessed memory, to be a brilliant and illustrious lamp. It was fitting, moreover, that He should elevate him upon a candlestick to shine for everyone. He indeed was distinguished in this city because of the special brilliance of his works, and in addition he diffused with the light of his merits all of the places which he reached through the fame of his name. As we remember his unconquerable faith in good works, his extraordinary rigor in despising the world, his unique and loving compassion, we believe that he undoubtedly reached martyrdom, even though he did not experience its sufferings. For not only the shedding of blood effects martyrdom, and not only the burning of flames gives the martyr's palm. That crown is reached, not only through death, but even through contempt of the body. It is possible to speak of the sufferings of the blessed dead without physical injury for them. To have battled the flesh, to have overcome evil desires, to have re-

---

1 St. Honoratus (feast January 16; Beck, *Pastoral Care* 312 at n. 97) was the founder of the celebrated monastery on one of the islands of Lerins, off the French riviera, opposite Cannes. He was later bishop of Arles, and his successor, St. Hilary, wrote his life.

sisted avarice, to have triumphed over the world is the best part of martyrdom.

(2) Now the good and merciful Lord has deigned to provide and prepare for this city not only the help of the martyrs, but also the protection of the supreme pontiffs. For this reason, with God's help let us strive as much as we can to give joy to our special patrons before God by our good deeds rather than to sadden them through our sins and negligences. Then the holy martyrs and distinguished bishops will be able to intercede for us with the Lord through their prayers and with confidence, if they see us always fulfilling God's precepts and devoted to good works. If, however—may God forbid—we are willing to be involved in wicked deeds, we indeed sadden them, but we also acquire for ourselves everlasting damnation. Just as we read that there is "joy in heaven over one repentant sinner,"[2] so as often as Christians commit some serious sin we believe that they sadden everyone because of the perdition they deserve.

(3) For this reason I beseech you again and again. As we think about the merits and protection of so many and such great martyrs or bishops, let us strive to show ourselves worthy of their good works, so we will not sadden them by our evil deeds. Then when the day of judgment comes, our joyful and happy patrons will offer us to the eternal judge and with confidence will utter that word of the prophet: "Look at me and the children whom you gave me, Lord."[3] Then, too, the shepherds along with their flocks will deserve to hear that blessed and desirable word: "Come. You have my Father's blessing! Inherit the kingdom prepared for you from the creation of the world."[4] May He Himself deign to grant this, who lives and reigns with the Father for ever and ever. Amen.

---

2 Luke 15.7.
3 Isa. 8.18.
4 Matt. 25.34.

*Sermon 215*

## ON THE ANNIVERSARY OF ST. FELIX[1]

To enlighten the human race, beloved brethren, our Lord lit many spiritual lamps in this world. Since worship and heavenly doctrine shine through holy men, one who has wished to see the light of truth is never wholly enveloped in the darkness of error. What, however, are these lamps, which our Lord permitted to dispel and illuminate the fog of faithlessness? First the patriarchs, then the prophets, afterwards the apostles, and finally the bishops of all the churches. Among these, divine compassion gave this city sublime Honoratus, of blessed memory, to be a brilliant and illustrious lamp. It was fitting, moreover, that He should elevate him upon the candlestick of this church to shine for everyone. Although he was distinguished in this city because of the special brilliance of his works, he also diffused with the light of his merits all of the places which he reached through the fame of his name. As we remember his unconquerable faith in good works, his extraordinary rigor in despising the world, his unique and loving compassion, we believe that he undoubtedly reached martyrdom, even though he did not experience its sufferings.

(2) For not only the shedding of blood effects martyrdom, and not only the burning of flames gives the martyr's palm. That crown is reached, not only through death, but even through contempt of the body. It is possible to speak of the

---

1 A second sermon on St. Honoratus, which well into section 2 is identical with the first (Sermon 214). The title reflects the work of later copyists, who, notes Morin, clumsily adapted the sermon to the cult of a St. Felix without removing even Honoratus' name. No St. Felix is recorded by Beck as being honored in the sixth-century Arles use (*Pastoral Care* 212). The section opening "2" appears twice in Morin's edition, for the second time at the paragraph beginning "Let no one believe . . ." (see Morin's note *ad loc.*).

sufferings of the blessed dead without physical injury for them. To have battled the flesh, to have overcome evil desires, to have resisted avarice, to have triumphed over the world is the best part of martyrdom. If we, too, want to arrive at fellowship with the martyrs or bishops, dearly beloved, let us meditate on imitation of the martyrs. For they ought to recognize in us something of their virtues in order that they may deign to beseech the Lord on our behalf. If we cannot suffer the torments which the holy martyrs endured, through their intercession, let us at least resist our evil inclinations. And since daily sins are not lacking to us, daily remedies should likewise not be absent.

Let no one believe that he possesses any happiness or true joy in this world. Happiness can be prepared for, but it cannot be possessed here. Two times succeed each other in their own order, "A time to weep, and a time to laugh."[2] Let no one deceive himself, brethren; there is no time to laugh in this world. I know, indeed, that every man wants to rejoice, but men do not all look for joy in the place where it should be sought. True joy never did exist in this world, it does not do so now, and it never will. For thus the Lord Himself warned His disciples in the Gospel when He said: "You will suffer in the world,"[3] and again: "While the world rejoices, you will grieve for a time, but your grief will be turned into joy."[4] For this reason, with the Lord's help let us do good in this life through labor and sorrow, so that in the future life we may be able to gather the fruits of our good deeds with joy and exultation according to that sentence: "Those that sow in tears shall reap rejoicing."[5]

(3) In this world, dearest brethren, through the sin of the first man we have been cast forth from the happy seat of paradise and have been, as it were, sent into exile. For this

---

2 Eccles. 3.4.
3 John 16.33.
4 John 16.20.
5 Ps. 125 (126).5.

reason we do not have a fatherland in this world, as the
Apostle says: "While we dwell in this body we are on a
journey away from the Lord."[6] Therefore let us not seek joy
in this world because, as it was said above, true joy can be
prepared for here, but it cannot be possessed here. Do not
seek on the journey what is being kept for you in your fatherland. Because it is necessary for you to fight against the devil
every day under the leadership of Christ, do not seek in the
midst of battle the reward which is being saved for you in
the kingdom. During the fight you ought not to look for what
is being kept for you when victory has been attained. Rather
pay attention to what the Apostle says: "Anyone who wants
to live a godly life in Christ can expect to be persecuted,"[7]
and again: "We must undergo many trials if we are to enter
the reign of God."[8]

(4) Through God's giving us the strength, we ought to live
in such a way that we may merit to return happily to our
chief fatherland where our forebears, the patriarchs, the
prophets, and the apostles, long to see and welcome us. There
our fellow citizens, the angels, that heavenly city of Jerusalem,
and Christ, the king of that city, await us with the outstretched
arms of love. If we have overthrown the devil and are filled
with good works, then we may happily return to them. For
you know, brethren, that all traders and travelers are anxious
on the road, in order that they may be free from care in
their native country, and they feel true joy when they merit
to reach their fatherland along with great gain. Thus we too,
dearly beloved, prepare our soul for joy whenever we deserve
to go to Christ. In the meantime let us rejoice only in hope,
but afterwards we are destined to possess joy in reality. There
are many people—so much the worse!—who in reverse order
think that they rejoice in the pleasure, delights, and dissipation of this world. What they seem to sow in joy they will

6  2 Cor. 5.6.
7  2 Tim. 3.12.
8  Acts 14.21 (22).

have to reap with tears and mourning, for He who spoke in the Gospel does not lie: "Woe to you who laugh now; you shall weep in your grief."[9] This is what was done by that poor rich man who "dressed in purple and linen."[10] Indeed, he had joy in this world, but he merited to find flames in hell. Lazarus, who lay at his door, felt sadness on the way but received true joy in his fatherland.

(5) For our part, dearest brethren, let us beseech God's mercy as much as we can, so that He may deign to inspire in us such a love of eternal life that we may want to love our fatherland more than the road to it. Let us think more about the future life than about this present one, and let us always strive so to live in the exile of this world that we may be able to come to the future judgment with a free, secure conscience and adorned with good works. With the help of our Lord Jesus Christ, to whom is honor and power for ever and ever. Amen.

---

9 Luke 6.25.
10 Luke 16.19.

## * Sermon 216

A HOMILY OF ST. AUGUSTINE ON THE NATIVITY OF ST.
JOHN THE BAPTIST[1]

Today we are celebrating the birthday of St. John, dearest brethren, something which we read has never been granted to any of the [other] saints. Only the birthday of our Lord and that of Blessed John are celebrated and honored throughout the world. A sterile woman bore the latter, a virgin conceived the former; in Elisabeth sterility was overcome, in blessed Mary the method of conception was changed. Elisabeth bore her son by knowing a husband; Mary believed the angel and conceived hers. Elisabeth conceived a man, and so did Mary; but Elisabeth conceived only a man, while Mary conceived both God and man. What did John want for himself? Why was he interposed? concerning whom was he sent ahead? For this reason John was great, and to his greatness even the Savior bears testimony when He says: "There has not appeared on earth a man born of woman greater than John the Baptist."[2] He surpassed and excelled everyone; he excelled the prophets, he surpassed the patriarchs. Anyone who is born of a woman is inferior to John. Perhaps someone may say: If John is greater than all the sons of women, he is greater than the Savior. Far be it from that. John indeed was born of a woman, but Christ was born of a virgin. The former

---

1 A sermon from which the Roman Breviary, in the office of St. John the Baptist, used excerpts, attributing them to St. Augustine, who for a long while passed as its author. Morin sees it as a cento drawn from Augustine, Pseudo-Ambrose, and Pseudo-Eusebius, in which, however, not only the ending but other elements as well bespeak the personal work of Caesarius. The feast here in question is the Nativity of St. John the Baptist (Beck, *Pastoral Care* 312 at n. 99); the martyrdom is celebrated in Sermon 218. A different recension of the sermon is published by J. Leclercq, O.S.B., in *Revue bénédictine* 58 (1948) 66-67 (cf. *ibid*. 59 [1949] 113 n. 1).
2 Matt. 11.11.

was brought forth from within a corruptible womb, while the latter was born through the flowering of an undefiled womb. Yet the birth of our Lord is considered along with that of John, so that our Lord may not seem to be outside of the reality of human nature. If John is compared with men, that man surpasses all men; none but the God-man excels him. John was sent ahead, before God. So great was the excellence in him, so great his grace, that he was considered as the Christ. What, then, did he say concerning Christ? "Of his fullness we have all had a share."[3] What does this mean, "we all"? The prophets, the patriarchs, the apostles, as many holy people as were sent ahead before the Incarnation or were sent after it, we all have shared in His fullness. We are the vessels, He is the fountain.

(2) If, then, we have understood the mystery, brethren, John is a man, Christ is God. Man should be humbled, but God should be exalted, according to what John himself said concerning our Lord: "He must increase, while I must decrease."[4] In order that man might be humbled, John was born on the same day that the days begin to grow shorter; in order that God might be exalted, Christ was born on the very day when the days begin to grow longer. It is a great mystery, dearly beloved, and for this reason we celebrate the birthday of John like that of Christ, because birth itself is full of mystery. Of what mystery but that of our lowliness, just as the birth of Christ is full of the mystery of our greatness? Let us become smaller in man, in order that we may grow in God; let us be humbled in ourselves, in order that we may be exalted in Him. The presumption of man should be humbled, in order that divine compassion may increase. The mystery of this reality was further fulfilled in the sufferings of both. The head of John was cut off in order that man might decrease, while Christ hung on the tree of the cross in order that God might be exalted.

---

3 John 1.16.                    4 John 3.30.

(3) If you bid us do so, we want to tell the ears of your charity briefly why our Lord and Savior said that blessed John was a lamp, and why he wanted him to be sent before Him. John was sent before Him like a voice before the word, a lamp before the sun, a herald before the judge, a servant before his master, a friend before the bridegroom. Because the darkness of sin and the night of unbelief had oppressed the whole world and it could not see the sun of justice, blessed John was sent ahead like a lamp. Thus the eyes of the heart, weakened by the inflammation of iniquity and unable to see the great and true light, first became accustomed to look at the light of the lamp as at slight brightness. Gradually, then, as the cloud of sins was removed and the moisture of unbelief disappeared, at the coming of Christ they could be gladdened rather than tormented by that heavenly light. Just as you encourage watery eyes to see if you show the slight brightness of a lamp and pain them if you bring a bright light, so it is with our Lord and Savior, who is the true light. If He had not first sent blessed John as a lamp, the entire world could not have endured His brightness. Allow John to speak and say: "I am a voice in the desert, crying out."[5] He was a voice, because he was filled with the spirit of God's word. Just as the utterance of a voice is transmitted by a speaker to a listener through some kind of instrumentality or vehicle, so John was the servant and bearer of the word when he spoke about Christ. St. John, I repeat, represented in himself a type of the law, which pointed out Christ from afar by signs and evidence, and for this reason he sent two of his disciples to Christ. Those two disciples who were sent to Christ by John perhaps are the two peoples, one of whom came to believe from the Jews and the other from the gentiles. John directed them to Christ; the law sent them to grace and wanted the truth strengthened through the ancient faith of the Gospel.

---

5 John 1.23.

(4) Now in order that we may be able to celebrate such a holy feast with not only bodily but also spiritual joy, dearly beloved, according to our strength let us prepare our souls to give alms and to observe peace with everyone. Out of love for God and a zeal for holy discipline, with all our strength let us strive to keep not only ourselves but our entire household and everyone who belongs to us from all scurrility or foul language. Moreover, let us not permit pleasure-seeking men to defile the sacred feast by singing voluptuous songs. St. John will be able to obtain for us whatever we ask only if he knows that we are celebrating his feast as peaceable, chaste, and temperate men, free from any immodest speech. It is through paternal solicitude that I am mentioning these truths, dearest brethren. Through the goodness of God I have such trust in your devotion that you will not only keep yourselves but also all who belong to you chaste and temperate, in every kind of upright conduct. Therefore in a spirit of gratitude to God I beg Him to allow you to persevere happily, since He gave you the grace to begin devoutly actions which are holy: who with the Father and the Holy Spirit lives and reigns, world without end. Amen.

### * Sermon 217

### ON THE NATIVITY OF ST. JOHN THE BAPTIST[1]

Today, dearly beloved, we are celebrating the birthday of John, who preceded the coming of our Lord. We do not recall that this has been granted to any [other] of the saints,

---

1 A sermon almost totally excerpted from a homily of "Eusebius Gallicanus." Morin notes as of special interest the three secular quotations contained in section 3.

and so I repeat that we are honoring his birthday with a unique and special celebration. Now because we cannot rightly extol him with the use of a human voice, we will speak in the remarkable words of our Lord's testimony when He said that "There has not appeared on earth a man born of woman greater than John the Baptist."[2] He Himself said this; so you can understand the magnificence of the praise from the dignity of the one who uttered it. Therefore while it is asserted that no one among the sons of women is greater than he, it is given to us to understand that John was the measure of human merits.

(2) "I am the voice of one that cries out in the desert."[3] This means: I am not the Word that was with God in the beginning and that was God, but I am rather a voice; in other words I am a minister of the Word, in order that through me He may reach the hearing and senses of men. For this reason the blessed Baptist exclaimed with equal humility: "He must increase, while I must decrease."[4] "He must increase," he says, because the Gospel of Christ is spread throughout the world; "while I must decrease," because the prophecy of John is completed. He who is to be lifted up on the cross must increase, while I who am destined to have my head cut off must decrease. The prophecy of John indeed came to an end because He who was foretold appeared. Therefore by his birth and life John presented a type of our Lord who was to come. John was born of an aged father, Christ of a virgin mother at a time when the world was declining; at a time, I repeat, which was barren in faith and good works. John came through a sterile woman who had despaired of bearing children, and Christ came through a virgin to the astonishment of nature. The former preached salvation, while the latter brought it; the former baptized unto repentance, while the latter gave new life in grace.

---

2 Matt. 11.11.
3 Isa. 40.3.
4 John 3.30.

(3) This is the same John who publicly condemned the wickedness of King Herod for seizing the wife of a man who was still living. By so doing John lost his life for the sake of justice, but he gained glory. In the meantime we prefer flattery and we sell the truth in order to gain the favor of men, or through fear of offending them, not fearing what was written in frightful words: "If you do not warn the wicked man about his evil conduct, I will hold you responsible for his death."[5] Many times even doctors of the Church are wont to stop rebuking sinners, not through carelessness but because they are afraid that the sinners will rush out to worse crimes as a result of the reproof. When bishops fail to preach for this reason, they cannot be guilty because of their silence. Just as good men sometimes correct themselves as a result of harsh reproof, on the contrary haughty men are always provoked to worse disaster by even the slightest admonition. Often preachers in church, not willingly but out of necessity, so far fail to rebuke sinners that by way of spiritual remedy and the exercise of charity they even bestow undeserved praise upon the proud. Thus while these men blush to think that what is said about them is false, they are encouraged to amendment of their life and to good works according to what is written: "For the wicked man is praised in the desires of his soul, and the unjust man is blessed."[6] Now because that statement of a wise man is true, "As genuine praise honors a man, so false praise rebukes him,"[7] it is not impossible with God that those who have begun to practice good works after they were invited through human praise, may be converted by Him to charity and to a good life. This

---

5 Ezech. 3.18.
6 Ps. 9 (10).3. Caesarius's Psalter differed here widely from the original that lies behind the *New American Bible*.
7 In Sermon 236.4 this quotation is described as "of worldly origin, to be sure, but exceedingly useful." By Sidonius Apollinaris (*Epist.* 8.4) it is attributed to Symmachus, but the work of the latter in which it appeared is lost; cf. *Monumenta Germaniae historica*, Auctores antiquissimi 6.1 p. 340.

is in agreement with what someone said concerning wise men: "When they have become accustomed to lead a good life, they will be ashamed to break the habit"; and again: "Let us talk about what is good, and our speech will be transformed into good-will."[8] Blessed John, however, with full and perfect liberty preferred to suffer injustice rather than fail to say what was right. For this reason, in his discourse in the Gospel blessed John himself touches our hearts with a salutary message when he says: "I am a herald's voice in the desert, crying: 'Make ready the way of the Lord, clear a straight path for our God.' "[9] If we cling to the word of truth and a love of justice within us, we will possess that way whereby Christ reaches the human heart. This is why he said, "I am the voice of one crying": the voice of the herald speaks of the judge, the shout of judges threatens.

(4) After this he also proclaims: "Every valley shall be filled and every mountain and hill shall be leveled."[10] This is the same thing which the Evangelist relates in different words: "Every one who exalts himself shall be humbled."[11] The time will come, dearly beloved, when the man who refuses to humble himself now in a salutary way will, without any remedy for it, be sorry that he was proud. A time will come when the humble will be lifted up into heaven, while the proud will be plunged into the depths of hell. A time will come when the rich people who now laugh at Christ's poor will be sorry that they all were avaricious. The order of man's condition will not always be kept the same as it is now. Lazarus will not always be tormented by hunger, and the greedy rich man will not always enjoy an abundance of luxuries. From a dunghill the one will quickly be lifted up into paradise by the angels, while the other one, who refused to give alms, unless repentance has come to his rescue, will

---

8 Both of the sentences quoted here are from an unknown source.
9 Luke 3.4; cf. Isa. 40.3.
10 Luke 3.5; cf. Isa. 40.4.
11 Luke 14.11.

be carried off from his luxurious banquet into hell. The man who has refused to give a morsel to the poor in this life will not merit to receive a drop of water in hell; the man who was unwilling to feed the poor from his luxurious banquet will feed the flames of hell with the marrow of his bones. For our part, brethren, let us labor as much as we can to bring down, through humility and meekness, what pride had made swollen and puffed up; to correct through the guidance of justice whatever injustice had perverted; to temper by the grace of goodness whatever had been provoked by wickedness. In the midst of these endeavors may Christ our Lord find in us the way which He Himself vouchsafed to confer upon us, and by which He leads us to our true country. Then He may deign to say concerning us: "I will dwell with them and walk among them; I will be their God."[12] If He has walked among us in this life, He will dwell among us in that other one: who lives and reigns for ever and ever. Amen.

## * Sermon 218

### ON THE MARTYRDOM OF BLESSED JOHN THE BAPTIST[1]

Through the revelation of the Holy Spirit, dearly beloved, the prophet Isaias foretold the character of blessed John, whose feast we are joyfully celebrating today, much before he was born. For this is what he said: "The voice of one that cries out in the desert, 'Prepare the way of the Lord! Make

---

12 2 Cor. 6.16; cf. Lev. 26.12, Ezech. 37.27.

1 As two sources of this sermon Morin identifies St. Ambrose's work *On Virgins* and a sermon of St. Augustine's (Caillau et Saint-Ives II.6; *Miscellanea Agostiniana* I 252–55). The sermon is important as reflecting early observance at Arles of this second feast of the Baptist (August 29; Beck, *Pastoral Care* 312 at n. 101); see Sermon 216 n. 1.

straight the paths of our God! Every valley shall be filled in,
every mountain and hill shall be made low; the crooked shall
be made straight, the rough places plain.' "[2] Now all of these
things have been fulfilled through divine mysteries, dearest
brethren. If we are unable to do everything, we want to suggest to your charity, as far as God deigns to give the grace,
what the prophet says about the subject that is useful for you:
"Every valley shall be filled in, every mountain and hill shall
be made low."

(2) "Every valley shall be filled in," he says, "every mountain and hill shall be made low." We realize, of course, that
this was never fulfilled according to the letter, for through
the preaching of blessed John no earthly mountains were
brought low nor any. . . .[3]

(3) Now let us return to the martyrdom of the blessed
Baptist. As the Gospel says, John was in chains. The law, too,
was covered and bound with mystery, and because of the
wickedness of an unbelieving people, it lay in darkness in
order that it might not openly show the light of the Resurrection. John remained in chains and in prison. The law, too,
was kept locked up in the minds of the Jews as though in
places of condemnation, and spiritual understanding was restrained by the letter of the law as in a hidden, secret place.
John was committed to prison; the law was confined within
the darkened hearts of unbelievers as in a prison. The fact
that he was delivered over to death seemed to indicate that
the letter of the law, a mere shadow, was destined to die at
the approach of the law of grace. Just as the method of his
death did not lack glory, so it was not without mystery. For
when the daughter of Herodias had danced for Herod and
under the pretext of reward had made her request, she said:
"Bring me the head of John on a platter."[4] Herod sent word

---

2 Isa. 40.3, 4.
3 The text is interrupted at this point and resumes with the opening
  of section 3.
4 Matt. 14.8.

to the prison and cut off the head of John, and when the young girl received his head, she handed it over to her mother. O evil deed, which is more wicked than every evil, dissipation joined to drunkenness! The head of such a great prophet is accepted as the reward for dancing.

(4) What wonder is it, dearest brethren, that a dancing girl killed the prophet? For we know that dissipation is always the enemy of justice, and that error ceaselessly persecutes the truth. Wantonness, moreover, associates with cruelty. The head of the prophet is brought to the table of Herod; this dish was due to his inhumanity. Blessed John had told him that it was not right for him to take the wife of a man who was still living, and for this one admonition Herod had him thrown into prison. O how bitter reproof is to sinners! in order that wickedness may not be rebuked, it is multiplied. O unhappy guilty conscience! while it avoids its witness, it adds to its offense. Even if there is no one to chide him, can there be lacking people who know his guilt? Look at the distance between injustice and justice, brethren. Even when the judgment of God delayed, even in this world Herod was blamed for so many years, while John was praised just as many years. Truly "the memory of the just will" always "be blessed,"[5] but "the desire of the wicked shall perish."[6] The sinner desperately loves his pleasure, even though it lasts to his damnation. For even before judgment day the torments of a wicked conscience rage within him, and after his transgression there is no chance for him to escape punishment, while he himself becomes a punishment of his guilt. See how the fire of his conscience will ceaselessly consume Herod, while the pleasures of paradise will delight blessed John.

(5) Let our minds, too, be aroused by the examples of the saints, for by imitating such deeds perhaps we will sometime attain similar good things. If it is not our fortune to end this life in defense of the truth, at least let it be our lot to

5 Prov. 10.7.
6 Ps. 111 (112).10.

amend our life after we have heard the truth. Let us speak on behalf of the truth, and whenever we know that it is in difficulty, let us hasten to defend it as far as it is possible, knowing most certainly that the defender of justice is going to receive the crown of martyrdom. For if Christ is the truth, doubtless the man who has borne witness to it will be a martyr of Christ. Now it often happens that even we ourselves do something contrary to truth and justice. For this reason let us not only rebuke others who do these things, but let us also punish ourselves with fasting, vigils, and prayers, as often as we act contrary to justice, and also redeem our sins with more generous almsgiving. Then while we are rebuking others and with God's help amending our own lives, if we do not merit to receive the martyr's crown, we will at least deserve to obtain the forgiveness of our sins. With the help of our Lord Jesus Christ, to whom is honor and glory for ever and ever. Amen.

## * Sermon 219

### ON THE FEAST OF ST. STEPHEN[1]

Although the passage from the Acts of the Apostles which was read to us today, dearly beloved, contains much by way of something to admire, it possesses no less by way of excellent mystery. "Look!" exclaimed St. Stephen, "I see an opening in the sky, and the Son of Man standing at God's right hand."[2] Notice quite carefully, brethren, why he testified that he saw the Son of Man and not rather the Son of God, when

---

1 This sermon, wrongly attributed to Faustus of Riez by his Vienna editor, is derived in the first part, states Morin, from a homily (64) of Maximus of Turin, but in what follows it is truly Caesarian.
2 Acts 7.56.

the blessed martyr saw our Lord Jesus Christ standing at the right hand of God the Father. He saw, of course, that he would bring more honor to the Lord if he said that he saw the Son of God rather than the Son of Man, but a specific reason required that He be shown in heaven in the same way as He was preached in the world. The stumbling block for the Jews consisted wholly in the fact that our Lord Jesus Christ, who was the Son of Man according to the flesh, was also said to be the Son of God. For this reason, then, Sacred Scripture aptly recalled that the Son of Man was standing at the right hand of God the Father. In order to confound the unbelief of the Jews, Christ, who was denied by infidels in the world, was shown to the martyr in heaven. Those whose faith was diminished by earthly wickedness were given testimony of Him by heavenly truth. According to the psalm which was read, "Precious in the eyes of the Lord is the death of his holy ones,"[3] if there can be any difference between the martyrs, the one who was the first seems to be special in comparison with all the others. For although St. Stephen was ordained deacon by the apostles, he preceded the apostles themselves by a blessedly triumphant death. Thus one who was lesser in rank became the first in suffering, and he who was a disciple in rank came to be the teacher through his martyrdom, fulfilling what the blessed prophet said in the psalm that was just read: "How shall I make a return to the Lord for all the good he has done for me?"[4] Stephen the martyr was the first voluntarily to requite the Lord for what he, together with the whole human race, received from the Lord. For death, which our Savior first deigned to suffer for all men, was first repaid to our Savior by Stephen. After this, Sacred Scripture adds something further and says: "He fell to his knees and cried out: 'Lord, do not hold this sin against them.' "[5] Notice the disposition of the holy man, dearly be-

---

3 Ps. 115 (116).15.
4 Ps. 115 (116).12.
5 Acts 7.60.

loved, and see the greatness and admirable quality of his charity. He was subject to persecution, and he prayed for his persecutors. In the midst of that hail of stones, when another might have forgotten even those who were most dear to him, Stephen commended his enemies to the Lord. For what did he say while he was being stoned? "Lord, do not hold this sin against them." He grieved more over their sins than he did for his own wounds; he mourned their wickedness more than his own death. And he acted rightly. Surely there was much in their sinful deed which should have been bewailed, while there was nothing to grieve over in his death. Eternal death followed their wickedness, while endless life succeeded his death.

(2) In some fashion, dearly beloved, let us imitate the faith of such a great teacher, the charity of such an illustrious martyr. Let us love our brothers in the Church in the same spirit in which Stephen then loved his enemies. Sometimes— so much the worse!—we not only fail to love our enemies, but we do not even preserve complete loyalty to our friends. Now someone may say: I cannot love my enemy whom I endure every day as an exceedingly cruel opponent. Whoever you are, you pay attention to what a man has done to you, and you do not consider what you have done to God. Since you have committed much more serious offenses against God, why do you not forgive a little to a man, in order that God may deign to forgive you a great deal? Remember what truth itself promised you in the Gospel, how and in what way it cautioned you, and what kind of an agreement it made with you. It said: "If you forgive the faults of others, your heavenly Father will forgive you yours; if you do not forgive others, neither will your Father forgive you."[6] You see, brethren, that by the grace of God it has been put into our power how we are to be judged by our Lord. If you forgive, it says, you will be forgiven. I have often said it, brethren, and I ought to

---

6 Matt. 6.14, 15.

do so even more frequently: no one should flatter or deceive himself. If anyone harbors hatred for even one man in this world, no matter what he has offered God in good works, he loses it all. The Apostle Paul does not lie when he says: "If I give everything I have to feed the poor and hand over my body to be burned, but have not love, I gain nothing."[7] This truth blessed John also confirms by saying: "Anyone who does not love his brother is among the living dead";[8] and again: "The man who hates his brother is a murderer."[9] In this passage every man should be understood as a brother, for we are all brothers in Christ. Therefore no one should rely upon chastity without charity, nor should anyone trust in almsgiving, fasting, or prayers. As long as a man keeps enmity within his heart, he will not be able to please God by those or any other kind of good works. If a man wants to have God merciful to him, he should not disdain to listen to good advice. Let him not listen to me, but to our Lord Himself: "If you bring your gift to the altar and there recall that your brother has anything against you, leave your gift at the altar, go first to be reconciled with your brother, and then come and offer your gift."[10] We, however, who have internal struggles and keep turning over treachery in our hearts, dare to approach the altar as though we had a good conscience, not fearing what is written: "He who eats and drinks without recognizing the body eats and drinks a judgment on himself."[11]

(3) Again someone may say: to love my enemies and to pray for my persecutors is a great trial. For our part we do not deny it, brethren. It is not a small task in this world, but in the future life the reward will be great. Through love for a man who is your enemy, you will become a friend of God, as a matter of fact, not only His friend but even His son, as

---

7  1 Cor. 13.3.
8  1 John 3.14.
9  1 John 3.15.
10  Matt. 5.23, 24.
11  1 Cor. 11.29.

our Lord Himself says: "Love your enemies, do good to those
who hate you; this will prove that you are sons of your
heavenly Father."[12] If a man who is rich and powerful wanted
to make you his adopted son in this world, how would you
serve him? What indignities at the hands of his servants, what
very difficult duties would you endure—and sometimes even
most disgraceful ones—in order that you might reach that
transitory, perishable inheritance? What, then, another man
suffers for the sake of earthly wealth, this bear for the sake
of eternal life. We are overcome by very definite reasoning,
because we truly can bear injuries for the sake of God, but
we refuse to do so. Now if a very powerful person injures us,
if he curses us to our face, we do not dare to give a harsh
reply, nor to react in the same way. Why is this? So that we
will not suffer at the hands of that powerful person still
greater injuries than we have borne. Love of Christ should
have exacted of us what fear of a man wrested from us. If
a powerful person rages against us, we are silent, we have
dared to say nothing; but if someone who is our equal or
perchance inferior to us insults us even slightly, like wild
beasts we rise up without any patience and without any
thought of God. Then we either vindicate the injury on the
spot or at least we prepare our minds for a greater reprisal.
Why is it that when a powerful person commits an injury
against us, we accept it patiently, but when someone lesser
than we does so, we are aroused by excessive wrath? Because
we have feared man in the former case, but in the latter we
refuse to fear God. For this reason I beseech you, brethren.
With God's help let us prepare our hearts as far as we can
for patience. Let us strive to act like doctors toward all
wicked men, and let us hate their evil deeds but not the men
themselves. Let us pray for all good men that they may always
rise to a better life, and for the wicked that through the remedies of repentance they may quickly have recourse to amend-

---

12 Matt. 5.44, 45.

ment of life. If we pray for this, He deigns to grant it to us, who lives and reigns with the Father and the Holy Spirit God for ever and ever.  Amen.

## * Sermon 220

### For the Feast of St. Stephen[1]

As often as we ought to appeal to your charity to love your enemies in accord with the Lord's precept, I am afraid that some people think about it and say that they can in no way at all fulfill it. Perhaps they are even willing to object to the point of saying that they cannot imitate Christ. Behold, man, I am speaking to whoever of you says that he is unable to imitate his Lord in love of enemies. Surely blessed Stephen was a man and not God. He was what you are, but he did what he did only with the help of God, Him whom you also ask. See, however, what he did. He was speaking to the Jews; he was angry and he loved them. I must show you both sides— his anger and his love. Listen to him in anger—they are the words of St. Stephen when he was addressing the Jews: "You stiff-necked people, uncircumcised in heart and ears, you are always opposing the Holy Spirit; was there ever any prophet whom your fathers did not put to death?"[2] You have heard him speak out in anger. I must show you the other side; also listen to him as he loves. When those men had become enraged, their anger kept getting more inflamed, and they were returning evil for good. Then they ran for stones and began to hurl them at the servant of God. Show your love here, holy Stephen. Let us see and observe you here, let us in

---

1 Augustine's Sermon 49 has been drawn upon in this sermon, especially in the opening and ending. Morin finds no trace here of Faustus, to whom his Vienna editor ascribes it.
2 Cf. Acts 7.51, 52.

this discern you as triumphant victor over the devil. Behold blessed Stephen looking up at Him who hung on the wood of the cross for him. Christ was crucified, Stephen was stoned to death. The former said: "Father, forgive them, for they do not know what they are doing."[3] And you, blessed Stephen, what do you say? Let me listen to you and see whether perhaps I can at least imitate you. First blessed Stephen stood up and prayed for himself when he said: "Lord Jesus, receive my spirit."[4] After he had said this, he fell on his knees, and when he had done this, he said: "Lord, do not hold this sin against them."[5] When he had said this, he fell asleep in death. O blessed sleep and true repose! Behold what it means to rest happily: to pray for one's enemies.

(2) I ask you, blessed Stephen, to deign to explain to me why it was that you prayed for yourself standing, but for your enemies when you had fallen on your knees. If you were in our presence, doubtless this is what you would reply: I stood when I prayed for myself because I did not work hard as I begged and pleaded for myself, since I served God by an upright life. A man does not labor strenuously in praying for a just man, and for this reason he stood when he prayed for himself. Then he came to the point of praying for the Jews who had killed Christ and the saints, and who were then stoning him. He fell on his knees, because he recognized that their wickedness was vast and excessive and could only be condoned with great difficulty.

(3) Therefore, dearly beloved, let us imitate blessed Stephen as far as God gives us the grace to do so. Let us not only love our friends but also our enemies, because there is nothing whereby we can so well redeem our sins, overcome the devil, and please God. The Lord Himself has said this: "Give, and it shall be given to you; pardon, and you shall be pardoned."[6]

---

3 Luke 23.34.
4 Acts 7.59.
5 Acts 7.60.
6 Luke 6.38, 37.

Again: "If you forgive the faults of others, your heavenly Father will forgive you yours,"[7] and so forth. See, brethren, the mercy of our Lord. He has put it in our power to determine on what terms we are to be judged on the day of judgment. If we forgive, we will be forgiven; if we do not pardon, we will not be pardoned. For this reason, dearly beloved, let us not only love our friends but also our enemies. Then we can come before the tribunal of the eternal judge with a secure conscience and say: Give, Lord, because we have given; forgive, because we have forgiven. We have done what you commanded; so now fulfill what you promised. He will grant this, who lives with the Father and the Holy Spirit for ever and ever. Amen.

## * Sermon 221

A HOMILY OF THE BISHOP, ST. AUGUSTINE, ON THE FEAST OF THE APOSTLES, JAMES AND JOHN; HE ALSO SHOWS HERE WHAT IS GOING TO HAPPEN TO THREE FRIENDS, AND HOW THE SPECK IS NOURISHED INTO A PLANK[1]

I entreat you, dearest brethren, not to receive our words with reluctance, and not to consider that it is superfluous for us to admonish you quite frequently with regard to love of enemies. The reason we do this is that we realize that there is no better remedy to heal the wounds of all sins. It should not seem foolish to you that we so often invite you to love your enemies, even on the feasts of the martyrs. We want this to happen because we know that all of the martyrs reached

---

7 Matt. 6.14.

1 The Augustinian source here is Sermon 49.5-7. Caesarius' authorship was established in Morin's mind by the language used in the beginning and ending.

the crown of martyrdom because of their exceedingly perfect charity. We rejoice with great admiration that this was also fulfilled in the case of blessed Stephen. I beg you to listen carefully, brethren. Understand that in the case of all wicked men we ought to harbor hatred for their vices rather than for the men themselves; we should love the man but hate the wickedness. Do not love the vice because of the man, nor hate the man because of his evil deeds. The man is your neighbor, but the vice is inimical to your neighbor; so then you love your friend if you hate the wickedness which harms him. You do this, if you have faith, because "the just man shall live by faith."[2] I will tell you what happens very often in human affairs. Sometimes a man who was the friend of both of you is inimical to your very dear friend. Two of the three friends begin to be enemies of each other; what does the one who remains in the middle do? One of those men who hate each other wants you to hate the one he hates along with him, and he says these words to you: You are not my friend, because you are a friend of my enemy. Furthermore what this one says to you about the other, that other one says to you about him. Originally there were three of you; two began to be in disagreement, and you alone remained. If you ally yourself with the one, you will have the other for your enemy, and if you join the latter, the former will be hostile to you; if you associate with both of them, both will complain. Behold the temptation. Perhaps you expect to hear from me what you should do. Continue to be a friend to both of them, and those who disagreed with each other may return to harmony through you. If you hear any evil about one from the other, do not carry the story back to either one, lest perchance those who are now enemies later become friends and betray those who were treacherous to them.

(2) I have spoken these truths out of regard for men, not because of the eyes of God. Behold, no one is betraying you;

---

2 Rom. 1.17.

it is God who sees you and who judges you. You have heard
a word from a man who is angry, afflicted, and resentful; let
it die within you. Why is it repeated? Why is it revealed? It
will not tear you apart if it stays inside of you.[3] By all means
speak to your friend who wants to make you an enemy of
your friend. Speak to him and treat him with soothing medicine, like a sick soul. Say to him: Why do you want me to be
an enemy of that man? He may respond: Because he is my
enemy. Do you, then, want me to be an enemy of your enemy?
I ought to be an enemy of your sin. The one to whom you
want to make me an enemy is a man. There is another enemy
of yours to whom I ought to be an enemy if I am your friend.
He will reply: Who is that other enemy of mine? Your wickedness. He will respond: What is my vice?—The hatred with
which you hate your friend.

(3) For this reason be like a doctor. A doctor does not love
a sick man if he does not hate his sickness; he fights against
a fever, in order to free the man who has been ill. Do not
love the vices of your friends, even if you love your friends.
If you approach any one of them and he asks you where you
are coming from, tell him: I spoke with your friend, whom
you consider your enemy. In compassion he says good things
about you, and grieves over the misfortune of your quarrel
because he longs to lay down his life for the sake of your soul.
After you have pacified the one, go to the other and you will
speak to him in these words: I am amazed at the insensibility
of your fury. For how do you suppose that he can be hostile to
you with a hardened heart, when he speaks such good things
about you? I heard his conversation about you myself, to the
effect that he is not undertaking any plots against you. Instead he rather grieves over your loss, because he has great
confidence in you. It is necessary for each one to do these and
various similar things, so that the prophetic saying may be
fulfilled in us: "Blessed are the feet that bring peace."[4] Most

3 Cf. Sir. 19.10 (9).
4 Cf. Isa. 52.7.

blessed John the Apostle, whose feast is celebrated today, threatens us in dreadful words when he says: "Anyone who hates his brother is a murderer, and walks in shadows."[5] James also says in a similar way: "The man who does not love his brother is among the living dead."[6] There are also many other words, not mine but those of our Lord, the prophets, and all the apostles, as well as those of this John whose feast is being celebrated today throughout the world. If a man despises Augustine, let him at least fear the Lord.

(4) Now do you suppose that I who am telling you this do myself practice what I say? I do, brethren, if I first practice it in my own case, and I practice it in my own case if I receive from the Lord the help to do it. I present my vices to my Physician as an object of hatred, my heart to be healed. Moreover I punish my sins as much as I can, I groan over them, I confess that they are within me, and see, I accuse myself. Do you, who were rebuking me, correct yourself. This is just, so that it may not be said to us: "Why look at the speck in your brother's eye when you miss the plank in your own? You hypocrite! remove the plank from your own eye first; then you will see clearly to take the speck from your brother's eye."[7] Anger is a speck, hatred is a plank; but you nourish the speck and it becomes a plank. Anger that lasts a long time becomes hatred, the speck that is nourished becomes a plank. Therefore in order that the speck may not become a plank, "the sun must not go down on your wrath."[8] You see and feel yourself livid with anger, and do you rebuke another who is angry? Remove your hatred, and correctly chide the wrath. There is a speck in his eye, a plank in yours, and how can an eye with a plank in it see the speck? I do not know with what boldness a man rebukes another who is angry for a moment, when he himself harbors hatred in his heart. A man

---

5  1 John 3.15 and 2.11.
6  1 John 3.14. This is a quotation from 1 John, not from James.
7  Matt. 7.3, 5.
8  Eph. 4.26.

who is momentarily angry but quickly appeased incurs a speck, to be sure, but he immediately removes it through repentance. But if a man retains hatred in his heart for a long time, by nourishing the speck he changes it into a plank. There is a plank in your eye because you were unwilling to remove the speck as soon as it appeared there. You slept with it and got up with it, you cultivated it within yourself, you watered it with false suspicions. By believing the words of flatterers and of those who brought evil reports to you about your friend, you nourished it. You did not tear out the speck, but with great diligence you formed a plank.

(5) Remove the plank from your own eye: do not hate your brother. Are you terribly afraid, or not? I tell you: Do not hate, and you are secure. You answer and tell me: What does it mean to hate? and what evil is there in a man's hating his enemy? You hate your brother, and if you think little of hatred, listen to Sacred Scripture: "Anyone who hates his brother is a murderer." Therefore if you hate, you are a murderer. You have not prepared poison, you have not gone out with a sword to strike your enemy, you have not provided the minister of a crime, you did not fashion the place or time or, finally, the deed itself. You only hated, and you killed yourself before you slew the other man. Learn justice, then, so that you will hate nothing except the evil deeds of a man. If you adhere to this and act justly so that you prefer to heal even vicious men rather than condemn them, then you will happily come before the tribunal of the eternal judge, not with the hatred of one to be damned, but with the love and peace of one who is to be crowned. With the help of our Lord Jesus Christ, who lives and reigns with the Father and the Holy Spirit for ever and ever. Amen.

## * Sermon 222

### ON THE FEAST OF THE HOLY INNOCENTS[1]

Today, dearest brethren, we are celebrating the feast of those infants who, the Gospel text tells us, were killed by King Herod, and for this reason our land, the fruitful mother of heavenly soldiers and such great virtues, should rejoice with the greatest exultation. Behold, the wicked enemy could never have helped the blessed infants as much by submission as he did by his hatred. As today's most sacred feast shows us, the grace of benediction shone forth in the blessed infants as much as cruelty against them abounded. For we heard a little while ago that when King Herod was pursuing Christ, thousands of happy boys were killed. As the prophet said, "Rachel mourns her children, she refuses to be consoled because her children are no more."[2] The blessed mother of the triumphant, the land of illustrious warriors, rich in children, for a short time seemed to the eyes of the foolish to be bereaved. But she never was in need of consolation, nor did she bewail the sons whom she acquired with enviable sorrows, even while she lost them. Blessed are you, Bethlehem, land of Juda, who suffered the cruelty of King Herod in the death of your sons, and at the same time merited to offer to God a white-clad group of peaceable, sinless infants.

(2) We are celebrating in a fitting manner the feast of those children whom the world brought forth to eternal life more blessedly than birth from their mothers' womb bore them. They acquired the dignity of eternal life before they received enjoyment from the present one. The precious death of the other martyrs has merited praise in their confession of faith;

---

1 Morin agrees with the opinion expressed long ago by the Maurists: that the sermon consists of excerpts from Augustine (Serm. 220) and "Eusebius Gallicanus" but comprises segments that savor of Caesarius.
2 Jer. 31.15; cf. Matt. 2.18.

the death of the infants has been pleasing in its consummation. Death itself, which put an end to their present life, afforded a beginning of glory for them at the very beginning of their life. The wickedness of Herod took them away as they were nursing at their mothers' breasts. Rightly are they called "the blossoms of martyrdom,"[3] since a kind of frost of persecution along with cold unbelief consumed them in their very beginning, like the first emerging buds of the Church. For this reason it is proper to give ceremonial honor to the infants who were killed for Christ's sake, not to grieve over them; to manifest our intention in the divine mysteries and not in tears, because the one who was the source of their being hated was also the reason for their crown. The same one who was the cause of hatred is also the reason for their reward. While Herod was planning murder for the infants, Joseph was advised by an angel to take Christ the Lord into Egypt, a land full of idols. After the persecution by the Jews and the intent on the part of a wicked people to kill Christ, Christ Himself deigns to cross over to the gentiles, who were given over to idols. Leaving Judea, He is carried to a world which did not know Him, to be worshiped.

(3) Because in Sacred Scripture, dearest brethren, we know that good and just men have always suffered persecution from the wicked, if we notice carefully, we will discover that those who perpetrate it suffer greater punishments than those who seem to suffer it. For every man who persecutes another in his body is recognized as first suffering persecution in his own heart. If he takes something of the wealth of the man whom he is persecuting, he causes a still greater loss to himself, because no one secures an unjust gain without a just loss. Where there is gain, there is also a loss: a gain in the money-coffers, but loss in one's conscience. When a man takes another's clothing he loses his honesty; if he acquires money, he loses his sense of justice. Men, however, do this because they refuse

---

3 Prudentius, *Cathemerinon* 12.125.

to pay attention to the last day. If they were willing to think continually about the day of their own death, they would keep their minds away from every wanton lust or wickedness. But because they are unwilling to think about this in a salutary manner now, afterwards they will have to suffer without any remedy. For the last day will come for them, judgment day, when it will not be possible for them to repent or to save themselves from eternal death by good works. The sinner is tormented even by this punishment, that when he is dying God will not be mindful of him, since while he was alive he forgot about God. The day of judgment will come, on which the foundations of the mountains will be moved, and the earth "shall burn to the depths of the nether world";[4] when "the heavens will be destroyed in flames,"[5] when "the sun will be darkened, the moon will not shed her light, the stars will fall from the sky,"[6] when sinners and all wicked men will be hurled "into the pool of fire, and the smoke of their torments shall rise forever and ever";[7] "wailing will be heard there, and the grinding of teeth."[8] The time will come, dearest brethren, when no good man will fare ill, and no wicked man well. The last day will come, I repeat, when good men will be separated from the wicked, the just from the unjust, those who praise God from those who blaspheme Him. The time will come when they will be separated in such a way that no good man, as has already been said, will fare ill, and no wicked man well.

(4) Why, then, is it not so now? Perhaps it is, but what is now in secret then will be made manifest. Read Sacred Scripture; walk with me, if you can, "into the sanctuary of God";[9] perhaps there, if I can, I will teach you. Or rather learn with me from Him who taught me that even now there is no good

---

4 Deut. 32.22.
5 2 Peter 3.12.
6 Matt. 24.29.
7 Apoc. 14.11; for first phrase, cf. *ib*. 20.9, 14, 15.
8 Matt. 8.12.
9 Ps. 72 (73).17.

for the wicked, and that things are better for the good than for
the wicked, even though the full enjoyment of good things has
not come yet, just as the final punishment of the wicked has
not come. If you carefully heed the law of God, perhaps you
understand with me that nothing is well for the wicked. I
beseech you, and I ask you: Why are things not well for you?
You are likely to reply: Poverty chokes me, trouble pursues
me, and perhaps also bodily pain and fear of my enemy. So
it is bad for you because you suffer evil circumstances, and
good for the man who endures himself as an evil person?
There is a great difference between suffering in the midst of
evil and being wicked. You are not what you suffer. You
suffer evil but are not wicked yourself; that other man does
not suffer evil but is wicked. Therefore do not be deceived;
it cannot happen that it is not well for you who suffer evil
and is good for the one who is evil. Now since he is wicked,
do you think that he does not also suffer evil when he endures
himself? It is bad for you because you in your body suffer
evil from another; is it well for him when he suffers himself
as evil within his heart? It is not good for you if you have an
unproductive farm, but is it good for him when he has a bad
soul? Be good, you who possess good things. Riches are good,
and so is gold, silver, a household, possessions—all of these
things are good. What makes you good is how you act with
them, not what they are. Have possessions which make you
good, not those which make you evil. What are these? you
say. Pass judgment and act justly. These are the good things
which you possess; be good yourself in the midst of your good
possessions. Blush at your possessions; do not be wicked in the
midst of them, lest you perish along with them. God, the
creator and regulator of all things, distributed the gift of
gold and silver to men precisely in order that by nature and
variety it might be a good in itself. An abundance of it, however, should not lift up a man, nor a lack of it crush him.
When offered, it blinds the wicked, and when it is taken away,

it torments them. This comes about because when money is acquired it gives a false joy, and when it is lost it leaves real sadness.

(5) Let us learn, then, to love true riches, that is, integrity and justice, peace and compassion. These are called just riches, because they are granted for good and just merits. They are also called true riches, because whoever possesses them will not want and like the Apostle is content[10] if he has food and clothing. Therefore it is wrong to consider as riches earthly riches, which do not take away poverty, since the more a man who loves them has, the more will he burn with the bitter want of avarice. How, then, are they riches, when a want of them increases as they increase, and since they do not bring satisfaction but arouse further desires on the part of their friends, the greater they are? Do you think a man is rich when, if he owned less, he would need less? Well, therefore, someone said: "Your love of money grows as fast as the money itself."[11] The fury of desire is augmented by an increase of money, for all avaricious and covetous men seem to be sick with dropsy. Just as a man with dropsy thirsts all the more, the more he drinks, so the avaricious or covetous man runs a risk by acquiring more and is not satisfied with it when it does abound.

(6) For our part, brethren, as we recall that we are "strangers and foreigners"[12] in this world, let us keep for ourselves on the journey of this life only what we need for food and clothing. Let us further direct as much as we can to eternal bliss through alms for the poor. Then when on judgment day the covetous and avaricious, because of the barrenness of their good works, merit to hear "Out of my sight, you condemned, into that everlasting fire,"[13] because of our good deeds we will be able to hear: "Come. You have my Father's blessing!

---

10 Cf. Phil. 4.11.
11 Juvenal, *Satires* 14.139.
12 Hebr. 11.13.
13 Matt. 25.41.

Inherit the kingdom prepared for you from the creation of the world. For I was hungry and you gave me food, I was thirsty and you gave me drink, I was naked and you clothed me."[14] To this blessedness may our Lord Himself lead us under His protection: to whom is glory for ever and ever. Amen.

## Sermon 223

### ON A FEAST OF HOLY MARTYRS[1]

As often as we celebrate the feasts of holy martyrs, dearest brethren, through their intercession we expect to receive temporal gifts from the Lord in such a way that by imitating those same martyrs we may merit to receive eternal rewards. In the pleasures of the feasts, the joys of the holy martyrs are proclaimed by the very people who follow the example of the martyrs. The solemn feasts of the martyrs are exhortations to martyrdom, so that we should not be ashamed to imitate what we are glad to celebrate. For our part we want to rejoice with the saints, but we are unwilling to bear the suffering of this world with them. The man who refuses to imitate the holy martyrs, as far as he can, will not be able to reach their bliss, as the Apostle Paul preaches when he says: "If we share in the sufferings, we will also share in the consolation."[2] Our Lord also said in the Gospel: "If you find that the world hates you, know it has hated me before you."[3] The man who is unwilling to suffer hatred with the head [Christ], refuses to be a member of His body [the Church].

---

14 Matt. 25.34, 35, 36.

1 Long used in the Roman Breviary as a work of St. Augustine's, but, says Morin, totally Caesarian. So also Serm. 227 below.
2 Cf. 2 Cor. 1.7.
3 John 15.18.

(2) Someone may say: Who is there who can follow the footsteps of the blessed martyrs? To this man I reply that we can imitate, not only the martyrs, but, with His help, even our Lord Himself, provided that we are willing to do so. Listen, not to me but to our Lord Himself when He proclaims to the entire human race: "Learn from me, for I am gentle and humble of heart."[4] Hear, too, the blessed Apostle Peter as he admonishes us: "Christ suffered for you in just this way and left you an example, to have you follow in his footsteps."[5] Behold, Christ says, "Learn from me," and blessed Peter says "to have you follow in the footsteps" of Christ. The Apostle Paul exclaims in a similar way: "Be imitators of God as his dear children."[6] What will we reply to these words, brethren, or what excuse will we be able to have? If someone tells you that you should imitate the powers which our Lord exercised, there is a reasonable excuse for you, because not everyone is given the grace to exercise those powers and to work miracles. But to live piously and chastely, to preserve charity with all men,[7] with God's help is easy for everyone. For our Lord Himself did not say, Learn from me to raise the dead to life, to give sight to the blind, or to walk upon the waters with dry feet. This He did not say, but what did He say? "For I am gentle and humble of heart"; and again: "Love your enemies, pray for your persecutors, just as your heavenly Father has his sun rise upon the good and the bad."[8] Again we read: "You must be made perfect as your heavenly Father is perfect."[9] Although there are many other ways in which we ought to imitate both God and the blessed martyrs, these are two special ones, namely, to be meek and humble of heart, and to love our enemies with our whole heart and strength.

---

4 Matt. 11.29.
5 1 Peter 2.21.
6 Eph. 5.1.
7 Cf. Titus 2.12; Rom. 12.18.
8 Cf. Matt. 5.44, 45.
9 Matt. 5.48.

(3) No one will ever be able to excuse himself in all honesty, brethren, from loving his enemies. Someone can tell me, I am unable to fast or keep vigils; can he say, I cannot love? He may say, I cannot give all my possessions to the poor and serve God in a monastery; how can he say, I am not able to love? If you say that you are not able to abstain from wine or meat, we believe you; but if you say that you cannot forgive those who wrong you, we do not believe it at all. Now because there remains no excuse for us, while we are commanded to practice almsgiving, not from our storehouses but from our heart, let us love not only our friends but also our enemies, so that we may merit to reach the eternal country on the path of this life. By these two precepts, that is, "You shall love God"[10] and "You shall love your neighbor,"[11] we can happily reach the heavenly country as it were on two spiritual feet, provided that we are willing to run on the path of true charity. On these feet the Apostle Paul was running when he said: "I do not run like a man who does not keep his goal in sight."[12]

(4) If a man loves his enemies, what our Lord said is fulfilled in him: "Love your enemies; this will prove that you are sons of your heavenly Father."[13] Choose now what pleases you. If you love your enemies, you will merit to be not only the friend but even the son of God; if, however, you are unwilling to love your enemies, you cannot have God merciful to you, because it is written: "Anyone who hates his brother is a murderer."[14] Elsewhere we read: "The man who does not love is among the living dead";[15] and again: "The man who hates his brother is in darkness; he walks in shadows, not knowing where he is going, since the dark has blinded his eyes."[16] In still another place it is written: "The paths of

---

10 Matt. 22.37.
11 Matt. 22.39.
12 1 Cor. 9.26.
13 Matt. 5.44, 45.
14 1 John 3.15.
15 1 John 3.14.
16 1 John 2.11.

those who harbor resentment for an injury lead to death."[17] Are these my words, dearest brethren? They are taken from the canonical Sacred Scriptures. Therefore in order that we may not be murderers or among the living dead, let us strive to love, not only our friends but also our enemies. Then we will be able to meet a kind and merciful Lord with an easy conscience, in accord with the bond of His pledge.

(5) Our Lord Himself said: "If you forgive the faults of others, your heavenly Father will forgive you yours; if you do not forgive others, neither will your Father forgive you."[18] Listen carefully, brethren, and realize that it is one thing to sin against God and quite another to sin against a man. When men offend *us*, we incur sin if we do not forgive them when they ask for pardon. If, however, someone sins against God, we make ourselves sharers in his sin if we are willing to forgive without using great severity. For this reason our Lord says: "If you forgive the faults of others, your heavenly Father will forgive you yours." I ask you, brethren, what can be said more discreetly, more kindly, or more pleasantly? Christ has placed it in our power, how we will be judged on the day of judgment. He did not say, Go to the east and search for justice; sail to the west, too, in order that you may receive pardon. What did He say? Forgive your enemy, and you will be forgiven; pardon, and you will be pardoned; give, and it will be given to you. He asks nothing of you outside of yourself; God directs you to your own self and to your conscience. He has placed within you what He requires. You do not have to search for remedies for your wounds. If you will, you can find forgiveness of your sins within, in the storehouse of your heart.

(6) Still you say: My enemy has compelled me to suffer such great wrongs that I can in no way at all love him. Are you heeding what a man has done to you and not paying attention to what you have done to God? If you examine and search

---

17 Cf. Prov. 12.28.
18 Matt. 6.14, 15.

your conscience carefully, without any comparison you have committed many more offenses against God than the man committed against you. With what kind of boldness, then, do you want God to forgive you much, when you do not agree to pardon a little? If you are willing to accept the spiritual remedies which we mentioned above, as you usually do through the goodness of God, very carefully keep them hidden in the closet of your conscience. Then with the Lord's help you will not fear the poisons of the devil, and the wounds of souls will never strike you through hatred or anger. If, perchance, they do creep up on you, through charity they will quickly be restored to their former healthy condition. With the help of our Lord Jesus Christ, who lives and reigns with the Father and the Holy Spirit for ever and ever. Amen.

## Sermon 224

### ON FEASTS OF HOLY MARTYRS: THAT THE SOUL SHOULD BE ADORNED WITH GOOD WORKS JUST AS THE BODY IS ADORNED WITH EXPENSIVE CLOTHING

As often as we celebrate the feasts of holy martyrs, dearest brethren, we do not so much confer adornments as acquire them. Although those who are venerated are established in eternal bliss, those who render the honor are more in need of the adornments than those who seem to be honored. Now because veneration of the blessed martyrs adorns us very much, dearly beloved, as often as we celebrate the feasts of holy martyrs, we ought to show ourselves such that we make ourselves worthy of the sacred solemnity. Wicked men usurp the adornments of the saints in an unworthy manner, and certainly they do not derive the merit of this deed if they do not imitate the observance of it. What we read in the Gospel about that wicked man who appeared under false pretenses and without a wedding garment in a lofty place at the sacred banquet of a marriage should be a source of fear to us. For this deed that man deserved to hear: "My friend, how is it you came in here without a wedding garment?"[1] And when that man remained silent, the waiters were told: "Throw him out into the night where there is weeping and gnashing of teeth."[2] We, too, should fear this, brethren, lest we come to a feast of holy martyrs with our wedding garment damaged and much sullied by the filth of dissipation. For this reason, as we very carefully examine our consciences, if we see in them anything scorched through anger, stained through evil desires, or defiled through drunkenness or avarice, let us hasten to heal or cure it through repentance and almsgiving. Let us fear that it may be said to us, too: My friend, with what boldness do you presume to celebrate a feast of the martyrs, when you have corrupted yourself with the stains of so many vices? Since you are full of darkness, with what boldness are you entering a brilliant assembly? With what kind of conscience are you rushing into a place of peace and charity, when you are raging with hatred? Just as it is a great honor for the prudent and chaste and compassionate to participate in feasts of martyrs, so on the contrary the punishment will be burdensome and intolerable for adulterers and drunkards and robbers, if they do not first amend their lives.

(2) Everyone who is adorned with expensive clothing and covered with precious stones and gold because of the vanity of this world, brings joy to himself on the feasts of holy martyrs, because of his body. But if interiorly within his heart he is defiled and corrupted with the stains of vice, he prepares grief for himself in his soul. For when the body is exteriorly directed to wickedness, then the unhappy soul within slips into ruin. Now someone may step forth and say: Should we, then, be clothed with old and stained garments on the feasts of the

---

1 Matt. 22.12.
2 Matt. 22.13.

saints? This is not true, dearest brethren. Our clothing should be kept bright, becoming, reasonably and moderately provided, not excessively expensive because of the vanity of this world. Thus we read in Solomon: "Never glory in raiment."[3] We also ought to fear the example of that rich man "who was dressed in purple and linen."[4] For the man who possessed purple garments in this world merited to find nothing but flames of fire in hell, and he did not deserve this because of the fact that he was rich, but because he was avaricious and without compassion. Finally, dearest brethren, what I am advising is not difficult, and what I am asking is not unreasonable. If you are not able to overcome the pleasure and ostentation of this life, at least do this. Let your soul be adorned with good works in the same way as your body is adorned with expensive garments; let your soul go forth as splendid in the sight of the angels as your body appears adorned before the eyes of men.

(3) See and notice, rational man, that God has impressed His image upon your soul. Therefore the soul ought to command, and the body obey. But—and this is worse—I and men like me want to act in the opposite way: we despise the mistress and adorn the handmaid. The maidservant, that is the body, is adorned with expensive garments and lives luxuriously, while the mistress is covered with the old clothing of vice. Sometimes the former is filled with delicacies even to the point of intoxication, while the latter is tormented by hunger since the food of good works has been taken away. What is it that you are doing, man? You exalt clay, and you despise gold; you adorn and satiate with pleasures the body which worms are going to devour in the grave, while you despise the soul which appears before God and the angels in heaven. Now the soul is of incomparably greater worth than the body; that is, the mistress deserves much greater attention

---

3 Sir. 11.4.
4 Luke 16.19.

than the handmaid. Although this is true, brethren, the only thing that we ask at present is that you store up for your soul by almsgiving and good works as much as you provide for your body in food and adornments when you are going to celebrate the feasts of martyrs. Otherwise perhaps the body, which was accustomed to be adorned, will be devoured by a multitude of worms when it is lying in the grave, while the soul will appear before the eyes of the divine majesty defiled with the stains of many sins.

(4) Far be it from us that this should happen, dearest brethren. We ought not to act in such a way that we come before the tribunal of the eternal judge with confusion and a guilty conscience, lest that terrible, exceedingly fearful sentence be directed to us: "Out of my sight, you condemned, into that everlasting fire."[5] May we rather so control our body in a reasonable way that we strive to adorn our soul with good works. Then we will merit to hear that other word: "Well done! You are a good and reliable servant. Come, share your master's joy!"[6] Above all, as I have frequently advised, as often as holy feasts approach, give alms more generously, recall to harmony those who are in disagreement, love temperance and chastity. Then when you come to the altar of the Lord with a secure and easy conscience, you will be able to receive a remedy and not judgment from the Lord's Body and Blood: with the help of Him who lives for ever. Amen.

*Sermon 225*

ON FEASTS OF HOLY MARTYRS

As often as we celebrate the feasts of martyrs, dearest brethren, we ought to consider that we are fighting under the

---

5 Matt. 25.41.
6 Matt. 25.21.

same king under whom they merited both to fight and to
conquer. We ought to reflect that we have been saved by the
same baptism by which they were saved, have been confirmed
by the same sacraments which they deserved to receive, and
carry on our foreheads the sign of the same commander whose
insignia they, too, happily bore. Therefore as often as we
desire to celebrate the feasts of holy martyrs, the blessed martyrs ought to recognize in us something of their virtues, in
order that it may please them to beseech the mercy of God
on our behalf. For "every living thing loves its own kind."[1]
If, then, like associates with like, the unlike is separated at a
distance. Behold, our special blessed patron,[2] whose feast we
are eager to celebrate with joy, was temperate; how can the
drunkard be associated with him? What companionship can
the humble soul have with the proud, the kind with the envious, the generous with the avaricious, the meek with the
angry? Without any doubt the blessed martyr was chaste; how
will an adulterer be able to associate with him? And since the
glorious martyrs lavished even their own possessions on the
poor, dearest brethren, how will people who rob the property
of another be able to be friends with them? The holy martyrs
endeavored to love even their enemies; how, then, will those
who often are unwilling to make a return of love even to their
friends have a part with them? Let it not grieve us, dearest
brethren, to imitate the holy martyrs as far as we can, in order
that we may merit to be absolved from all our sins through
their merits and prayers.

(2) Now someone says: Who is there who can imitate the
holy martyrs? If not in everything, at least in many things we
both can and ought to do so with the help of God. You cannot endure the flame of fire? you can avoid dissipation. You
are unable to stand the torturing claw which tears one to

---

1  Sir. 13.19 (14).
2  Morin suggests that Caesarius has the local martyr St. Genesius in
   mind; cf. Beck, *Pastoral Care* 287-89 and index, p. 405 *s.v.*

pieces? despise the avarice which encourages wicked business deals and evil profits. If easy circumstances overwhelm you, how will harsh ones fail to break you? Peace also takes hold of its martyrs; for to overcome anger, to reject envy as the poison of serpents, to resist pride, to repel hatred from one's heart, to bridle superfluous desires of the appetite, not to give way to immoderate drink—all this is a great part of martyrdom. Whenever and wherever you see the cause of justice oppressed, if you give testimony in its behalf, you will be a martyr. Because Christ is both truth and justice, whenever either justice or truth or chastity is in difficulty, you will receive the reward of the martyrs if you have defended it with whatever strength you possess. And since in our tongue a martyr is interpreted as a witness, one who has borne witness to the truth doubtless will be a martyr of Christ, who is the truth.

(3) It is clear, brethren, that both truth and justice could defend themselves in this world without our help, but they allow themselves to be in difficulty because they want to test the merit of our faith, or rather because they desire to afford us an opportunity for merit. Provided that we defend justice and truth in this life, they will deign to come to our defense afterwards in the future life. If you defend them here in your country, they will repay you with a reward and give you consolation in life eternal, and there will be fulfilled in you what is written: "Blest are they who show mercy; mercy shall be theirs."[3] Therefore each one should cry aloud on behalf of chastity, peace, justice, and truth. He should cry out in their defense, as much as he can, whenever he sees them unjustly in trouble. If a more powerful man is persecuting truth, beseech him. If it is a person that is your equal who despises justice, advise him to remove himself from injustice; if he is unwilling to do this, as the Apostle says, do not take food with anyone of this kind.[4] If the person who is not doing what is right is your

3 Matt. 5.7.
4 Cf. 1 Cor. 5.11.

subject or of lesser rank than you, rebuke and punish him; if you can, even reprove him with severity. By beseeching, by giving advice, and by rebuke fulfill your own self in them, for God will demand His image of them.

(4) Not only the clergy, that is, bishops, priests or other ministers, will have to render an account if they refuse to preach, but also all lesser clerics and even the laity to whom God has deigned to give understanding. If they neglect to do so, as I said above, and fail to admonish or to rebuke, they should not doubt that they are going to bear the blame for them on the day of judgment. But I am not a bishop or a priest, someone may say; what business is it of mine how each person acts? he is going to render an account for himself. It is true that he will be rendering an account for himself, but you will not be altogether free from blame, if you have kept silent. In Sacred Scripture we read the precept that if anyone sees his neighbor's animal lying in the mud, he should not pass by without lifting him up.[5] You are commanded to pull out the ass or the ox which is lying in the mud. Do you, then, see a Christian like yourself, who was redeemed by the blood of Christ, lying in the sewer of drunkenness and wallowing in the mud of dissipation, and remain silent? Do you pass by and not stretch forth the hand of mercy by shouting to him or rebuking him or instilling fright in him? If he neglects to listen to you, mention it to the priest somewhat secretly, in order that he may accomplish by his authority what you were unable to obtain by your humble admonition. Know for a most certain fact that unless you first in secret and with great love admonish sinners, and later publicly do so if you have been rejected, that sentence must be directed to you: "If you do not warn the wicked man about his wicked conduct," it exclaims to careless bishops, "I will hold you responsible for his death."[6]

---

5 Cf. Exod. 23.5; Deut. 22.4.
6 Cf. Ezech. 3.18.

(5) In order that we may fulfill what the Apostle says, dearest brethren: "Help carry one another's burdens; in that way you will fulfill the law of Christ,"[7] let us always admonish each other in charity. As often as any one of us sins, let us willingly and patiently accept the reproof of a neighbor or a friend, because of what is said: "Reprove a wise man, and he will love you; rebuke a foolish man, and he will hate you."[8] Therefore I beseech you, brethren, to chide, rebuke, and reprove those who you know are dancing, leading songs, uttering disgraceful words voluptuously or drunkenly on the holy feasts. Admonish one another to observe chastity several days before the feasts of martyrs, and if you know that any are harboring hatred or scandal, recall them to harmony. Dispose yourselves to give alms, too, and have something ready to spend that you are giving for the salvation of your own soul. If you give alms in a cheerful and joyous spirit, there will be fulfilled in you what was written: "God loves a cheerful giver."[9] If, through the inspiration of God you willingly listen to these truths and endeavor to fulfill them faithfully, as you usually do, dearest brethren, you will approach the feasts of holy martyrs with joy and exultation both physically and spiritually. Then you will come to the altar of the Lord with a free and secure conscience, without any anger, with a pure heart and a chaste body.

(6) As I advised your charity already last year, dearest brethren, so I beseech and exhort you again. As often as we approach the more special celebration of the feasts of saints, if any want members of their household to be baptized, about ten days before or at least a week before, they should come to church with those who are to be baptized, and should approach for the anointing with oil and the imposition of hands. Above all, especially, those who want their children baptized should fast as far as their strength allows, and they

7 Gal. 6.2.
8 Cf. Prov. 9.8.
9 2 Cor. 9.7.

should come to vigils rather frequently. Thus in proper order their children will receive the sacrament of baptism, and the parents will obtain the remission of their sins. Although it is much better for those who are to be baptized to be kept for the Paschal feast, nevertheless because of emergencies due to human weakness, the gift of baptism cannot be denied, especially to those catechumens who quite often are ill. By the same reasoning, as I already said, fasting and vigils should precede it, and they should not delay coming beforehand for the oil and the imposition of hands, in accord with the regulations of the Church. If a man willingly listens to our advice and devoutly wishes to fulfill it, because of his obedience we are confident that in the mercy of God the good Lord will deign to grant him a reward both in this life and in the future one. Who lives and reigns with the Father.

* *Sermon 226*

A SERMON OF ST. AUGUSTINE ON THE MARTYRS AND ON GRACE[1]

Our Lord Jesus Christ gave great assurance to His witnesses, that is, to the martyrs who, on account of their human weakness, were worried that perhaps they would perish by confessing Him and by dying. He did this by telling them: "Not a hair of your head will be harmed."[2] Are you, whose hair will not be harmed, afraid of perishing? If superfluities of yours are protected in this way, under how much protection is your soul? A hair, which you do not feel when it is cut,

---

1 In this sermon, sections 1-5 are the work of Augustine (Serm. 333), to which Caesarius has added sections 6 and 7. These sections, Morin tells us, stand in close relation to definitions of the Council of Orange held in 529.
2 Luke 21.18.

does not perish; does the soul, through which you feel, perish? To be sure He foretold that they were going to suffer many difficult circumstances, in order that by His prediction He might make them stronger. They said, then, to Him: "My heart is steadfast."[3] What does this mean, "My heart is steadfast," except that my will is strong? In their martyrdom the martyrs had their will steadfast, but "their will was made steadfast by the Lord."[4] As they thought about the future harsh and difficult evils, He added: "By patient endurance you will save your lives."[5] By patient endurance, He said, for patient endurance would not be there if your will were not in it. "In patient endurance," but where does ours come from? Both what is had by us and what is given to us are ours, for if it were not ours, it is not given to us. How do you give something to another, unless it comes to belong to the one to whom you are giving it? That confession is revealed: "Will not my soul be subject to God? For from him comes my patience."[6] He Himself tells us: "In patient endurance." Let us also say to Him: "From him comes my hope." He made it yours by giving it to you; do not be ungrateful by attributing it to yourself. Do we not say in the Lord's prayer that what is from God is ours? Every day we say: "Our daily bread." You already said "our"; you also say "give us."[7] Look at "our," and look at "give us"; it becomes ours by His giving it. If it becomes ours through His gift, it becomes foreign to us if we are proud. You say "our," and you say "give us"; why, then, do you attribute to yourself what you did not give yourself? "Name something you have that you have not received."[8] "Our," and "give us," you say. Recognize the giver and admit that you receive, in order that He may deign to give willingly to you.

---

3  Ps. 56 (57).8.
4  Cf. Prov. 8.35.
5  Luke 21.19.
6  Ps. 61 (62).2, 6.
7  Matt. 6.11.
8  1 Cor. 4.7.

If you who are begging are not in need, why are you also proud? Or do you not beg when you ask for bread? Christ, who is equal to the Father, is our eternal bread, Christ in the flesh is our daily bread; He is eternal without any time, He is daily in time. Moreover, He is "the living bread that came down from heaven."[9] The martyrs are strong and courageous, but "bread fortifies the hearts of men."[10]

(2) Now let us listen to the blessed Apostle Paul. As he was approaching his sufferings and was trusting in the crown prepared for him, he said: "I have fought the good fight, I have finished the race, I have kept the faith. From now on a merited crown awaits me; on that Day the Lord, just judge that he is, will award it to me—and not only to me, but to all who have looked for his appearing with eager longing."[11] The Lord, just judge that He is, he says, will render to me a crown. Therefore He owes what He is going to give; that is why the just judge will render it. After examining his deeds, He cannot refuse the reward. What deeds does he examine? "I have fought the good fight" is the deed; so, too, is "I have finished the race" and "I have kept the faith"; "From now on a merited crown awaits me" is the reward. You do nothing with regard to the reward; you do not act alone in the deed. Your crown comes from Him, but the work is yours, although it does not happen without His help. When the Apostle Paul, who was first Saul, was an exceedingly cruel and fierce persecutor, he merited nothing good at all but rather a great deal of evil; he deserved to be damned, and not chosen among the elect. Then suddenly, while he was doing evil and meriting evil, he was thrown to the ground by a voice from heaven. The persecutor was cast to the ground, and the preacher was lifted up. Listen to him admitting his own condition: "I was once a blasphemer, a persecutor, a man filled with arrogance,

---

9 John 6.41.
10 Ps. 103 (104).15.
11 2 Tim. 4.7, 8.

but I have been treated mercifully."[12] Did he say there: "The just judge will give an award to me"? "I have been treated mercifully," he said; I deserved evil but received good. "Not according to our sins does he deal with us."[13] I obtained mercy; what was due to me was not given to me, for if what was due had been rendered, punishment would have been given. I did not receive what was due to me, he says; I have been treated mercifully. "Not according to our sins does he deal with us."

(3) "As far as the east is from the west, so far has he put our transgressions from us."[14] Turn away from the west, and turn to the east. See the one man, Saul and Paul: Saul in the west, Paul in the east; a persecutor in the west, a preacher in the east. Sins kill in the former place, and from the latter arises justice. In the west is the old man, in the east the new; Saul in the west, Paul in the east. How did this happen to Saul, the cruel man, the persecutor, the one who was not yet a shepherd? For he himself said: "I am a ravenous wolf, of the tribe of Benjamin."[15] It was said in prophecy: "Benjamin is a ravenous wolf; mornings he seizes the prey, and evenings he distributes the spoils."[16] First he consumed it, and afterwards he fed upon it. He ate it, and then he fed on it again. Read that he ate: read the book of the Acts of the Apostles.[17] He had received letters from the high priests that he should bring in bound for punishment those whom he found following the way of Christ. He went out raging, breathing out murder and blood: behold he ate. It is still in the morning, and vanity is under the light of the sun; evening comes to him, when he is struck by blindness. His eyes are closed to the vanity of this

---

12 1 Tim. 1.13.
13 Ps. 102 (103).10.
14 Ps. 102 (103).12.
15 Cf. Rom. 11.1. The words, "a ravenous wolf," are not part of Paul's statement in Romans; in adding them Caesarius draws upon the Genesis verse to follow.
16 Gen. 49.27.
17 Cf. Acts 9.1ff.

world, but other interior vision is illuminated. What was a
vessel of perdition a little before becomes a vessel of election,
and behold there is fulfilled "He will distribute the spoils."
Divisions of His spoils are read daily. See how he divides them.
He knows what is fitting for each one; he divides them,
he does not squander them at random or haphazardly. He
divides them; that is, he distributes and separates them, he
does not dispense them at random and without any system.
He speaks "a certain wisdom among the spiritually mature";[18]
but to those who are not able to take solid food he divides
and says: "I fed you with milk."[19]

(4) Behold, a man does this, who a little before did—what?
I do not want to mention it. Or rather, let me recall the
wickedness of the man, in order that I may prove the mercy
of God. The one at whose hands Christ suffered, suffers for
Christ. Paul is made out of Saul; a true witness is created out
of a false one. The one who was scattering gathers, and he
who was attacking defends. How did what we are saying
happen to Saul? Let us listen to his own word. You ask how
this happened to me? he says. "I have been treated mercifully."[20] This did not come to me from my own self: "I
have been treated mercifully." "How shall I make a return to
the Lord for all the good he has done for me?"[21] For He did
not return evil for evil; He clearly made a return, but not
evil for good; He rendered good for evil. How, then, shall I
make a return? "The cup of salvation I will take up."[22]
Surely you made a return? I still received. Now with suffering
obviously approaching, I will return good for good, not good
for evil. Now our Lord first owed evil for evil, but He was
unwilling to render evil for evil; He returned good for evil.

---

18  1 Cor. 2.6.
19  1 Cor. 3.2.
20  1 Tim. 1.13.
21  Ps. 115 (116).12.
22  Ps. 115 (116).13.

By rendering good for evil, He found a way of returning good for good.

(5) See that He found no good in Paul, who was first Saul. Although He found nothing good in him, He let the evil go and made a return of good. When He first rendered good things to him, He excelled. By giving the good things with which He would repay good, behold He returned a reward for that good, good deeds. He rendered good things to the one who was fighting a good fight, to the one finishing the race, to the one keeping the faith. But with what good deeds? Those which He Himself gave. Or did He not give you the grace to fight the good fight? If He did not give it Himself, what is it that you say in another place: "I have worked harder than all the others, not on my own but through the favor of God"?[23] Behold, again you say: "I have finished the race." Did not He Himself give you the grace to finish the race? If He did not give you the grace to finish the race, why is it that you say in another place: "It is not a question of man's willing or doing but of God's mercy"?[24] "I have kept the faith." You kept it, yes, you have kept it; I admit it and confirm it. I confess that you have kept it, but "unless the Lord guard the city, in vain does the guard keep vigil."[25] Therefore with His help and by His grace you have kept the faith. Grant pardon, Apostle, I know nothing that is yours except evil. Grant pardon, Apostle; we say it because you have taught us. I hear you admitting it, I do not find you ungrateful. We have not known anything devised by you entirely, except evil. Therefore when God crowns your merits, He crowns nothing except His own gifts.

(6) Let no arguments uproot this faith and true devotion; so no one will be lifted up of his own free will because of his good works. Each one should accept the gifts which he receives in such a way that he recognizes the one who gives

---

23  1 Cor. 15.10.
24  Rom. 9.16.
25  Ps. 126 (127).1.

them and is not ungrateful to the giver, haughty to his physician, still out of his mind, or at least not reasonable in himself. Let no arguments uproot from your hearts this faith and
true devotion, I repeat. Preserve what you have received. For
what do you have that you have not received? This is what
it means to confess God, to say what the Apostle Paul said:
"The Spirit we have received is not the world's spirit."[26] The
spirit of this world makes men proud and haughty, and it
causes them "to think they amount to something, when in fact
they are nothing."[27] But what does the Apostle say, contrary
to the spirit of the world? What does he say against the spirit
of this world which is haughty, proud, puffed up, arrogant,
without substance? "The Spirit we have received is not the
world's spirit but God's Spirit."[28] How do you show this?
"Helping us to recognize the gifts he has given us."[29] Let us,
then, listen to our Lord when He says: "Apart from me you
can do nothing";[30] and that other word: "No one has anything unless it is given him from on high."[31] Also: "No one
comes to me unless the Father who sent me draws him";[32]
and "I am the vine, you are the branches; no more than a
branch can bear fruit of itself apart from the vine, can you
bear fruit apart from me."[33] The Apostle James also declares
this when he says: "Every worthwhile gift, every genuine benefit comes from above, descending from the Father of the
heavenly luminaries."[34] This, too, the Apostle Paul exclaims
and says, to correct the presumption of those who glory in
their own free will: "Name something you have that you
have not received; if, then, you have received it, why are you

---

26 Cf. 1 Cor. 2.12.
27 Gal. 6.3.
28 1 Cor. 2.12.
29 *Ibid.*
30 John 15.5.
31 John 3.27.
32 John 6.44.
33 John 15.5, 4.
34 James 1.17.

boasting as if it were your own?"[35] And again: "It is owing
to his favor that salvation is yours through faith, this is not
your own doing, it is God's gift, so let no one pride himself
on it."[36] And still again: "It is your special privilege to take
Christ's part—not only to believe in him but also to suffer
for him; God, who has begun the good work in you, will carry
it through to completion."[37]

(7) As we carefully and faithfully reflect on these truths and
others like them, let us not agree with those who exalt free
will into pride and try to destroy rather than to elevate us.
With all humility let us consider what the Apostle says: "It is
God who begets in you any measure of desire or achieve-
ment."[38] Let us give thanks to our Lord and Savior who
healed us when we were wounded, without any preceding
merits of our own. He has reconciled enemies, redeemed men
from captivity, led them from darkness into the light, recalled
them from death to life. As we humbly confess our weakness,
let us implore His mercy, so that He may deign, not only to
preserve in us, but also to increase the gifts and benefits which
He has condescended to grant us. For according to the psalmist
His mercy overcomes all things, who with the Father and the
Holy Spirit lives and reigns for ever and ever. Amen.

---

35  1 Cor. 4.7.
36  Eph. 2.8, 9.
37  Phil. 1.29, 6.
38  Phil. 2.13.

*Sermon 227*

### ON THE FEAST OF A CHURCH[1]

As often as we celebrate the feast of an altar or of a church, dearest brethren, if we pay attention carefully and devoutly, and live both piously and justly, everything that is done in the churches built by hands is fulfilled in us as in a spiritual structure. The one who said "For the temple of God is holy, and you are that temple,"[2] did not lie; likewise when he said: "You must know that your body is a temple of the Holy Spirit, who is within you."[3] Now since we have merited to become the temple of God through His grace and without any preceding merits of our own, dearest brethren, let us put forth as much effort as we can, with His assistance, so that our Lord may not find in His temple, that is, in us, anything to offend the eyes of His majesty. Let the dwelling of our heart be freed of vices and filled with virtues; let it be closed to the devil and open to Christ. Let us labor in such a way that we may be able to open for ourselves the door of the heavenly kingdom with the keys of good works. Just as this door to life is closed to us by evil deeds as by locks and bolts, so without any doubt it is opened by good works.

(2) For this reason, dearest brethren, each one should examine his own conscience. When he knows that he has been wounded by some wicked deed, he should first strive to cleanse his conscience by prayer, fasting, and almsgiving and thus presume to receive the Eucharist. If the man who recognizes his own guilt withdraws from the sacred altar, he will immediately obtain the pardon of divine mercy. Just as "whoever exalts himself shall be humbled," so on the contrary "who-

---

1 See Serm. 223 n. 1.
2 1 Cor. 3.17.
3 1 Cor. 6.19.

ever humbles himself shall be exalted."[4] If the man who
realizes his own guilt, as I said, is willing to remove himself
humbly from the altar of the church in order to amend his
life, he will not be afraid of being entirely excluded from
that eternal and heavenly banquet.

(3) I beseech you, brethren, listen carefully. If no one dares
to approach the table of a powerful man with torn and
stained clothing, how much more so should he withdraw from
the banquet of the eternal king, that is, from the altar of the
Lord, if he has been struck by the poison of envy or hatred
or is filled with the fury of anger. He should do this with
reverence and humility, because of what is written: "First be
reconciled with your brother, and then come and offer your
gift";[5] and again: "My friend, how is it you came in here
without a wedding garment?"[6] A text of the Gospel passage
tells us that a certain man prepared a wedding feast for his
son, and when he entered, he saw everyone reclining. As he
saw there a man who was not wearing a wedding garment, he
said to him: "My friend, how is it you came in here not
properly dressed?" Then when that man remained silent, he
said to his servants: "Bind him hand and foot and throw him
out into the night where there is weeping and gnashing of
teeth."[7] See what kind of sentence a man will deserve to hear
if he dares to approach the Lord's nuptial banquet, that is,
His altar, as a drunkard or an adulterer, or harboring hatred
in his heart. May God turn this sentence away from us,
dearest brethren, and grant that we may never be willing to
commit those wicked deeds. If we have committed them, let
us without any delay strive to heal these wounds through
repentance and peace, and let us hasten to wash them away
by more generous almsgiving. Unless we do this, when we
come before the tribunal of the eternal judge with the wounds

---

4  Matt. 23.12.
5  Matt. 5.24.
6  Matt. 22.12.
7  Matt. 22.13.

of our sins, we may be separated from that eternal Church and from that heavenly Jerusalem, by an unending separation.

(4) I beseech you, brethren, consider this. If today a man is thrown out of the assembly of this church because of some wicked deed, in how much grief and tribulation will his soul be? If it causes unbearable pain to be thrown out of this church, where the one who is rejected can eat and drink and speak with men and has the hope of deserving to be called back again to the church, how much pain do we think there will be if, because of his sins, a man is separated from that Church which is in heaven, segregated from the assembly of the angels and the company of all the saints? For such a man it will not be enough punishment for him to be cast outside, but in addition he will be shut out into the night, to be consumed by an eternal fire. The man who has merited to be shut out of that heavenly Jerusalem will not only have for punishment the fact that he will not be able to eat or drink, but he will also suffer the flames of hell, "where there is weeping and gnashing of teeth."[8] There will be the wailing of lamentation and repentance without any remedy, that worm too which does not die, and the fire which is not extinguished;[9] there death is sought as an end to torment, and it is not found. Why is death sought and not found in hell? Because those who are unwilling to accept life in this world when it is offered to them will seek death in hell and will not be able to find it. There will be night without the light of day, bitterness without pleasure, darkness without light. There neither riches nor parents nor spouses nor children nor neighbors will be able to help a man. There the sinner will find nothing except what he sent over from this life through abundant almsgiving and by living chastely and piously.

(5) As we meditate on these truths, dearest brethren, let us strive with God's help to approach the altar so chastely, soberly, and peaceably that we may not merit to be excluded

---

8 *Ibid.*          9 Cf. Mark 9.47, 43, 45.

from that eternal altar. The man who comes to this altar with a chaste body and a pure heart and with a sincere and pure conscience will arrive at that altar which is in heaven by a happy crossing. Finally, dearest brethren, what I am suggesting to you is not burdensome or difficult; I am telling you what I see you often do. When they desire to communicate, all men wash their hands, and all women show their splendid garments when they receive the Body of Christ. What I am telling you is not burdensome, brethren. Just as men wash their hands with water, so they should cleanse their consciences with almsgiving. In the same way, just as women show their splendid clothing when they receive the Body of Christ, so they should show a chaste body and a pure heart and receive Christ's sacraments with a good conscience. I ask you, brethren, is there anyone who wants to put his clothing in a chest that is full of dirt? Now if expensive clothing is not put into a chest full of dirt, with what boldness is Christ's Eucharist received into a soul which is stained with the filth of sins? Because we have begun to speak in the most precise examples, I am also suggesting what you already know very well. I do not think that there is a man, who keeps precious garments locked up in a chest, who agrees to enclose within it either a live coal or any kind of spark. Why is this, brethren? Because he is afraid that the clothing which he wears on a feast may be burned. I ask you, brethren, if a man does not want to put a spark of fire in his chest of clothes, why does he not fear to kindle the flame of wrath in his soul? We know clearly and plainly why this happens. We do not put fire into a chest of clothes, because we love our garments; but we do not extinguish the fire of wrath because we not only fail to love our soul but even harbor hatred for it. This is according to what is written: "The lover of violence hates his own soul."[10]

---

10 Ps. 10 (11).6 (5).

(6) As we reflect on these examples more carefully, dearest brethren, with God's help let us strive to protect more diligently our interior chests, that is, our consciences, as far as we can. Then when judgment day comes, we may appear in that eternal and blessed church, where no wicked person will ever be able to dwell, and from which there will never be an exit for the just, and we will not be cast outside into the night with our old clothes. Covered with the robe of immortality, adorned with the jewels of chastity and justice, and covered with the bright light of almsgiving, may we rather deserve to hear: "Come. You have my Father's blessing! Inherit the kingdom";[11] and also: "You are a good and reliable servant; come, share your master's joy."[12] To this joy may the Lord lead us under His protection: who lives and reigns for ever and ever. Amen.

## Sermon 228

### ON A CHURCH, OR ON THE CONSECRATION OF AN ALTAR

As your holy charity knows very well, brethren, today we are celebrating the consecration of an altar. We rejoice rightly and deservedly, when we celebrate the feast on which the stone where the divine sacrifice is consecrated was blessed and anointed with oil. But when we celebrate these feasts, dearest brethren, we ought to pay careful attention and strive with all our might, so that what is visibly worshiped in churches or on the altars may be invisibly fulfilled in us. Although the churches which we see made of wood and stone are holy, still the temples of our heart and body are much more precious in the sight of God, because the former were made by carnal

---

11 Matt. 25.34.
12 Matt. 25.21.

man, while the latter were fashioned by the creator of the world. Churches are constructed of wood and stone by the talents of man, but the temples of our bodies and souls are formed by the hand of the divine artist Himself. Finally, as it is written: "Your hands have made me and fashioned me";[1] and again: "Before I formed you in the womb I knew you."[2] The fact that we are temples of God the Apostle Paul clearly shows when he says: "The temple of God is holy, and you are that temple."[3] Our Lord also says through the prophet: "Ever present in your midst, I will walk among them."[4] Now God desires both to dwell in and walk among us, as you see, dearest brethren. Let us, then, with His help strive always to occupy our heart with good thoughts and continually keep our bodies chaste, cleansed of all the filth of dissipation, in order that it may please God to dwell in us.

(2) We read that two altars were set up in the temple built by Solomon,[5] one outside, and one within. On the one that was outside, the sacrifice of animals took place, while on the one inside, the burning of incense was offered. Let us see, brethren, whether there are two altars set up in ourselves, the one that of the body and the other that of the heart. God, finally, asks a twofold sacrifice of us: the one, that we be chaste in body; the other, that we should be pure of heart. For this reason good works are offered on the exterior altar, that is, in our body. May holy thoughts emit a sweet fragrance in our hearts, and let us continually do what is pleasing to God on the altar of our heart. We celebrate the consecration of an altar with joy and in a right order of things at the time when we offer the altars of our heart and body purified in the sight of the divine majesty and with a good conscience. I do not know with what boldness or with what kind of a conscience a man desires to rejoice at the consecration of an altar, if he

1 Ps. 118 (119).73.
2 Jer. 1.5.
3 1 Cor. 3.17.
4 Cf. Lev. 26.12.
5 3 (1) Kings 8.64; 6.20 and elsewhere.

does not strive to preserve purity on the altar of his heart. For our part, brethren, let us endeavor to live in such a way that we may always merit to celebrate a twofold feast. Just as we rejoice visibly at the consecration of a church or of an altar, so let us invisibly merit to feel spiritual joy as the result of bodily chastity and purity of soul.

(3) Notice this, too, brethren. On that altar which we read was dedicated by Solomon, a continual flame was kept burning every day; may the divine goodness also effect this in us. For this reason God should be entreated and appeased, not only by our prayers, but also by good works, so that on the altar of our heart He may always light that fire of His, concerning which He Himself said: "I have come to light a fire on the earth; how I wish the blaze were ignited!"[6] Now there are two fires, obviously one of evil desires and one of charity. The one is on the side of God, the other on the side of the devil; the one consuming all evil, and the other destroying everything that is good. For this reason each one should examine his own conscience, and if he sees the fire of passion burning, with God's help he should hasten to extinguish it. Nothing good can remain in him if the fire of evil desires is burning, just as on the contrary no evil will remain in the man in whom the fire of charity burns. The flame of evil desires in the heart of a sinner as on a sacrilegious altar devours everything good and exhales an odor of sweetness for the devil, but in the holy soul as on a sacred altar the flame of charity consumes whatever evil is present and burns for God the fragrant incense of repentance.

(4) Because each one's heart is the altar of either God or the devil, as I already said, everyone should examine his own conscience, and if it is consumed by the fire of passion it should be relieved by the cooling effect of almsgiving, for it is written: "Just as water quenches a flaming fire, so alms atone for sins."[7] If a man is consumed with evil desires, he should

6 Luke 12.49.
7 Cf. Sir. 3.33 (29).

remove wicked deeds from himself and try to practice what
is good. However, if a man is on fire with the flame of charity,
this should always be increased through good works, and he
should nourish within himself the fire which Christ has
deigned to enkindle in him. Just as the man in whom the
fire of passion burns is immediately inflamed with the fire of
charity if he desists from his wicked deeds, so on the contrary
if the man who is filled with the light of charity is careless,
charity quickly grows cool and wicked passion is ignited. For
this reason the man who is wicked should not despair, because
he can quickly recover; likewise the man who is good should
not stay careless or presume in any way on his own virtue,
lest his joy be turned into grief.

(5) Therefore, dearest brethren, let us with God's help
strive to preserve bodily chastity and purity of heart as far
as we can, for it is by these means that the fire of charity or at
least of repentance is always kindled and nourished. If a
man does not observe chastity in his body and purity in his
mind, as often as the sacred feasts come he seems to experience
joy in his body, but in his heart he enjoys nothing but grief.
For what kind of joy can a man have with such a conscience,
when the devil rather than Christ is proved to dwell in his
soul that is possessed by many vices? What kind of joy can a
soul have, if it is on fire with the fury of anger, dimmed by
the darkness of evil desires, filled with the biting smoke of
pride, struck by the poison of envy, or stained with the filth
of dissipation?

(6) For our part, dearest brethren, even if some sins creep
up on us, as is wont to happen, with God's help let us strive
as much as we can, through fasting, vigils, prayers and almsgiving, to cleanse what is dirty, to restore what was destroyed,
to build up what had fallen, and to rebuild the temple of the
living God. Then when the Lord comes He will find nothing
in us to offend the eyes of His majesty, because it is written
of Him: "Here I stand, knocking at the door; if anyone arises

and opens the door, I will enter his home and have supper
with him, and he with me";[8] and again: "I and my Father
will come and make our dwelling place with him."[9] How
happy is that soul, in which the Father and the Son, when
they come, deign not only to dwell and abide, but also to have
supper! The fact that He says "I will have supper with him,
and he with me," means that if we reinstate Him in this world
through our good works, He will renew us in the future life
by His gifts, according to what is written in the Gospel:
"Come. You have my Father's blessing! Inherit the kingdom:
for I was hungry and you gave me food";[10] and "As often as
you did it for one of my least brothers, you did it for me."[11]
In order that we may merit to be delivered from hearing the
evil words in which it will have to be said "Out of my sight,
you condemned, into everlasting fire,"[12] and may be able to
hear that desirable word, "Come, you have my Father's blessing! Inherit the kingdom," let us preserve in ourselves purity
of heart and chastity of body. Let us also dispense more
generous alms to the poor, because He does not lie who said:
"Blest are they who show mercy; mercy shall be theirs."[13]
For this reason we repeatedly recommend to you the misery
of the poor and of strangers, hoping that this plea will prevail
with you on their behalf, and that our admonition or preaching will not be in vain. At the command of Christ we bring
a delegation of the poor into your presence, and if your charity willingly listens to me pleading in their behalf, doubtless
Christ will hear me when I pray for you. God has placed me
like a mediator between the poor and you. It seems to me
that your prayer will be heard by Christ in the same way in
which my prayer has been heard by you on behalf of the need

---

8 Apoc. 3.20.
9 John 14.23.
10 Matt. 25.34, 35.
11 Matt. 25.40.
12 Matt. 25.41.
13 Matt. 5.7.

of strangers. This did Christ Himself promise when He said: "Give, and it shall be given to you; pardon, and you shall be pardoned."[14] May He deign to grant this, who lives and reigns for ever and ever. Amen.

### Sermon 229

## ON THE FEAST OF A CHURCH[1]

Through the goodness of Christ, today we are celebrating with joy and exultation the feast day of this temple, dearly beloved, but it is we who ought to be the true, living temple of God. Deservedly, Christian people devoutly celebrate the sacred feast of their mother, the Church, through whom they realize that they have been spiritually reborn. For we, who were "vessels fit for the wrath" of God through our first birth, have merited to become "vessels for mercy"[2] through the second one. The first birth brought us forth to death, but the second one recalled us to life. All of us, beloved, were temples of the devil before baptism; after baptism we have merited to be the temples of Christ. If we reflect somewhat carefully on the salvation of our soul, we recognize that we are the true and living temple of God. God not only "dwelleth in buildings made by human hands"[3] or in those constructed of wood and stone, but above all in the soul which has been made according to the image of God and was formed by the hand of

---

14 Luke 6.38, 37.

1 The authenticity of this sermon, Morin states, has been established by its inclusion in an eighth-century homiliary in Würzburg (Mp. th. f. 28). See below, n. 5.
2 Rom. 9.22, 23.
3 Acts 7.48.

the Creator Himself. Thus the blessed Apostle Paul said: "The temple of God is holy, and you are that temple."[4]

(2) These temples are made of wood and stone[5] in order that the living temples of God may gather there and come together into one temple of God. A single Christian is one temple of God, and many Christians are many temples of God. Also notice, brethren, how beautiful is the temple which is constructed from temples; just as many members form one body, so many temples form one temple. Now these temples of Christ, that is, devout Christian souls, are scattered throughout the world, but when judgment day comes they will all be gathered together and will form one temple in eternal life. Just as the many members of Christ form one body and have one head, Christ, so also those temples have Christ Himself as their inhabitant, because we are members of Him who is our head. Thus the Apostle says: "May Christ inwardly dwell in your hearts through faith."[6] Let us rejoice because we have merited to be the temple of God, but let us be afraid that we may violate the temple of God by evil deeds. Let us fear what the Apostle says: "If anyone destroys God's temple, God will destroy him."[7] God, who could without any difficulty form heaven and earth by the power of His word, deigns to dwell in you, and for this reason you ought to act in such a way that you cannot offend such an inhabitant. Therefore let God find in you, that is, in His temple, nothing filthy or dark or haughty. If He suffers an injury there, He quickly withdraws, and if the Redeemer departs, the devil immediately draws near. What will be the condition of that unhappy soul, when it is deserted by God and possessed by the devil? Such a soul is deprived of light and filled with darkness; it is drained of

---

4 1 Cor. 3.17.
5 The text gives two different versions of section 2. We have followed the version that Morin took from the Würzburg homiliary (cf. above n. 1). This, the longer one, includes most of the other.
6 Eph. 3.16, 17.
7 1 Cor. 3.17.

all sweetness and saturated with bitterness; it destroys life and finds death; it acquires punishment and loses paradise. Now since God has willed to make out of us a temple for Himself and deigns to dwell in us continually, with His help let us strive as much as we can to lay aside what is superfluous and to gather what is useful. Let us reject dissipation, preserve chastity, despise avarice, seek compassion, scorn hatred, and love charity. If we do this with God's help, brethren, we continually invite God into the temple of our heart and body.

(3) For this reason, beloved, if we want to celebrate a feast of the Church with joy, we should not destroy the living temples of God within us by evil deeds. I will tell you what everyone can understand. As often as we come to church, we ought to prepare our souls to be such as we want to find the church. You want to find the church shining; do not defile your soul with the filth of sin. If you want a church to be full of light, God also wants your soul not to be in darkness. What our Lord says, should happen, that the light of good works shine forth in us in order that He who is in heaven may be glorified. Just as you enter this church, so God wants to enter your soul, as He promised: "I will dwell with them and walk among them."[8] Just as we do not want to find pigs or dogs in church, for they cause us to shudder, so God should not find in His temple, that is, in our souls, any sin which might offend the eyes of His majesty.

(4) As often as you desire to celebrate the feast of a temple, you ought to come to church temperately and peaceably. For this reason several days beforehand, observe chastity even with your own wives and according to your means give alms to the poor. Also present the offerings which are consecrated on the altar, pay tithes from your resources, receive strangers, and recall the discordant to harmony. If we come to the feast of a church and the solemn festival of the saints in such a spirit, we will merit to obtain in its entirety whatever we

---

8  2 Cor. 6.16.

have justly willed to ask of God. Above all it is necessary for
you to come to church with pure hearts, just as you come
with bright garments, for it does you no good to appear glittering in the eyes of men, if you are filthy in the sight of the
angels. To be sure, brethren, when we want to enter church
and communicate we first wash our hands. Now as we wash
our hands with water, it is just as necessary for us to cleanse
our souls through charity and almsgiving, according to what
is written: "If you give alms, all will be clean for you."[9] And
again: "Just as water quenches a flaming fire, so alms atone
for sins."[10] A sheen on our body is not at all profitable for
us, if purity is not preserved in our heart. If it is wicked and
disgraceful to approach the altar with dirty hands, how much
worse is it to receive the Body and Blood of Christ into a
soiled soul? If you are unwilling to put your clothing into a
chest full of mud, how have you dared to take Christ's sacrament into a soul that is full of sin? Surely when women come
to the altar, they all wear glittering clothing in which they
receive the sacrament of Christ. This they do justly and properly, but they should pay attention and reflect that, just as
they wear bright clothes, so they should show that their souls
are bright. If they do otherwise, Christ's sacrament will suffer
injury in them. In order that we may deserve to receive our
Lord's Body and Blood as a remedy and not to our judgment,
with His help let us labor as much as we can that they may
not suffer injury in us because of our evil deeds. Every man
who leads a wicked life does an injury to Christ. Just as you
do not want to suffer damage to your house, so God, too, does
not want to suffer any damage to His dwelling, that is, to your
soul. Therefore if you do not spare yourself on your own
account, at least do so for the sake of God who has deigned
to make you His temple. All men who are drunkards, adulterers, envious or proud, injure Christ; all thieves and perjurers,
all men who fulfill vows to trees or fountains, everyone who

9 Luke 11.41.
10 Sir. 3.33 (29).

consults magicians and soothsayers or sorcerers on their own account or for the sake of their household—all who are men of this kind eject Christ from their hearts and bring in the devil. What will be the nature of that unhappy soul who despises life and chooses death, who scorns light and seeks darkness? All Christians of this kind, as I said, even though they come to church, communicate at the altar, and are seen to sign themselves with the cross quite frequently, are proved to serve, not Christ, but the devil, unless they have amended their lives through repentance. On the other hand Christians who are chaste, humble, temperate and kind, who come to church rather often, practice almsgiving, observe peace and charity, and do not bear false testimony—in such men the temple of Christ is kept intact, and Christ is known to dwell in them.

(5) For this reason, brethren, with God's help let us avoid serious sins. As for the small sins of which we cannot be free, let us resist them by daily almsgiving and redeem them by continuous prayer, so that, as I said, Christ who desires to dwell within us may not suffer any injury. There are two who want to dwell within us, Christ our Lord and the devil our adversary; both of them knock at the door of our heart. Do not reject Christ, if you want to be unafraid of the enemy; cling to the lawful king, and you will not fear the cruel tyrant; hold fast to the light, and darkness will not dare to approach you; love life, in order that you may be able to avoid death. Therefore let us fill our soul with the sweet perfume of chastity, brighten it through almsgiving, and adorn it with the flowers of various virtues, in order that we may invite Christ our Lord in faith, feed Him with hope, and give Him to drink with charity. As often as there are solemn feasts, let us come to church, not only with a chaste body but also with a pure heart. Above all let us preserve in our heart hatred for no man, for he who harbors hatred for even a single person should listen to the Scriptures say: "Anyone who hates his brother is a

murderer."[11] Now if the man who hates his brother is a murderer, with what boldness does he presume to communicate at the altar of the Lord? Therefore if a man has injured another, he should quickly ask pardon, and if he has suffered an injury, he should immediately forgive, in order that we may be able to say to God with assurance in the Lord's prayer: "Forgive us the wrong we have done as we forgive those who wrong us."[12]

(6) The sacrament of baptism can be denied to no man, dearest brethren, especially if bodily sickness seems to demand it. However, it is good and proper for those who are in good health to be kept for the Paschal feast. In accord with the regulations of the Church, these people should fast and keep vigils during the days of Lent and should approach for the anointing with oil and the imposition of hands. If a man wants his son to be baptized on a certain feast, it is proper for him to come to church with him at least seven days before, to fast and keep vigil there. He should also have his son come for the anointing with oil and the imposition of hands, as was said above, and so he will receive the sacrament of baptism in the right order of things. Men who do this both have their sons receive the sacrament of baptism and acquire pardon for their own sins, while they are watching and fasting. If a man is unwilling to do this and brings his son to the sacrament of baptism just on time, he should know that he is committing no slight sin, as we have said, because he has refused to bring him for the anointing with oil and the imposition of hands. Know that you yourselves are a surety before God, dearest brethren, for the infants whom you have received in baptism. For this reason, then, endeavor to advise and rebuke them always, so that they may live chastely and justly and temperately. Above all show them the creed and the Lord's prayer, and encourage them to good works, not only by words but also by examples. While men who live chastely

11 1 John 3.15.
12 Matt. 6.12.

and justly and temperately give the example of a good life to others, they will receive a reward both for themselves and for the others. On the contrary, too, those who lead a wicked life and observe neither chastity nor justice, receiving "bribes against the innocent"[13] as often as they hear cases, will have to endure eternal punishments for as many people as the number of those to whom they gave the example of an evil life. Let us rather trust in the mercy of God, that He will inspire us to live in such a way that we may not be able to incur punishment because of our evil deeds, but rather to reach eternal rewards on account of our good deeds. With the help of our Lord Jesus Christ, to whom is honor for ever and ever.

*Sermon 230*

## ON THE CONSECRATION OF A BISHOP[1]

The office of bishop is a good work, dearest brethren, as the blessed Apostle says: "Whoever wants to be a bishop aspires to a noble task."[2] Now when "task" is heard, labor is understood. Therefore whoever desires the office of bishop with this understanding, wants it without the arrogance of ambition. To express this more clearly, if a man wants not so much to be in authority over the people of God as to help them, he aspires to be a bishop in the true spirit.

(2) Now my sermon is directed to you, beloved brother, at whose election so many people today rejoice in Christ. And they rejoice correctly and rightly, for it redounds to the honor and advantage of all the faithful, when they have such a bishop, by whose assistance many people are helped and by

---

13 Ps. 14 (15).5.

---

1 Morin notes the close resemblance of this sermon to Caesarius' admonition to the bishops (Serm. 1).
2 1 Tim. 3.1.

whose example they are inspired. Because you are not ignorant of what we think about the sincerity of your soul as a result of our previous knowledge of you, you know that we very justly demand that you prove what we have assumed about you. For this reason, dearest brother, I advise you with a unique and singular charity, that authority may not be lacking to your humility, that gentleness may offset your firmness, mildness temper your justice, and patience restrain your freedom of action. Avoid pride, into which it is natural for anyone to fall, and pursue humility, in which everyone ought to grow. Let your beloved self not be ignorant of the laws of the Church, in order that you may keep the rights of your authority within the rules and regulations of the Fathers. To be sure it is said "that the law is not aimed at the good man,"[3] because he fulfills the norm of the precept by the judgment of his will. True love holds within itself both the authority of the Apostles and canonical sanctions, and let your pious will always pursue examples of these.

(3) As for you, the brothers and sons for whom the divine goodness has deigned to provide such a worthy bishop, know and understand how grave a burden weighs upon the neck of bishops. Everyone of the people will have to render an account for himself alone, but a far different condition exists for the Lord's bishops, since the souls of all men are going to be required of them. To them the Holy Spirit pronounces the terrible words: "If you have warned the wicked man about his wicked conduct, you shall have your life";[4] and again: "Cry out full-throated and unsparingly, lift up your voice like a trumpet blast; tell my people their wickedness, and the house of Jacob their sins."[5]

(4) Again and again my sermon is directed especially to you, at whose appointment we know that so many people rejoice in Christ. I know that you cannot be ignorant, dearest

---

3 1 Tim. 1.9.
4 Cf. Ezech. 3.19.
5 Isa. 58.1.

brother, as to how all of the Lord's bishops are going to render
an account for the souls of everyone. For this reason, with the
Lord's help courageously cling to patience in great fear and
trembling. In addition, if grief and trouble, even perils and
reproaches from an unlearned people are stirred up as the
result of a spirit of animosity, bear them with courage and
constancy. Look rather to our Lord and Savior, the true shepherd who condescended to suffer, not only tribulation but even
death, for the sake of His sheep. It is necessary for you to bear
many adversities, if you want to preserve right doctrine and
continuously to preach the word of God as it is expedient to do.
The precepts of justice are always bitter to men who lead a
wicked life, and for this reason I exhort you today in the sight
of God and His angels, and I declare with the voice of the
Apostle: "Devote yourself to the reading of Scripture, to
preaching and teaching."[6] "I charge you to preach the word,
to stay with this task whether convenient or inconvenient—
correcting, reproving, appealing—constantly teaching and
never losing patience."[7]

(5) Mark and see to it that involvement in worldly affairs
not keep you so occupied that you are unable to have time
for the word of God. Instead, fear what is written: "The burdens of the world have made them miserable,"[8] and another
text: "No one serving as God's soldier becomes entangled in
worldly affairs, that he may please the one under whom he en-
listed."[9] Christ did not appoint you today to be the cultivator
of fields but to be the shepherd of souls. Because to you is
directed today that word of our Lord and Savior in which He
exclaimed three times, "Tend my sheep,"[10] assume the office
of preaching in such a way that you may not be unable to
have time for the word of God and to provide the spiritual
food of souls to your flock because you are choked by present

6 1 Tim. 4.13.
7 2 Tim. 4.2.
8 On this quotation see Serm. 196 n. 2.
9 2 Tim. 2.4.
10 John 21.17.

cares. Entrust to your children the worldly transactions which must be taken care of, in order that your soul may be occupied only with those matters of business through which salvation is imparted to all men. Just as you will incur the guilt of sin if you assume worldly cares and neglect study of the word of God, so it will be a serious sin for each of your children if they refuse to relieve the needs of the Church. Like true, excellent Christians, those children of the Church should strive to handle and direct with justice everything that pertains to the world, leaving to you only solicitude for doctrine. For if you are busy with worldly concerns, you both deceive yourself and leave the flock entrusted to you to be devoured by wild beasts. For this reason keep yourself free for this one task, to teach your children, fitly and without ceasing, the things whereby they may attain eternal salvation. The people entrusted to you should listen to you, too, with such great reverence that they may recognize that you are their advocate and herald.

(6) Again I admonish you, dearest brother, to restore with manifold interest before the tribunal of the eternal judge, the talents which our Lord today has entrusted to you to be multiplied by you like a good businessman. As far as you can, see to it that you do not bury the talent you received, like the useless servant. In other words, do not extinguish the light of doctrine because you are involved in worldly occupations. Instead, always tremble more and more, fearing that if you refuse to take time for the word of God, perhaps you will deserve to hear: "You worthless, lazy servant! Why didn't you deposit my money with the bankers, so that on my return I could have had it back with interest?"[11] May God avert from us what follows: "Throw this worthless servant into the darkness outside, where there will be wailing and gnashing of teeth."[12] Behold with what kind of sentence men will be

---

11 Cf. Matt. 25.26, 27.
12 Matt. 25.30.

condemned, if they are so much involved with occupations of this world that they are unwilling to listen to the Apostle when he says: "Devote yourself to the reading of Scripture, to preaching and teaching";[13] and that other text: "Do not forget that for three years, night and day, I never ceased warning you individually even to the point of tears."[14] If the Apostle preached the word of the Lord day and night to the people entrusted to him, in order that he might absolve himself in the sight of God, what will happen to us if we neglect to serve the salt of doctrine to the sheep entrusted to us on feasts or on Sundays? For this reason, with God's help let us labor as much as we can to spend on the people committed to our care the spiritual coin of the Lord, not only in church, but also in assemblies, at banquets, and wherever we are. For our part let us distribute this coin, because when He comes He is going to demand interest. If we do this faithfully, we will be able, when we come before the tribunal of the eternal judge, to say with assurance, along with the prophet: "Look at me and the children whom you have given me."[15] Then in return for the multiplied interest of the talents we will merit to hear: "Well done! You are a good and reliable servant; come, share your master's joy!"[16] May He Himself deign to grant this, who lives and reigns for ever and ever. Amen.

---

13 1 Tim. 4.13.
14 Acts 20.31.
15 Isa. 8.18.
16 Matt. 25.21.

## * *Sermon 231*

### A SERMON OF ST. AUGUSTINE ON HIS BIRTHDAY[1]

This day admonishes me, brethren, to think more carefully about my burden. Although I must reflect upon it by day and by night, nevertheless this day of anniversary impinges it upon my mind in such a way that I cannot omit thinking about it. The more the years come on, or rather the more they depart, and the closer they bring us to the last day which surely and without doubt is going to come at some time or other, the more intense is my reflection. The more full of anxiety, too, are my thoughts as to what kind of account I can render for you to the Lord our God. There is a difference between each one of you and us, because you will have to render an account of practically only yourselves, while we will have to do so both for ourselves and for all of you. For this reason my burden is greater. If it is carried well, it also brings greater glory, but if it is borne unfaithfully, it hurls one into the most severe punishment. Now what should I especially do today, except commend to you my danger, in order that you may be my joy? It is a source of danger to me, if I notice how you praise me but do not pay attention to how you live. However, God, under whose eyes I am speaking, or rather under whose sight I think, knows that I am not so much pleased by the praise of people as troubled and dis-

---

1 The title of the Augustinian original from which this sermon is in large part drawn (Sermo Frangipane 2; *Miscellanea Agostiniana* I 189-94) carries the words "de proprio natali" ("on his own feast," literally "birthday"). The word "birthday," both there and in the similar title of the present sermon, means the day of the bishop's consecration or the anniversary of that day. In adapting Augustine's sermon for his own use, Caesarius shortened and somewhat modified the original (e.g., see n. 4) but added a termination of his own. Before the discovery of the Frangipane sermon, the present sermon was thought to be by Augustine; the Maurists numbered it 339 among the genuine sermons of Augustine.

turbed as to how those who praise me live. I do not want to
be praised by people who are leading a wicked life, I detest
and abhor it; it is a source of grief to me, not of pleasure. If
I were to say that I do not want to be praised by people who
are leading a good life, I would be lying; but if I say that I
desire it, I am afraid that I may be more eager for something
empty rather than for what is of solid value. What, then,
shall I say? I neither want to speak freely nor am unwilling
to do so. I do not want to speak freely lest I be exposed to
danger because of human praise; I do not want to fail to do
so, lest the people to whom I am preaching be displeased.

(2) Mine is the burden which you just heard about when
the prophet Ezechiel was read. It is not enough that the day
itself admonishes us to reflect on the burden; in addition such
a lesson was read to excite in us a great fear, so we will think
about what we are carrying. Unless the One who imposed the
burden on us carries it with us, we fail. This is what you
heard: "When I bring the sword against a country, and the
people of this country select a man to be their watchman,
when he sees the sword coming he warns the people; but if
the watchman sees the sword coming and remains silent, so
that the sword comes and slays a sinner, I will hold the watchman responsible for that person's death, even though that
person is taken because of his own sin. However, if he sees the
sword coming and blows the trumpet to warn the people,
anyone hearing but not heeding the warning and therefore
slain by the sword shall be responsible for his own death, and
the watchman will save himself. You, son of man, I have
appointed watchman for the children of Israel."[2] He explained
why he said the sword, why he said a watchman, and what
death he spoke about. He did not permit us to excuse our own
neglect because of the obscurity of the lesson. "I have appointed you watchman," he says. "If I tell the wicked man
that he shall surely die and you are silent, he shall die for

---

2 Cf. Ezech. 33.2-7.

his guilt. He will die for his guilt" rightly and justly, "but I
will hold you responsible for his death. But if you warn the
wicked man that he shall surely die and he heeds not the
warning, he shall die for his guilt, but you shall save yourself."[3]

(3) Lighten my burden, brethren, and carry it with me.
Lead a good life. The Lord's birthday is approaching,[4] and
we have companions in poverty who must be fed, and kindness must be shown to them. For you, these words of mine
are spiritual food; I do not suffice to feed everyone with the
visible food which can be touched. I feed men from the same
source from which I am fed; I am a servant, not the head of a
household. I bring food to you from the same source on which
I live myself, from the treasury of the Lord, from the banquet
of that head of the household "who for our sake made himself
poor though he was rich, so that we might become rich by
his poverty."[5] If I were to give you bread, when the bread had
been broken you would each carry away with you only crumbs;
even if I were to distribute a great deal, very little would come
to each one of you. But as it is, what I am saying all of you have
entirely, and each one has it all. Did you divide the syllables
of my words among you? Did you carry away with you individual words of the sermon which was preached? Each one
of you heard the whole thing, but let each one see how he
heard it, because my work is to dispense, not to exact.

(4) If I do not dispense my money but keep it, the Gospel
frightens me. I might say: Why am I concerned to be a
nuisance to men, to say to the wicked: Do not lead an evil
life, act this way, or stop acting this way? What business is it
of mine to be burdensome to men? I have heard how to live,

---

3 Cf. Ezech. 33.7-9.
4 These words, Morin discovered, are a Caesarian addition; any use of
   them to fix the time of the year in which Augustine was consecrated
   was a mistake (see Morin, in *Revue bénédictine* 40 [1923] 366-67).
   As for the provision of a meal for the poor, Augustine's text fixes this
   for the very day on which the sermon was delivered. Caesarius omits
   the word *hodie* ("today"), since, as Morin suggests, he probably meant
   to postpone the meal until the approaching feast of Christmas.
5 Cf. 2 Cor. 8.9.

let me teach others as I have been directed and commanded, as I have heard; how does rendering an account for others affect me? The Gospel frightens me. There is something, the height of carefree leisureliness, at which no one could surpass me. Nothing is better, nothing more pleasant than to examine the divine treasury when no one is making a noise; it is pleasant, it is good. But to preach, to rebuke, to reproach, to build up, to be concerned about each one—this is a great burden, a huge weight of responsibility, a great effort. Who would not flee from such effort? But the Gospel terrifies me. A certain servant went forth and said to his master: "I knew that you are a hard man; you reap what you never sowed";[6] I kept your money, I refrained from spending it; so take what belongs to you. Judge whether something is missing; if it is intact, do not be hard on me. But he said: "You worthless servant! I shall condemn you on your own evidence."[7] Why is this? You said that I am greedy; why did you neglect what would be profitable to me? I was afraid to spend it, lest I lose it: this is what you say. Very often it is said: Why do you rebuke me? He passes over what you say, he does not hear you. For my part, he repeats, I refrained from spending your money, for fear that I might lose it. "On my return I could get it back with interest."[8] I had appointed you to dispense, not to exact return; you were to exercise dispensation, and leave to me the work of exaction. Every man who fears this should see how he receives it. If I myself am afraid as I dispense it, should the man who receives it be free from anxiety?

(5) The man who was wicked yesterday, let him be good today. This is my work of dispensation: the man who was wicked yesterday should be good today. He was evil yesterday, and he is not dead. If he died as a wicked man, he would have gone to the place from which he could not return. He was an

6 Cf. Luke 19.21.
7 Luke 19.22.
8 Luke 19.23.

evil man yesterday, but he lives today. Let the fact that he lives be a source of good to him, let him not lead a wicked life. For this reason why does he want to add the wickedness of today to yesterday? You want to have a long life, but do you not want a good one? Who would bear lengthy evil, or a long meal? Has mental blindness made man so insensible, and is the interior man so deaf that he wants to possess all good things except his own self? Do you want to own a farm? I deny that you want to have a bad farm. Do you want to have a wife? You do not want any but a good one, and no house except a good one. Why run through cases one by one? You do not want to have a bad shoe, and still you want to have an evil life? Just as though a bad shoe would hurt you more than a wicked life. When a bad or tight shoe hurts you, you sit down, you take off your shoe, you throw it away or fix it, or you change it so it will not injure your toe; then you put on your shoe. A bad life is one whereby you destroy your soul. But I see clearly how you are deceived. A harmful shoe causes pain, but a hurtful life produces pleasure; the former causes injury, the latter pleasure. However, what brings pleasure for a moment, afterwards causes worse pain. On the other hand what causes momentary pain in a salutary manner, afterwards delights with infinite pleasure and an abundance of joy, according to what is written: "Those that sow in tears shall reap rejoicing";[9] and that other text: "Blest are the sorrowing; they shall be consoled."[10]

(6) As we pay attention to these truths more carefully, let us reflect on what is written concerning dissipation and evil desires: "The lips of an adulteress are sweet for a time," it says, "but in the end she is more bitter than gall."[11] Now since our life in this world is known to be, as it were, a road, it is necessary for us to reach rest as the result of our labor, rather than labor as the result of rest. It is better for us to

9 Ps. 125 (126).5.
10 Matt. 5.5 (4).
11 Cf. Prov. 5.3, 4.

work for a short time on the way, in order that afterwards we
may be able happily to reach eternal joy in our fatherland.
With the help of our Lord Jesus Christ, who lives and reigns
with the Father and the Holy Spirit for ever and ever. Amen.

## * Sermon 232

### A Homily of the Bishop, St. Augustine, on His Birthday[1]

Anxiety stemming from my position always bothers me and
has, ever since the day when there was placed upon my shoul-
ders that burden of which it is difficult to render an account.
Nevertheless I am moved much more by reflection on this
burdensome weight, whenever the anniversary day of it re-
news its former memory. This puts it before my eyes in such
a way that I hold onto what I had already received before,
and approach it as if I were about to undertake it today. What
is feared in this office, except that we may find greater pleasure in what is a source of danger in our honor than in what is
fruitful for your salvation? Therefore let me be helped by
your prayers, so that He who did not disdain to carry me
myself may deign to carry my burden along with me. When
you pray for this, you also pray for us, for this burden of mine
about which I am now speaking, what else is it but you yourselves? Pray for strength for me, just as I pray that you may
not be troubled. The Lord Jesus would not call it His burden, unless He were carrying it with the one who bears it.
Do you also support me, so that in accord with the Apostle's

---

1 A second sermon preached by Caesarius for an anniversary of his
   consecration (cf. Serm. 231 n. 1). In this case, however, Augustine's
   original—which appears to have given Caesarius everything but his
   conclusion—has never come to light. The Maurists, while recognizing
   the Caesarian style of the conclusion, presented this sermon as No. 340
   among Augustine's sermons.

precept we may carry one another's burdens and so fulfill the law of Christ.[2] If He does not bear it with us, we collapse; if He does not carry us ourselves, we die. When it frightens me that I am responsible for you, then I am consoled by the fact that I am with you. For I am your bishop; I am also a Christian along with you. The former is a name for an accepted office, the latter is the name for a grace received; the one is a source of danger, the other of salvation. We are tossed about by a tempest, as it were, on the vast sea of our work, but when we recall through whose Blood we have been redeemed, at the tranquillity of this thought we enter a kind of haven of security. While we labor in the task which is ours, we find rest in common benefits. Therefore if it affords me greater pleasure that I was bought along with you than that I have been placed over you, then, as the Lord commanded, I will more abundantly be your servant. Thus I will not be ungrateful for the price whereby I merited to be your fellow servant.

(2) I ought to love our Redeemer, and I know why He said to Peter: "Peter, do you love me? Feed my sheep."[3] This He said once, a second time, and again a third time. Love was questioned, and labor was commanded, because where love is very great, labor is very slight. "How shall I make a return to the Lord for all the good he has done for me?"[4] If I should say that the return I make is that I feed His sheep, even this I do "not on my own but through the favor of God."[5] Therefore in what will I be found the repayer, when I am anticipated everywhere? However, because we freely love and because we feed His sheep, we seek a reward. How does this happen? how fitting is it that I freely love Him in order that I may feed them, and I demand a reward because I do so? This should not happen at all; in no way at all should a

---

2 Cf. Gal. 6.2.
3 John 21.17.
4 Ps. 115 (116).12.
5 1 Cor. 15.10.

reward be sought of one who is loved freely, unless the reward is the very one who is loved. Now if we have made this return, that we feed His sheep because of the fact that He redeemed us, what have we rendered through the fact that He made us be shepherds? Truly we are wicked shepherds— may this be far from us—through our own wickedness, but we cannot be good shepherds—and may He help us to be this—except through His grace.

(3) Therefore, my brethren, "we beg and exhort you not to receive the grace of God in vain."[6] Do you make our ministry fruitful. "You are God's cultivation";[7] exteriorly receive the planter and waterer, but interiorly accept the giver of increase.[8] The unquiet should be rebuked, the discouraged comforted, the weak supported,[9] the contradictory refuted, plotters avoided, the illiterate taught, the slothful aroused, the contentious restrained, the proud repressed, those in despair encouraged, the quarrelsome brought to peace, the needy given help, the oppressed brought to freedom, the good commended, the wicked tolerated, and everyone loved. Help us by prayer and submission in this great, manifold and diversified treatment of varied circumstances. In this way it will give us pleasure, not so much in being in authority over you as in helping you.

(4) Just as it is expedient for us to implore God's mercy for the salvation of your souls, so you ought to pour forth prayers to the Lord on our behalf. We should not consider that what we know the Apostle did is unfitting. To so great an extent did he long to be commended to God through prayer that he himself besought the people and said: "Pray for us."[10] Therefore we ought to say what can both encourage ourselves and instruct you. Just as we must reflect with great fear and anxiety on how we may fulfill the office of bishop

6 Cf. 2 Cor. 6.1.
7 1 Cor. 3.9.
8 Cf. 1 Cor. 3.6.
9 Cf. 1 Thess. 5.14.
10 2 Thess. 3.1.

without reproach, so you should observe that you ought to strive to practice humble obedience in everything that has been commanded you. So let us pray, dearly beloved, that my episcopacy may be profitable for both you and me. It will be useful to me if I preach what should be done; it will be advantageous for you if you practice what you have heard. If we ceaselessly pray for you with the perfect love of charity and you do the same for us, with the Lord's help we will happily reach eternal bliss. May He deign to grant this, who lives and reigns for ever and ever. Amen.

## Sermon 233[1]

### To the Holy Monks, Beloved Brothers in Christ, Who Are Located at the Monastery in Blanzac

Your venerable and saintly father, Arigius,[2] humbly but with almost indiscreet prompting asked me to deliver a sermon of exhortation to your holy selves. While he wants to provide you with what you now almost do not need, he is seen to engender embarrassment in us. For what are we going to tell you verbally that you do not already fulfill in glorious deeds? Should we tell you, "do not love the world," when we know that you despise the world with all of its desires in total faith and devotion? Are we going to tell you to despise its adornments, when through the goodness of God you have

---

1 Morin's collection closes with the six fully authentic sermons "To monks" (or [Serm. 237] "To God's servants or handmaids"), of which this is the first.

2 The abbot Arigius named in the first line is otherwise unknown. This composition started as a letter to Arigius's community; later reworked and shortened, it passed into various collections as a sermon. I have followed Morin's suggestion that Arigius's monastery (*monasterium Blandiacense*) was located at Blanzac (département Charente), where there was an ancient monastery dedicated to a "St. Artemius."

already rejected them as filth and dung? Can we tell you to
give alms out of your possessions, when you have devoutly
offered to the Lord, not only your wealth but also your very
selves? Are you to be admonished to stop serving your appetite for food and drink, when we see that you ceaselessly
engage in fasting and vigils? Can we preach that you should
flee from quarrels and occasions of sin, when we see that you
have devoutly and happily fled to the haven of the monastery
from the sea of this world, which is dangerous and restless
because of its mighty waves?

(2) Although we rejoice at all these blessings which God
has conferred on you, and, since through the goodness of God
you devoutly practice them, we by no means presume to admonish you, still there is something which we might not
unfittingly mention to your charity. With the help of God
may you fulfill steadfastly to a glorious end what you have
faithfully begun through His inspiration, for not he who has
begun but "whoever holds out till the end will escape death."[3]
Since you have begun to build a spiritual structure with the
help of Christ, after laying the groundwork of humility you
ought to place the foundation of genuine devotion upon the
rock. Although a building may be lofty and vast, it will
quickly fall into ruin unless it has a firm foundation. This is
also the case with a spiritual structure, dearly beloved. Whatever good things a man may possess, if he is unwilling to have
the foundation of true humility, he will not be able to stand.
As the Apostle says: "No one can lay a foundation other than
the one that has been laid, namely Jesus Christ."[4]

(3) There are two buildings and two cities constructed since
the beginning of the world. Christ builds the one, the devil
the other; the humble one constructs the one, the proud one
the other. The one is humbled in order that it may rise steadfastly; the other is raised up in order to fall disastrously. Those

---

3 Matt. 10.22; 24.13.
4 1 Cor. 3.11.

who are built on the structure of Christ are lifted up from
the depths to the heights; those on the structure of the devil
are hurled from the heights into the depths. Therefore each
one should examine his own conscience, beloved brethren. If
he sees pride dominant in himself, a man should not doubt
that he is being unhappily built, or rather thrown down, in
the city of the devil. However, if genuine humility reigns
within him, he should rejoice that he is being built upon
Christ, and happily cling to Him.

(4) The sons of God and of the devil are not distinguished
from each other except through humility and pride. Whenever you see a proud man, do not doubt that he is a son of
the devil; whenever you see a humble person, you should
believe with confidence that he is a son of God. In order that
you may realize that this is true, listen to the Scriptures say:
"The beginning of pride is man's stubbornness in withdraw-
ing his heart from his Maker";[5] and "Whoever exalts himself shall be humbled, but whoever humbles himself shall be
exalted."[6] What the devil has cast down through pride, Christ
has lifted up through humility, because He set forth the healing of humility for the wound of pride. Therefore if we want
to avoid the poison of pride, we ought continually to draw
in the antidote of humility. Let us listen to the Lord say:
"Learn from me, for I am gentle and humble of heart."[7] He
did not say: Learn of me to create the world, to revive the
dead, and to perform the other miracles; but He did say "for
I am gentle and humble of heart."

(5) Let us therefore cling to humility above all things,
dearly beloved; not only that which sometimes is shown only
outwardly, but that which is kept within one's conscience.
There are people who are wont to show humility both in their
words and in their heart when things are tranquil, but if, as
often happens, some storm of tribulation or of an obstacle

5 Sir. 10.14 (12).
6 Matt. 23.12.
7 Matt. 11.29.

arises, through their unbridled speech and stiff neck the pride
which was concealed in their heart is expressed vocally. Why
does this happen, brethren? Because that man did not have the
foundation of true humility. The humility which he first
promised through his bodily actions he did not possess within
his heart, "for the mouth speaks whatever fills the mind."[8]
You seek to reach without cause what you refused to store
away when you might have done so. Our hearts, dearly beloved, are like vessels, which can in no way at all be empty.
Every man is known to be full of either good or evil. Just as
when a vessel is fanned, there is shown what kind of substance
is within it, so when a man is fanned by correction or difficulty, as usually happens, he immediately shows what he is
filled with, because as I said: "The mouth speaks whatever
fills the mind." The humility which he promised at first was
only on his lips but was not in his conscience. When a man
has been corrected for a just reason, with cruel fury he replies
exceedingly bitter words. That pride was not born just then
but was revealed then in truth. Discipline or holy correction
did not make the man proud but showed what kind of a man
he had been for a long time. So on the contrary, if the humble
and saintly soul sometimes hears either unjust or just rebukes,
as is wont to happen, through the inspiration of Christ he
humbles himself still more, and through the operation of the
Holy Spirit he exclaims that the rebuke he hears is less than
he deserves. Thus the man who conceals his pride within his
heart emits an exceedingly foul stench when he is brought
into the breeze, while the one who is gentle and humble
exudes a very sweet odor.

(6) Let us therefore be humble, dearly beloved, not only
toward our superiors, but also to our equals, so that God may
not resist the proud or humble those who are exalting themselves, and lest men who are puffed up with pride not be able
to walk on the narrow road. Receive whatever you are com-

---

8 Matt. 12.34; Luke 6.45.

manded by your superiors in the same way as if it were brought from heaven by the mouth of God. Refute nothing, discuss nothing, and do not presume to murmur at all interiorly, because you came to the monastery to serve, not to rule, to obey rather than to command. Whatever you or others are seen to be commanded, consider it all holy, just, and useful. Strive not only to restrain your own tongue from deadly murmuring, but also not to listen willingly to another who is doing this. Instead, endeavor to mitigate the wrath of the other person, as far as you can, by pious and salutary advice. What is worse, there are some devil's co-workers, and when these men see people aroused by excessive wrath, they immediately try to strike them with poisonous advice to render them all the more angry. Such men are on the left side and are being built in that ruinous city of the devil. However, through the kindness of Christ, there are other men, concerning whom the Apostle says: "We are God's co-workers."[9] Co-workers of God are those who, when once they see the poison of pride creeping into the heart of a brother, with all haste try to destroy it with the medicine of true humility. Just as those others, the inciters of the wicked, merit redoubled punishment because of their own ruin and their destruction of others, so these humble and kindly souls achieve double glory. Through their bad advice the former try to kill Christ, not only in themselves but also in the hearts of others; holy, humble souls, on the other hand, persecute the devil both in themselves and in others.

(7) As I already suggested above, brethren, we should therefore trust in true humility, not false humility. Let us show ourselves to all as a medicine and a bright light, so that what the Lord said may be fulfilled in us: "In the same way, your light must shine before men so that they may see goodness in your acts and give praise to your heavenly Father."[10] If there is no true charity and humility, we should not trust

9 1 Cor. 3.9.
10 Matt. 5.16.

or confide in the religious habit alone, lest we be like whited sepulchres. Let no one deceive himself, brethren, because "none of us lives for himself alone and none of us dies for himself alone."[11] You will possess eternal rewards with so many men and because of as many as the number of those to whom you showed the example of true humility and perfect charity But if—far be it from us!—you have given to others for theii imitation a model of pride, anger, murmuring, or disobedience, you will suffer the punishment of hell, not only for yourself but also for those whom you destroyed. Perhaps you say: The commands which are given to us by our superiors are excessively harsh and foolish. Have you not read: "For the sake of the words of your lips I have kept hard ways"?[12] Have you not also read that "Strait and narrow is the road that leads to life"?[13] Have you not heard the Apostle say: "We must undergo many trials if we are to enter into the reign of God"?[14] And have you not listened to the prophet say: "With the rod and stripes you will be chastised, daughter of Sion, lest my zeal depart from you"?[15] And that other text: "Whoever is dear to me I reprove and chastise";[16] elsewhere, too: "God scourges every son he receives."[17] Even if the commands which are given to you are difficult, will you be able to make them easier by murmuring? Practice obedience with humility; if you cannot do this, ask pardon for your weakness with humility. The commands of a superior seem difficult to you; how much harsher will be the advice of the deceiver? The commands given by superiors seem severe to you; how much harder are the things which avarice commands its advocates? How laborious and how perilous are the journeys it compels them to endure! Now since they accept all that with patience for the sake of temporal money, why do you not

11 Rom. 14.7.
12 Ps. 16 (17).4.
13 Matt. 7.14.
14 Acts 14.21 (22).
15 Cf. Jer. 6.7, 8.
16 Apoc. 3.19.          17 Hebr. 12.6.

suffer with equanimity for the sake of eternal life? Have you
not read: "Better wounds from a friend than deceitful kisses
from an enemy"?[18] And that other text: "The just shall reproach me in mercy and he shall reprove me; but let not the
oil of the wicked," that is, the compliments of a flatterer,
"anoint my head."[19] For a superior rebukes in order to correct, but the devil flatters in order to destroy. The advice of
the devil, as the prophet says, "anoints the throat for a
moment, but in the end is more bitter than gall."[20] In a
very short time he leads the proud and wicked to death on a
broad and spacious path. Christ our Lord, on the contrary,
leads the humble and obedient to life on the strait and
narrow path. Both of those roads, the wide one and the narrow
one, have an end and are very short; labor is not long on the
narrow road, nor is joy lengthy on the broad one. Those
whom the broad way of wickedness delights, after brief joy
will have endless punishment; on the contrary those who
follow Christ on the narrow way, after brief tribulations will
merit to reach eternal rewards. If a layman who is in the
world possesses pride, it is a sin for him; if a monk is proud,
it is a sacrilege. You ought to show yourselves living so holy
a life, so justly and piously in such a way that your merits
may not only suffice for you but also obtain pardon in this
world for other sinners. If we do not bridle our tongue, our
religion is not true but false;[21] and it would have been better
not to have made a vow than after the vow not to do what was
promised.[22]

(8) I am not suggesting these truths to you, brethren, because I think that you are men of this kind. I am presuming
to speak in the spirit of a man who knows fear rather than of
one giving a rebuke, according to what the Apostle says:

---

18 Prov. 27.6.
19 Cf. Ps. 140 (141).5.
20 Cf. Prov. 5.3, 4.
21 Cf. James 1.26.
22 Cf. Eccles 5.4.

"Work with anxious concern to achieve your salvation."[23] I
have not said this because you are acting in that other way,
but I have mentioned it so that you may not do so if the devil
perchance overtakes you. We hold such an opinion of you
that we believe that we are rather helped by your prayers, so
that as a result of your supplications we will be able to reach
the haven of true happiness in the midst of the storms and
tempests of this life. Therefore as I mention your exceedingly
fruitful and salutary state of soul, I beseech you to commend
me to the Lord by your holy prayers, and to grant pardon
to my presumption on behalf of your charity: with the help of
our Lord Jesus Christ, to whom is honor and glory for ever
and ever. Amen.

## Sermon 234

### ANOTHER SERMON OF ST. CAESARIUS TO MONKS

Your saintly and venerable father, in abasing himself—if he
will permit such an expression—with indiscreet humility, has
caused me not a little embarrassment. With admirable charity
he strove to enjoin upon me, or rather to wrest from me, that
I should address to your saintly souls a sermon of exhortation.
As I consider both my own merits and your manner of life,
and at the same time when I observe your holiness and my
own conscience, I do not know what to choose. If I remain
silent, I will appear disobedient to your charity, but if I
presume to say something, I will incur the mark of temerity.
But I ask you, brethren, what shall I suggest to you in words,
when I rejoice greatly that you fulfill everything by your
deeds? With what boldness does a sick man presume to preach
to those who are in good health? How can one who is guilty

23 Phil. 2.12.

of many negligences admonish saintly men? How can one who is fond of sleep stimulate those who keep vigils? With what kind of conscience does one who is satiated with a continuous abundance of food rebuke men who are fasting? From what source can a beggar offer true bread to those who thirst after justice? With what truths can I admonish you, brethren? Am I to tell you that you should despise the world, when you have rejected it and all its pleasures with the whole strength of your soul? Shall I tell you that you ought to throw away the hindrances of the world, when I see that you despise all its desires with the most ardent devotion? Am I to give you advice that you should give generous alms, when I know that out of love for Christ you have rejected all the wealth of the world, and when I see that you have given the Lord not only all your possessions but your very selves? Will I perchance be able to preach to you that you should be humble toward your neighbors and friends, when you not only faithfully but even joyfully bend yourselves beneath the yoke of Christ? Will I perhaps be able to recommend charity to you, when I see that you love, not only your friends, but even your enemies? Are you to be advised to practice obedience, when you strive never to fulfill your own will but to fulfill the command of God and of your superiors? Or can I admonish you to avoid the disease of anger, when I rejoice that you are holding fast to the foundation of patience? Do I dare to say that your holy selves should not be occupied with idle gossip, when I know that you are busy with reading and prayer, and that you meditate on the law of God by day and by night? Only this one thing remains, then, dearest brethren, since the Lord has deigned to gather you and put you in a holy monastery as in a haven of rest and refreshment as if in some part of paradise. By your continuous prayers may you strive to obtain for us that we who are ceaselessly tossed about by the waves of this world and are exhausted by many storms on the sea of this life, under the leadership of Christ may reach the haven of a blessed life through the favor of your prayers, after overcoming the whole tide of vice. Then when the crown of glory is given to you in the presence of the eternal judge, pardon for our sins will also be granted to us.

(2) In order that I may not seem to be disobedient to your saintly father in all respects, with great humility and patience I presume to suggest that you should maintain perseverance in the holy work which you devoutly practice with God's help, until a happy end. Not he who has made a beginning, but "whoever holds out till the end will escape death."[1] For this reason it is necessary that men who are regulated by a holy life, are also endowed with the wings of many virtues, like spiritual doves, and are adorned with the pearls of good works, should be able to say with the prophet: "Had I wings like a dove's, I would fly away and be at rest."[2] Devout souls can accomplish this, if they practice humility and obedience with steadfast fidelity. Whatever other good deeds a man may possess, if he does not have the wings of those two virtues, that is, humility and obedience, he will not be able to soar on high. Every devout soul which wants to avoid and escape the birds of prey that are flying around and the diabolical hawks, that is, spiritual vice, should through God's gift preserve within himself the wings of those two virtues which we mentioned above. For neither virginity nor vigils nor fasting nor even prayer or reading will be able to help the servants of God, if there is in them no perfect obedience nor true humility.

(3) It should not seem incongruous to anyone that I have recommended humility and obedience particularly and have not added to these charity, which is the mother of all virtues. This is not true, dearest brethren. Since obedience and humil-

---

1 Matt. 10.22; 24.13.
2 Ps. 54 (55).7. Below, in the interpretation of this verse, "spiritual vice" appears to be an allusion to Eph. 6.12.

ity are proved to be the fruit of charity, how can they exist without it, for they cannot even arise except from it? True humility and genuine obedience never have existed and never will be able to do so without charity. Just as there is no fire at all without heat or brightness, so charity cannot exist without humility and obedience. Now as we observe true charity along with perfect humility and obedience, let us not trust anything, as it were, on our own merits. No one should extol himself as the result of his own endeavors, but he should trust in divine grace; no one should think that virginity or reading or prayer or vigils or fasting without charity and obedience has any value. Just as the body cannot live without the soul, so the rest of the virtues may have some form without charity, but they cannot have true value. Fasting without charity is like a lamp without oil; it can smoke, it can produce a smell or stench, but it cannot give light. There is no need for us to presume to admonish you any further in words, as I already said, because we know that through the goodness of God you accomplish it in reality by your actions. Through continuous reading and by the inspiration of God you know what you ought to think and say and do.

(4) Now if, with God's help, you strive to fulfill everything that you read, if you love your saintly and venerable father with your whole heart, showing pious and humble obedience in everything that he commands through the inspiration of God, without any doubt you will happily reach eternal bliss along with your holy father. But because through the goodness of God you are secure and free from all serious offenses, you should always be anxious about small, lesser sins. I am talking about those sins concerning which blessed John the evangelist admonishes us when he says: "If we say, 'We are free of the guilt of sin,' we deceive ourselves; the truth is not to be found in us."[3] As a result of this it is also written: "The

---

3  1 John 1.8.

just man falls seven times in a day and rises again."[4] With
God's help we both can and should be without serious offenses,
but no just man ever was or ever will be able to live without
small sins. We are continuously troubled and tormented by
these as by flies buzzing around, and in accord with this we
already said above: "The just man falls seven times in a day
and rises again." Very often sins creep up on us through
thoughts or desires or speech or action, as the result of necessity, through weakness or out of forgetfulness. If a man thinks
only of serious sins and strives to resist only these but has
little or no care about small sins, he incurs no less danger
than if he committed more serious offenses. Therefore let us
not think little of our sins because they are slight, but let us
fear them because they are many. Drops of rain are small, but
because they are very many, they fill rivers and submerge
houses, and sometimes by their force they even carry off
mountains. Concerning these it is written: "He who scorns
little things will fall little by little";[5] and again: "Who can
detect failings?"[6] Who is there who guards his heart with
such great vigilance that no idle word ever proceeds from his
lips? However, an account must be rendered for this on the
day of judgment. Who is there who does not lie, although
Scripture says: "A lying mouth slays the soul"?[7] Who is there
from whose mouth an evil word does not sometimes issue,
although it is written: "No slanderers will inherit God's
kingdom"?[8] Who could even count the sins which we consider
small or almost nonexistent, even though Sacred Scripture
testifies that we are going to be severely punished for them?
For this reason, with God's help and in accord with the text
of Solomon, let us keep our hearts with all watchfulness. If we
are unable to escape or avoid small sins entirely and are

---

4 Prov. 24.16.
5 Sir. 19.1.
6 Ps. 18 (19).13.
7 Wisd. 1.11.
8 1 Cor. 6.10.

overtaken by them rather slowly, let us hasten either to purge them or to redeem them by sighs and groans as often as we are overcome.

(5) As I suggest these truths, I seem to admonish your holy selves needlessly. However, through the goodness of God what is written is fulfilled in you: "Instruct a wise man, and he becomes still wiser";[9] and again: "The virtuous must live on in their virtue and the holy ones in their holiness!"[10] Again and again with all humility I beseech you to commend me continuously to the Lord in such a way both by your holy and illustrious merits and by your prayers, that my merits may not sadden you in the future life, because your pious manner of life gives me much joy in this world. When you receive glory from God, the just judge, through your prayers may I merit at least to obtain the forgiveness of my sins, as I asked up above: with the help of our Lord Jesus Christ, to whom is honor and glory for ever and ever. Amen.

*Sermon 235*

## To Monks

Whatever the nature of the sermon I preach to your community, brethren, at the request and even the bidding, with charity, of your saintly father, I do so, not because of some kind of presumption, but out of true and honest charity. Although through the goodness of God you are so perfect that you do not at all need our admonition, still, at the bidding of charity which knows no fear, with true humility and perfect charity we presume to suggest and advise even what we know you are fulfilling very well. But since we realize that we

---

9 Prov. 9.9.
10 Apoc. 22.11.

are not yet fit to be your disciples, it is not without embarrassment that we are seen to arouse teachers to a holy task. Although we are tepid, we are compelled to advise the fervent; although we are unskilled, we are instructing learned men; although we are exhausted on the sea of this world by its great waves, we are uttering words of preaching to men who have already happily reached port.

(2) Because ships are wont to exert effort even in the safest port after the waves of the sea have been overcome and mastered, dearly beloved, and because they are almost overwhelmed unless great caution is taken, we are advising you with the greatest humility and immense respect. Since Christ has freed you from all serious sins as though from dangerous waves, you who are established in a haven of rest and blessedness should continually hasten to remove the slight negligences and as it were the small sins which gather in the soul in the same way in which drops of water run into the bottom of a ship through very small chinks. With Christ's help you should do this with all watchfulness. Just as a ship is filled and sunk by the smallest drops of water, after it has escaped the waves of the sea, provided that it is not emptied of the bilge water in port, so if a monk has neglected to remove the slight daily offenses which creep up on him from the depths of his soul, he incurs the danger of shipwreck right in port. This can happen when he has come to the port of a monastery after overcoming and mastering the storms of life and the vices of this world, like dangerous waves.

(3) Perhaps someone may say: How can a soul be emptied of bilge water? Surely by prayer, fasting, vigils, and by showing true charity, genuine humility, and real obedience. I beseech you, brethren, notice that just as a ship is emptied of bilge water with a bucket, so the soul is freed of all sins by the Lord's prayer, if a man says, and says truly: "Forgive us the wrong we have done as we forgive those who wrong us."[1] If

---

1 Matt. 6.12.

a man mercifully forgives all who sin against him, no trace of sin will remain in his soul. But notice, brethren, and consider carefully what I said: if he forgives anyone who sins against him. I did not say that you should forgive the man who sins against God, but the man who has offended you is the one whom you should forgive. Sometimes—which is worse—we grant pardon to the man who has offended us, slowly or reluctantly, while we quickly forgive the man who has offended God. If we want to act justly, we should never forgive the man who has sinned against God without the severest penalty, lest he give an example of perdition to others while he is being pardoned through indiscreet piety. Each one should show himself merciful in his own case, for the Lord said: "If you forgive the faults of others, your heavenly Father will forgive you yours."[2] When someone presumes to commit a sin against God, he ought to suffer a monastic penance. This should be done in a kind and devout spirit, so that through rebuke he may be corrected in this life in such a way that he may not perish in the future. For every sin which is not corrected in this world will be punished in the future life. Sacred Scripture speaks thus about the son and the servant: "Beat him with the rod," it says, "and you will save him from the nether world."[3]

(4) For this reason let us not only beware of serious sins, as I suggested above, but let us also spurn small daily negligences as the poison of the devil. There are some people who are weakened by excessive unconcern after their religious profession, because they seem to have left the world. In such people is fulfilled that sentence of our Lord in which it is said: "How I wish you were one or the other—hot or cold! But because you are lukewarm, I will spew you out of my mouth!"[4] What does it mean that He said, How I wish you were one or the other—hot or cold? This means that it would have been

2 Matt. 6.14.
3 Prov. 23.14.
4 Apoc. 3.15, 16.

better for you to have remained cold in the world or to be
fervent in the monastery. Now because you have withdrawn
from the world and still have refused to acquire spiritual
warmth because of your carelessness, you have become lukewarm and will be vomited from the Lord's mouth, scarcely
ever to be recovered again. For this reason, dearest brethren,
with God's help carefully listen to the sentence of Sacred
Scripture in which it is said: "With closest custody guard your
heart."[5] There should be rejoicing over the monk who has
come to the monastery and in a meek and humble spirit wills
to practice meekness, obedience, and patience. So on the
contrary there should be grief over the one who seems to have
left the world only bodily but is known to have remained
faithlessly in it or unhappily to have returned to it. Such a
man practices pride instead of humility, anger instead of
patience, contempt instead of obedience; he emits the poison
of wickedness instead of the medicine of charity. To people of
this kind applies that true and exceedingly dreadful sentence
of blessed Peter: "It would have been better for them not to
have recognized the road of holiness than to have turned their
backs on it once they had known it";[6] and again: "The dog
returns to his vomit,"[7] "and a sow bathes by wallowing in the
mire."[8]

(5) You should not despair of such men, brethren, because
through your prayers God is able to kindle the spark of repentance and to consume with a salutary fire all worldly
pleasure like thorns and thistles of malice. Surely this is that
fire about which our Lord Himself said: "I have come to light
a fire on the earth. How I wish the blaze were ignited!"[9] Therefore pray, dearly beloved, not only that God may grant you
perseverance in doing good, but also that those who are care-

---

5  Prov. 4.23.
6  2 Peter 2.21.
7  Prov. 26.11.
8  2 Peter 2.22.
9  Luke 12.49.

less He may consider worth lifting up from the pit and dig-
ging out of the snare. If those who are lukewarm and careless
are corrected through your prayers or through the advice you
give in charity, the Lord will deign to give you a twofold reward because of your own salvation and the amendment of
their life. Men who are good should not extol themselves as
though this were due to their own merits, nor should those
who are careless despair of God's mercy. The former should
preserve God's gifts with humility, while the latter should
hasten very quickly and with much contrition to the medicines
of repentance and amendment. If the man who is good begins
to become proud, he will quickly be humbled; if the man who
is proud humbles himself, through the mercy of God he will
be exalted. It is so important that a man not allow himself
to be oppressed any longer by the exceedingly harsh yoke of
the devil, and not to be hardened in sin by persevering in it
through too much dangerous carelessness; instead, he should
take refuge *in repentance*[10] so quickly that he leaves no trace
of sin within himself. A poultice or clamp is best applied to
wounds that are still fresh. If there is the prompt intention of
arising to the heavenly physician, no trace can remain on the
one who has fallen, because beneath the hand of the almighty
physician disease quickly disappears and the sick man is
promptly healed.

(6) Again and again I beseech you, brethren. I also admonish you to strive continually to practice obedience, humility, and charity, not only to your superiors and equals, but
also to your inferiors. For if humility and true charity are not
in a man, he loses everything, no matter what good qualities
the servant of God endeavors to possess in abundance. Do not
murmur, for it is written that murmurers "were destroyed by
the serpents."[11] Do not slander your brothers, for it is written:

---

10 The italicized words give the probable sense of a short phrase that
   has dropped out of the manuscripts.
11 1 Cor. 10.9.

"If one slanders his brother, he will be rooted up."[12] Do not retain anger in your heart, for it is written: "A man's anger does not fulfill God's justice."[13] Do not harbor hatred for one another, because of what is written: "Anyone who hates his brother is a murderer."[14] But there is no need for us to teach your saintly charity any longer in words, because we both know and rejoice that you fulfill everything for the glory of God in your actions. This alone we ask in particular, that since God has deigned to put you in a place of peace and tranquility, you may pray to God more abundantly on our behalf, for the storms and innumerable floods of this life afflict us. Then if glory is not given to us, because we do not deserve it, at least through your prayers the forgiveness of our sins will be granted.

### Sermon 236

## A SERMON TO MONKS

I wonder that my lord, your father, is abasing himself with such great humility, dearly beloved, that he wants a sermon of exhortation addressed to your learned ears by one as ignorant as I am. Because of this admirable humility he desires the drops of a very small brook to be given by me, as though from a dry little rivulet, to you, who are living fountains in Christ. What, then, am I, "poor and afflicted,"[1] to do? Where will I be able to find something to serve you who are thirsting for justice? Where, I repeat, am I to seek what I do not have in my possession? Although your own blessed humility as

---

12 Cf. Prov. 20.13 (20).
13 James 1.20.
14 1 John 3.15.

1 Ps. 68 (69).30.

well as that of your saintly father almost cannot be raised any higher because of the merits of your virtues, it finds in this humility a source from which it can be increased. We bless our Lord, who considers this holy institution and the wonderful life of this place worthy to grow and to be erected on a hill of greater glory. O happy, blessed abode of this island, where the glory of our Lord and Savior is augmented by such holy and spiritual gains, and the wickedness of the devil is lessened by such great losses. O blessed and happy island of Lerins, I repeat, for although it seems to be small and flat, it is known to have sent countless mountains up to heaven! This it is that nourishes excellent monks and supplies outstanding priests throughout all the provinces. Those whom it has received as sons, it makes fathers; the little ones it nourishes, it makes great; those whom it receives as beginners, it makes kings. Christ is wont to lift up to the lofty heights of virtue on the wings of charity and humility all those whom this happy and blessed abode has received.

(2) What was accomplished in almost all of the inhabitants of this place is proved not to have been fulfilled in me because of the resistance of my faults.[2] Although this holy island, like a loving mother and uniquely special nurse of all good men, formerly received my littleness with pious arms and strove to educate and nourish me for a considerable length of time, although it brought the others to the height of virtues, because my hardness of heart contradicted it, it was unable to take away my negligences. For this reason I am begging with all humility, and with heartfelt contrition I am asking that what is deservedly denied to me may be supplied through your prayers. As a special pupil of yours may I merit to be helped by the support of your prayers in such a way that the fact that I was raised in this holy place may not bring judgment to me but progress. For my part, dearest brethren, while I do not

---

2 For Caesarius's life as a monk on the island of Lerins, see Vol. I pp. vi-vii. It was to the monks of Lerins that this sermon was preached.

presume to contradict the request of your saintly father, I
incur a mark of considerable temerity. When I consider who
dares to speak and to whom, or what kind of a person presumes to teach what great men, consciousness of my lowliness
makes me tremble beneath the weight of great embarrassment.
Ignorant as I am, what am I going to say to men who are
exceedingly learned? What am I to say to saintly people,
when I myself am guilty of many negligences? In the dark as
I am, what shall I say to men who are brightly illumined;
lukewarm as I am, what am I going to say to the fervent? What
shall I teach those who are established in a very fortunate
harbor, when I am in the middle of the sea, exhausted by the
very great waves of this world? Above all, since I am starved,
where will I find something that I can worthily offer those
who are fed with Christ's delicacies? Nevertheless I trust that
through your prayers I have already discovered what I should
do. What should I show except the sacrifice of a humbled
and contrite heart, so that what a supply of good deeds cannot accomplish in me may at least be obtained by humility
itself. Behold, I am preparing the receptacle of my heart for
the divine water flowing into it through you. For in truth I
recognize that you are the ones concerning whom our Lord
is read to have said: "Who believes in me, from within him
rivers of living water shall flow."[3] Now since we rejoice and
believe that from you as from spiritual fountains living waters
flow, water the dry, satisfy the starving, refresh the weary,
wash him who is defiled by many negligences, like good and
spiritual disciples of that heavenly physician offer the favor
of your prayers and extend the medicine of your lofty merits.
Now because we rejoice that you fulfill in deeds what we are
only preaching in words, obtain for us the grace that we may
merit in some measure to share in your works, because of our
special love for you. And since not only men in the world but
even the angels in heaven congratulate you on your manner of

---

3 John 7.38.

life, strive through your holy prayers to bring it about that
when glory is given to you before the eternal judge because
of your merits, at least the pardon of our sins may be granted
to us.

(3) In order that I may not seem to contradict entirely the
entreaties of your saintly father, with great humility and respect I presume to mention things that you already possess.
For I beseech you, and advise your saintly souls with humble
charity always to strive to bestow true love on my lord, your
father, and to practice the obedience of perfect charity. Then
just as you rejoice in the Lord because of the merits of your
saintly father, so he may always give Him thanks for your
advancement. Now since the whole world both admires and
loves your deeds because of your holy and spotless obedience,
and since you know that you are indebted to the whole human
race, it is necessary that you repay the honor and love which
you receive from everyone by your continuous prayers and
spotless life. In almost all places from the east to the west
where the Christian religion is practiced, your manner of
life for the glory of God is preached with most illustrious
fame. It is rightly required of you that what is believed in
your case should also be proved. With the Lord's help, then,
do what you have always done, and preserve charity, humility,
meekness, and obedience in such a way that what is believed
about you in the whole world may be augmented by the
deeds of an ever spotless life. Then whoever has merited to
see you will be able to give verbal utterance to the sentence
uttered by that queen who wanted to seek out Solomon as a
type of the Church. When each one of you like living temples
of Christ, adorned with the pearls of good works, filled with
the holocausts of prayers, and fragrant with the spices of virtues has merited to be contemplated, then immediately break-
ing forth with the voice of exultation, may he exclaim and
say with that queen: "The report I heard in my country"
about the life of this saintly community "is true." Behold

now in truth "I have discovered that they were hardly telling me the half";[4] for I have merited to see with my eyes much greater things than I first heard with my ears. When anyone merited to seek and to behold you like angels placed on earth, he rejoiced at such things and uttered words with his own lips. Then he happily announced throughout the whole world: Consider and see how much glory is added to you and how precious and holy a joy is produced for the universal Church throughout the entire world.

(4) Above all, brethren, with a most watchful heart always fear that there may creep into our minds the thought that we believe human praise alone suffices us for a blessed life. Then we do not consider what kind of men we are, but rather what kind we are seen to be by others, and by neglecting the merits of virtue may perhaps think only about our reputation. Let us rather reflect on that thought, of worldly origin, to be sure, but exceedingly useful: "As genuine praise honors a man, so false praise rebukes him."[5] One of the wise men also said this: "If your praises are true, they are published abroad; if they are false, they are insults."[6] But the accomplishment of so holy and so excellent a perfection will depend upon a considerable effort of soul. For without effort, who can withdraw his tongue from slander, put an end to murmuring or idle conversations, reject impure thoughts with an exceedingly vigilant heart, refrain from cursing or swearing as from deadly poison, resist vanity, and repress wrath? Without great compunction of heart, who is there who has rejected and refused the seeking of honor or the desire for clerical office out of a love for true humility? Without effort, who could ever submit his pious neck to holy obedience, never find fault with the will of a superior, retain hatred in his heart against no man, love not only brothers but all men, and even his persecutors, out of love for Christ; pray for the good, so that they may always be

---

4 3 (1) Kings 10.6, 7.
5 For this quotation see Serm. 217 n. 7.
6 The source of this quotation is unknown.

augmented with holy deeds; pray for the wicked, so that they may merit to reform more quickly? Without effort, who will be able to apply himself to prayer or have time for reading? Who, I repeat, will accomplish all these things without the grace of God and great purpose of heart?

(5) Until all of these things are put into habitual practice, brethren, they seem to be difficult. To speak still more truthfully, as long as they are thought capable of fulfillment by human strength, so long are they considered impossible. But when they are believed able to be obtained from God and capable of fulfillment through His grace, they are proved to be, not hard or difficult, but light and sweet, according to what the Lord said: "For my yoke is easy and my burden light."[7] Since this yoke is already happily carried and sweetly borne by you, pray that our little self may also merit to receive it and to carry it with humility until the end. Then when glory is given to you in that eternal bliss, pardon of our sins will be granted to us: with the help of our Lord Jesus Christ, to whom is honor and glory for ever and ever. Amen.

## Sermon 237

### A SERMON TO GOD'S SERVANTS OR HANDMAIDS ON GIVING A GOOD EXAMPLE

If you notice carefully, beloved brethren or venerable daughters, you realize clearly that no man lives for himself alone, nor does he die for himself only. The blessed Apostle Paul confirms this in similar words when he says that "None of us lives for himself alone and none of us dies for himself alone."[1]

---

7 Matt. 11.30.

---

1 Rom. 14.7.

Every man will reach eternal rewards with and on behalf of
as many souls as the number of those to whom he gave the
example of a holy life. On the contrary, too, the man who
has shown the example of an evil life and of wicked actions
will suffer endless punishments with and on behalf of as
many men as the number of those whom he provoked to
wicked deeds by his own evil habits. Not only should we
refrain from giving the example of a wicked life to others, but
we should continually invite them to humility, charity and
obedience by pious and salutary advice. Let us not be of the
number of those who by their perverse advice are wont to
supply the food of pride to any brothers or sisters who are
angry or irascible, telling them that they should not abase
themselves so much in abject humility, and that they are
suffering harsh and foolish commands. Let us not be of the
number of those who not only refuse to heal wounds that
have been inflicted by exceedingly bitter tongues, but even
strive to injure those that are healthy. By their murmuring
and disparagement such men are wont not to serve Christ, but
through disobedience and wrath to serve the devil.

(2) The devil is a shrewd and cruel enemy, and with the
cunning of old tricks and manifold talents, by means of exceedingly evil persuasion he makes souls slothful and tepid
and careless, and he even compels them to serve him through
the destruction of others. Concerning such men it is written:
"How I wish you were one or the other—hot or cold! But
because you are lukewarm, I will begin to spew you out of
my mouth!"[2] Such souls, which have been prepared for disobedience and pride, the devil makes blind to the light of
truth and charity. Like a very strong hunter and a very clever
bird-catcher, he equips and prepares even devout souls, as if
to capture decoys for himself. Just as bird-catchers are wont
to make blind and deaf pigeons they have previously caught,
so that the rest of the birds, flocking to them, can be captured

2 Apoc. 3.15, 16.

in the nets which have been set out, in the same way the ancient enemy is wont to act in the case of tepid clerics and careless monks or slothful virgins. When he has closed their eyes to patience and extinguished the fire of compunction and the flame of true charity and has persuaded them to glory in the religious habit alone, as I have already said, he disposes and prepares them as an example, decoys for the destruction of others. Then when simple souls and those who are less careful imitate them, they are seized in different kinds of snares and nets. On judgment day such men will have to render an account, not only for themselves but also for the others whom they have called away from pious humility and obedience through the example of their wicked life.

(3) The ancient enemy, who always is wont to envy the just first encourages God's servants or handmaids whom he knows are lukewarm and careless to be occupied with idle gossip, invites them to disobedience through murmuring or detraction, and makes them very sluggish in listening to reading. Then when he has introduced into their hearts insensibility and, so to speak, the dross of tepidity, he prepares them for any kind of wicked deed and compels them unhappily to serve all sorts of vice and carelessness, according to what truth has said: "Everyone who lives in sin is the slave of sin,"[3] and "Anyone is the slave of that by which he has been overcome."[4] Just as spiritual and saintly souls, inflamed by the ardor of charity, are impelled by the Holy Spirit and are continually ready for every good work, according to what the Apostle says: "All who are led by the Spirit of God are sons of God,"[5] so on the contrary careless and tepid souls are possessed by that opposite spirit about which it is written: "When an unclean spirit has gone out of a man, it wanders through arid wastes searching for a resting place; failing to find one, it goes back to find the house empty and swept. Next it returns

3 John 8.34.
4 2 Peter 2.19.
5 Rom. 8.14.

with seven other spirits far worse than itself; the result is that
the last state of the man is worse than the first."[6] These, no
doubt, are the things suffered by clerics, monks, or virgins who
are proud, disobedient, and lukewarm. When at the beginning
of their life they abandoned the ways of this world and with
a fervent spirit fled to the service of holy religion, through the
grace of God they were rid of all their sins. But afterwards,
when they did not put forth zeal because of carelessness and
sloth and were not filled with spiritual graces through the
help of God, the vices which had departed found them empty,
returned with many more,[7] and compelled them to return to
their vomit. Then was fulfilled in them what is written: "As
the dog that returns to his vomit becomes hateful, so is the
sinner that returns to his sin."[8] Concerning such men the
Apostle Peter exclaims in a terrible way: "When men have
fled a polluted world and then are caught up and overcome
in pollution once more, their last condition is worse than their
first. It would have been better for them not to have recognized the road to holiness," he says, "than to have turned
their backs on the holy law handed on to them, once they had
known it. How well the proverb fits them: 'The dog returns
to its vomit,' and, 'A sow bathes by wallowing in the mire.' "[9]
This is what happens to those who return to gluttony after
abstinence, to sleepiness after vigils, to pride after humility, to
disobedience after obedience, to wrath after patience. They
return like a dog to its vomit, and like a sow to the mire of
dissipation.

(4) Whoever recognizes that he is this kind of a person,
while there is still time for reform, should with crying and
groaning strive to apply the medicine of humility to this
wound of pride, and he should hasten to receive the antidote

---

6 Luke 11.24, 25, 26.
7 There is a small lacuna in the text. A suggestion found in the margin
   of one of the manuscripts has been used in filling it.
8 Cf. Prov. 26.11.
9 2 Peter 2.20, 21, 22.

of obedience against the poison of murmuring and wrath. Before his soul departs from the light of this life subject to many sins, he should seek for himself a remedy against the day of need, and while there is time to gather it and to reform, strive to prepare the oil of humility and charity for his lamp, which has been extinguished through pride. Then when the lamp of virginity has been lit, in the midst of the holy virgins the oil of charity will abound in the vessel of his soul, for bodily virginity is of no value if charity and humility have departed from the heart. Saintly souls and those which want to be like them observe these truths, to be sure, and do not cease to practice them. But there are other souls which live, not spiritually, but carnally, for they submit their unhappy necks, not to humility, but to pride. They do not gather spiritual honey like bees, but like wasps they spread cruel poison, when they are disobedient to their superiors, when they are aroused by flames of wrath, when they store up hatred within their hearts, when by their murmuring they cause shipwreck to both themselves and others who have been forced out of the port of obedience by the wind of pride and disturbed from the tranquillity of patience. Thus souls which had left the waves of the world at the beginning of their life and had recourse to the peace of the monastery, because of the excessive fury of pride are shown to have incurred shipwreck right in port because of the storms of wrath. Better than such men are those who are seen to serve the world, because a humble wedded life is much better than haughty virginity; those who with God's help protect themselves in the midst of the sea are more praiseworthy than those who sink in port because of too much carelessness and a false security.

(5) Happy, then, are those souls that through the gift of Christ strive to fill their hearts with the spices of different virtues in such a way that nothing but charity and humility ever proceeds from their lips, nothing but chastity and meekness and obedience. As a result of this, they both provide

eternal rewards for themselves and afford the example of a
saintly life to others. On the contrary there also are miserable
and unhappy souls which should be mourned with every fountain of tears. These are so corrupted by an evil life that from
their lips proceeds, not the medicine of Christ but the poison
of the devil, because of their shameful life. Although such men
are covered outwardly with the religious habit as "in sheep's
clothing," they are known to be interiorly "wolves on the
prowl."[10] As long as they are carried along without reproof,
like snakes and vipers, by the habit of their body they are
seen to show a false humility. But when there is even a slight
admonition, then with the removal of the false humility the
pride which had been concealed will be revealed. Then it is
known in truth that one thing was spoken with the lips and
another concealed in the heart; false humility was fashioned
in the body, but the poison of pride was hidden in the mind.
Now with all humility and paternal solicitude we have suggested all these truths to your charity, more in fear than because we think anything pernicious about you. We have
willed to present before your eyes the carelessness of tepid
souls, in order that you may spiritually rejoice and give thanks
to God for the graces which have been conferred on you
through the divine gift. May you also continually beseech
God's mercy on my behalf and for people like me who are
still oppressed by many negligences, so that when a crown
is given to you before the tribunal of Christ for your perseverance in good works, at least the forgiveness of sins may
be granted to us through your intercession: with the help of
our Lord Jesus Christ.

---

10 Matt. 7.15.

*Sermon 238*


A SERMON TO BE READ TO MONKS DURING THE DAYS OF LENT


Love for your way of living, beloved brethren, tells me that with God's help I should make known to you some words that have been gathered from the books of Sacred Scripture. But what can a poor man dispense to those who are rich? With God's help you yourselves learn through reading what you can give to others, but for the sake of those who are slothful in reading, something must be said. Why do they perhaps not understand, if they do read? However, if with the assistance of the Lord we are willing to review the psalms from memory rather frequently, dearly beloved, and if we daily strive to introduce the lessons of the Apostles into our hearts, you all know very well that what is done with great effort is achieved more brilliantly, and what is kept well in mind is sung more elegantly. I am saying from memory, so no one can excuse himself, lest he find an accuser whom he cannot refute. One says that he is unable to get ready, and another says: I want to, but I have a poor memory. Behold, you are instantly held to be guilty, because of your lying; see that you are confounded in the very act. Why do you excuse yourself? Do not offer false testimony against yourself. You have a room which the Lord made; open it, and hide your Lord's coin there. He wants you to put it away now, while you have the space. Put forth effort, gather it; let your room be open to wisdom and closed to foolishness. You have; you have received. Listen to a faithful witness, the prophet, when he says: "The Lord has given me a well-trained tongue,"[1] "that I may learn to reject the bad and choose the good."[2] What He gave to him, brethren, He has transmitted to us. If you ask what kind of a

---

1 Isa. 50.4.
2 Isa. 7.15.

tongue, He Himself tells you. You already received a well-trained one; why do you excuse yourself? Think about yourself, think about your soul; let your heart put forth effort within you. Why do you allege that it is hard and foolish, when you received a well-trained one? Because you are lukewarm, you make the excuse that you cannot. If you do not get it ready, what are you going to reply to the Lord when He says: Eat me, and drink me? When you get it ready, you eat; when you cling to it, you will drink.

(2) Let each one of you get ready what is good, dearly beloved, because here one must live on it, and in the future life it will be the source of joy. If we return to our psalms rather frequently, brethren, we shut off the approach to worldly thoughts; the spiritual song dominates, and carnal thoughts depart. The psalms are the weapons of the servants of God. The man who clings to the psalms does not fear the enemy, for our Lord says concerning this adversary: "Your adversary is the devil."[3] He suggests adverse thoughts, in order that he may kill us if he can; on the other hand we have right thoughts, if we read the psalms aloud quite frequently. He says, Be proud; I repeat with the psalm what our Lord says: "He shall not dwell within my house who practices pride";[4] and elsewhere: "God resists the proud";[5] also in Solomon: "A proud man knows nothing, has a morbid passion for contention."[6] He would not encourage pride, if he knew that it had a place among the servants of God in paradise. This is why he especially exhorts monks to be proud, in order that they may afterwards be excluded from the place from which he was expelled. If he had not been proud, he would have kept his preeminence in heaven. He encourages quarrels, he excites hatred, he himself stirs up people, but do you like the true psalmist resist him by saying: "O Lord, set a watch before

---

3 1 Peter 5.8.
4 Ps. 100 (101).7.
5 James 4.6.
6 1 Tim. 6.4. This text is not from Solomon as Caesarius indicates.

my mouth, and let not my heart incline to evil words."[7] Elsewhere he also says: "I said, 'I will watch my ways, so as not to sin with my tongue; I will set a curb on my mouth while the wicked man is before me.' "[8] If the servant of God frequently has such a guard on his tongue, he breaks the web of the exceedingly wicked enemy without delay. Do not be malicious toward one another for the Lord detests this vice, as He says: "I hate the assembly of evildoers."[9] Let us, then, amend vices of the flesh, dearly beloved, for the sake of beauty of soul, in which there is the image of Christ. I speak the truth, brethren, that if we want to observe all these things, we will also say to the one who is tempting us: Do not persuade me, devil, to defile the image of my God by listening to you. He suffered for me, He was covered with spittle for me, He was struck with blows on the cheek for me, He was scourged for me, He was hung on a cross for me. This the servant of God should say to his tempter: Truly, you are not persuading me to do what you are urging.

(3) You have admired patience, brethren; now listen to liberality. The noble Joseph returned charity for hatred. When he saw his brothers, or rather his enemies, and when he wanted to be recognized by them, with pious grief he gave witness to the affection of his love. As he affectionately kissed them, he moistened the neck of his brothers with the stream of his tears and washed away the hatred of his brothers with the tears of charity. He did not remind himself that he had been sent down to violent death by them but returned good for evil. He had not yet read the precepts of the Apostle up to that point, but he already showed an example of charity. Nevertheless, they were ever afraid in his presence. Why? Because they had been abased by the poison of envy. In truth, brethren, what does envy do for the unhappy man who is envious except interiorly tear him to pieces within his soul,

---

7 Ps. 140 (141).3, 4.
8 Cf. Ps. 38 (39).2.
9 Ps. 25 (26).5.

with poisonous claws? What does he receive as a result of his
hatred except darkness of soul and the destruction of his
judgment? While a man wants to injure another, he torments
himself. It is not right for monks to be jealous or envious, as
the Apostle says: "As long as there is bitter jealousy among
you, are you not of the flesh? And is not your behavior that
of ordinary men?"[10] Servants of the Lord, however, should
always be anxious to do and think and say the things which
will not displease the Lord but will always be profitable for
the better.

(4) Above all let us cling to the affection of charity, dearly
beloved, so that Christ may not reject us but may praise us
and invite us to eternal reward, saying: "Come. You have my
Father's blessing! Inherit the kingdom prepared for you."[11]
O how fortunate is that servant who is invited by our Lord to
His kingdom! It is such that a man frequently has in his
hands the means whereby he may fulfill the will of His Lord;
that is, the sacred reading, holy thoughts within his heart, and
continual prayer should be his. As often as the enemy ap-
proaches to tempt us, he should always find us occupied with
good works. Especially in these holy days of Lent no one
should excuse himself, because the more we are invited to
God's work, so much the less do we now engage in activity. We
have these holy days, and if anyone of you refuses to exert
effort faithfully on a remedy for his soul, there will be no
excuse for him. Lent comprises one-tenth part of the year,
and many fruits for the soul are gathered into that tenth part.
Therefore I do not want you to excuse yourselves, dearly
beloved, because something in which you fall short at another
time is not made good now. Provide what each one of you
considers necessary; the man who likes psalms or readings or
vigils should keep vigil or read or make progress or pray or
sing. You all have something that you can do for the good of
your soul. The days seem few, but the benefits that are reaped

---

10 1 Cor. 3.3.              11 Matt. 25.34.

during them are of long duration. Pray more now, chant the psalms more, read more, keep more vigils; and if you do not want to do this, you still are compelled to do so, either by the sound of the commandments or in response to the word of your superior.

(5) But you, O servant of God, no one advised you to come here. You came, and so why are you growing lukewarm? Why are you looking for someone to admonish you? You listen to the commandments; why do you delay? Why do you lag behind? Hurry, and run. You are called to a good life; why are you looking for another? Do not be ashamed, be the first to enter, and there you will be found by the One whom you are awaiting. Now that you have come, why are you in a hurry to leave? You have come to a table, not your own, but that of your Lord. Stand firm, and fulfill your ministry. That is the source of your life and your clothing; you are a servant, and you should not leave. Why do you flee from the Lord? What does He tell you? Receive the reward of your service. Let it be a source of pleasure to you that you are serving such a master, who does not know how to become angry. Listen to what He commands you. It is not bitter or harsh; and even if it is difficult, you are a servant. Why do you despise it? Hurry for liberty's sake so that when He has conferred a favor upon you, you may possess liberty with a secure conscience. Already you are considered among the first, already you are called sublime, already you happily exult in the house of your Lord, and you say: "Happy they who dwell in your house! continually they will praise you."[12] May He deign to grant this, who lives and reigns for ever and ever. Amen.

---

12 Ps. 83 (84).5.

## Additional Sermon[1]

A SERMON OF ST. AUGUSTINE ON THE GOSPEL TEXT WHICH SAYS: "ASK AND IT SHALL BE GIVEN TO YOU."[2]

We ought to do what our Lord advised us in the Gospel, dearly beloved, for thus He spoke: "Ask, and you will receive; seek, and you will find; knock, and it will be opened to you."[3] For everyone who asks receives, who seeks finds, and who knocks has the door opened to him. Notice the three things which He mentions: ask, seek, and knock. Let the man who asks bring humility, the one who seeks offer diligence, and the one who knocks bring perseverance. One asks with the lips and seeks with the eyes. What does it mean to ask, except to do so in prayer? And what does it mean to seek except that we do so when we meditate? Finally, what does it mean to knock except that we do so when we perform good deeds with our hands? May God open to us because we knock through good deeds, for this is what it means to knock "before God."

---

1 The Latin text remained in manuscript until published in 1953 by Anna Maria Giorgetti Vichi, *Academie e biblioteche d'Italia* 21 (1953) 335-42, from a 13th-century MS at Rome, Biblioteca Vallicelliana, Tomo VII, fol. 336ᵛ-337ʳ (reduced facsimile, *ibid.* between pp. 336 and 337). This scholar's attribution, based primarily on impressive external evidence, was accepted by Dom Cyrille Lambot (Vicchi p. 341 n. 2) and (with an "it seems") by Abbot Dekkers (*Clavis*2 No. 1008). As known to the Maurists in a 9th-century manuscript (now lost), the piece had a title calling it a "sermon of St. Augustine's"; from the extant table of contents of the lost manuscript Morin, who died in 1946, knew the incipit of the sermon (ed. of Caesarius's sermons, p. 933 [CCL 104.983]). No Augustinian sermon now known appears to be close enough to justify the claim made in the title. Augustine's Sermon 61 has the basic Scripture text in common but little more; in Sermon 105 (sect. 6 and 7), however, there are significant parallels with sections 5 and 6 of the new sermon. In Dom Morin's arrangement of the sermons of Caesarius, the new sermon would seem to find a place among the sermons on Holy Scripture, that is, after No. 148. The present division into sections is new.
2 The title here translated is that reported from the 9th-century manuscript known to the Maurists but now lost.
3 Matt. 7.7; Luke 11.9.

(2) This is what the Scripture says in another place, in the Psalms: "On the day of my distress I sought the Lord; by night my hands were stretched out before Him, and I was not deceived."[4] On the day of my distress I sought God; I did not seek gold or silver or the world, but God alone. No one wishes to suffer distress, and therefore the tribulation which compels a man to seek God is a good thing. Did he say: On the day of my pleasures I sought God? Perhaps,[5] when he had pleasures to enjoy, [he would have said] "I did *not* seek God." God sent him distress, not in anger but rather in pity. God did not abandon him but wished to be sought by him. That is why he said: "On the day of my distress I sought God." We know for a fact that many men do not seek God when things go well with them, but when they are in distress, they do seek Him. And so tribulation is good for them, prompting, as it does, a searching on their part; then follows the finding and their distress is removed.

(3) Notice, too, what the psalmist said. When he told them: "On the day of my distress I sought God," he also added: "My hands were stretched out"; further, "by night" and also "before Him." What is distress? What does it mean to stretch out one's hands, and what does it mean to do so before God? There is distress when we suffer annoyances, and stretching out of hands [when we engage] in good deeds. Searching by night occurs in this world when the truth has not yet shed light. Truly this world will pass away and find Christ. And when Christ comes, He will be like the sun shining in the hearts of all men. Why did he add "before Him"? The man who stretches out his hands performs good deeds. However, the man who thus performs good deeds in order to please men does not do so before God; that is, in order to please Him

---

4 Cf. Ps. 76 (77).3.
5 [We have tentatively emended the *fore* of the MS to *forte.*—Ed.] For a similar first-person utterance in a third-person context, see below section 3 at n. 7.

rather than men.[6] Quite rightly, then, "I was not deceived" follows; a man who has sought God in this way [may say:] "I have not been deceived."[7] He has found what he was seeking, and therefore he has told us: "Ask, seek, knock."

(4) Then see what comes next in the Gospel: "Would one of you hand his son a stone when he asks for a loaf? or a poisonous snake when he asks for a fish? or a scorpion if he asks for an egg? If, then, you who are sinful know how to give your children good things, how much more will your Heavenly Father give what is good to those who ask Him."[8] Are we going to suffer the day of tribulation as long as we live in this world, because we are traveling away from the Lord? It is a day of distress as long as it is a time of sojourning, even if it is well with us according to the world. For the tribulation passes away only when the sojourning is finished. And only then will this traveling be ended when we are united with the holy angels in our heavenly fatherland and live forever with our king, the Lord Jesus Christ. There, indeed, we shall love and praise and rejoice; we shall rejoice and we shall see.

(5) There are three virtues pertaining to the Lord which the holy Apostle forms within us.[9] They are the same qualities which are necessary in this world—faith, hope, and charity; faith, that we may believe, hope, that we may have expectations, and charity, that we may love. Faith, moreover, is signified by the fish. Just as a fish swims in the water and draws life from it, so also is it with respect to baptism. Faith is received and lives in the world. And now the egg—why does it represent hope?[10] Because the chick is not yet seen, but still there is hope of it. For thus the Apostle speaks: "Through

---

6 [Possibly a few words have dropped out here that would yield the sense: ". . . before God; ⟨he who does so before God does so⟩ in order . . ."—Ed.]

7 See n. 5.

8 Cf. Matt. 7.9-11; Luke 11.11-13.

9 [The translation supposes a *quae* instead of the *q(ui)* of the MS. Possibly also *d(omi)ni* is not in place here.—Ed.]

10 [The context requires a question and answer here, but the punctuation of the MS does not indicate such an arrangement.—Ed.]

hope we were saved. Hope that is seen is not hope, for does anyone still hope for what he sees? But if we hope for what we do not see, we await it with patience."[11] Our patient waiting warms the egg. See how much patience a hen possesses when she is warming an egg. She hardly gets up from it to eat a little and return;[12] she has patience beforehand so that afterwards she may find joy from her young.

(6) Charity, which overcomes all things, is compared to bread, for without bread no meal is possible; in other words, without God. Surely the man who does not possess charity loses his life. How is it that bread is set out first on the table? The first course is also placed on the table, but after that it disappears from it. Other courses are served and are removed, but bread stays until the very end. Therefore let us ask, seek, and knock, so that our Lord may give us in this world what He knows is good for us and, in the future one, may grant the eternal life which He promised. Who lives and reigns for ever and ever. Amen.

---

11 Rom. 8.24-25.
12 ["to eat . . . return": the translation supposes here "*ut* . . . manducet . . . redeat," instead of "*uel* . . ." In the MS *uel* is represented by the common abbreviation, which could easily have come from a misinterpreted *ut* in the exemplar.—ED.]

# Appendix

Here follow additional notes to the sermons included in Volumes I and II; they are based on Morin. See above, p. 3.—ED.

**3** Morin here gives the Athanasian Creed in the form—"homiletic," writes Morin, "and somewhat freer"—in which, in a Zwiefalten manuscript, it follows item 2 above. Cf. *Revue Bénédictine* 44 (1932) 212ff.

**9** In this address Morin believed he had found the form of the Apostles' Creed used by Caesarius, whose characteristic diction he finds in several of the passages which surround the text of the Creed. For a full statement of Morin's arguments, see *Revue Bénédictine* 46 (1936) 178-89.

**10** Accepted as Caesarian by Morin after long hesitation. Formerly it stood as Sermon 244 in the Augustine Appendix (PL 39.2194-96). The expression *excarpsum* ("selection") used in the title appears in four or five other Caesarian homilies; cf. e.g., Sermon 20.

**11** In this sermon, which is drawn mainly from some preacher of Southern Gaul, Morin notes the indubitably Caesarian conclusion.

**18** Morin points to borrowings, in sections 5 and 6, from Augustine, Sermon 82.14, where also we have the crow's "Caw, caw" (*cras, cras* [tomorrow, tomorrow]). The conclusion is easily recognized as Caesarius's own.

**20** This *excarpsum* (cf. above, on Sermon 10) is drawn from an *Admonitio* published in 1934 by Morin (*Revue Bénédictine* 46 [1934] 5-15; Dekkers, *Clavis* No. 763), which is perhaps to be ascribed to a *De vita Christiana* addressed to a certain Fatalis by a Breton bishop, Fastidius.

**21** Published by the Maurists, Sermon 385, as a doubtful sermon of Augustine's, but the original has been reworked by Caesarius, who added on his own an introduction and conclusion.

**24** Whether this adaptation of a (possibly lost) Augustinian original reproduces the words of the model or only the sense is disputed.

**28** Another sermon found by Morin to contain Augustinian elements in the body of the work and a genuinely Caesarian conclusion.

**36** In the early part of this sermon, there are two versions of the Latin text. In the translation that of the "Collectio Clichtovea" has been followed.

**58** This sermon has been assigned to Faustus of Riez, but Morin, with others, gives it rather to Caesarius. There are some borrowings from Eusebius Gallicanus.

**62** This short piece may stem in origin from Faustus of Riez. In two manuscripts, however, it is joined with Caesarian homilies on penance, and Morin reasonably holds that it was reworked by Caesarius.

**63** Not readily proved to be Caesarius's on stylistic grounds, this sermon was widely transmitted among the bishop's sermons and was surely well known to him. It is important for the understanding of the Church's early penitential discipline and so deserves, states Morin, to be added, if only as an appendix, to the genuinely Caesarian sermons on penance.

**70** Delivered apparently about the year 508, when Arles was being besieged by the Franks and Burgundians in league against the Goths. The sermon contains clearly Caesarian elements, but, notes Morin, sections 1 and 2 are drawn from the *De tempore barbarico* of the fifth-century Carthaginian bishop Quodvultdeus (Dekkers, *Clavis* No. 412; cf. Morin in *Revue Bénédictine* 16 [1899] 257ff.)

**90** The sermon consists mainly of borrowings from Pelagius, Cyprian, and Augustine (Sermon 343). Morin, following Casimir Oudin, is sure that the assembly was made by Caesarius, who toward the end adds material of his own.

**92** A sequel to the preceding, this sermon is drawn mainly from St. Ambrose's *De Ioseph;* only the introduction and conclusion are the original work of Caesarius himself.

**93** Essentially the work of an unknown, early preacher, but a few passages of possibly Caesarian origin appear in it. Morin was strongly tempted not to include it in his edition.

**94** As the Maurists saw, this sermon contains excerpts from Origen's first homily on Exodus (in Rufinus's translation). Section 4, the extended conclusion, is Caesarius's own.

**97** Morin has no doubt that this sermon, formed in part of borrowings from Origen's homilies on Exodus, was put together by Caesarius.

**99** Sections 1 and 2 are drawn in large part from Origen, but the recapitulation and conclusion in section 3 are clearly by Caesarius.

**100** A sermon drawn mainly from Augustine's Sermon 8; yet the hand and art of Caesarius may be seen in the assembling of the extracts; e.g., in the use (section 4) of the quotation, "The burdens of the world . . ." (see above, Sermon 196 n. 2), not found in the Augustinian original. The version here followed is that of two homiliaries; a widely different version, drawn from a 14th-century biblical collection in Oxford, is given as Sermon 100A.

**100A** See the note in Vol. 2 *ad loc.* and above on Sermon 100. In this version the quotation "The burdens of the world . . ." does not appear.

**102** Comprising much drawn from Origen's homilies on Exodus, this sermon is Caesarian not only in its introduction and conclusion but, notes Morin, in other parts as well.

**103** Another sermon drawn largely from Origen on Exodus (*Hom.* 11) but comprising characteristic Caesarian elements, among them the conclusion (sect. 6); the sermon promised there for the next day may be Sermon 199 below.

**105** Less a sermon, Morin declares, than an assembly of material for one, this is drawn from Origen's 16th homily on Leviticus. The assemblage, however, is the work of Caesarius. Morin notes the abrupt ending, caused perhaps by the preacher's sense of having already spoken too long.

**108** Like Sermon 105, drawn from Origen (in this case *Hom.* 8 on Exodus) but furnished with unmistakably Caesarian additions.

**109** The version followed in the translation is mainly the one reported by Morin from manuscripts at Reims and Épinal.

**110** Another Caesarian accommodation of an Origenian original (*Hom.* 9 on Numbers), handed down, however, under Jerome's name.

**111** Only a few characteristic phrases serve to show that it was Caesarius who produced this further adaptation of Origen (again, *Hom.* 9 on Numbers).

**113** Yet another piece drawn by Caesarius from Origen (*Hom.* 13-15 on Numbers) and provided with a conclusion of his own. Of the versions set out by Morin the translator follows that of the Oxford biblical collection mentioned above in the note on Sermon 100.

**117** St. Ambrose's name is given in the title because the sermon consists almost entirely of the prologue of that writer's *De Spiritu Sancto*. The recapitulation (sect. 6), however, is a sign that the piece as it stands was produced by Caesarius.

**118** The basis of this work appears to be a lost sermon by St. Augustine. In reworking his original, Caesarius introduced material so clearly in his style as to show that here again it is he who has preserved sermon material of Augustine's which but for the reworking would never have survived at all.

**123** The source of sections 2-4 is a work against five heresies now assigned to Quodvultdeus (Dekkers, *Clavis* No. 410) but early attributed to St. Augustine. The opening section is Caesarian, however, as is the adaptation of the older text.

**131** Though the Maurists could not determine the identity of the "learned and pious" author, Morin after long uncertainty became convinced that Caesarius is the author, drawing on a number of sources.

**132** From Caesarian traits in the body of the sermon—to say nothing of the characteristic opening section—Morin is surprised that the Maurists had nothing to say about Caesarian authorship.

**133** Again Morin is amazed that the Maurists, while recognizing much derived from Augustine's *Enarratio* on Ps. 49.27-30, did not see that the whole piece proclaims the authorship of Caesarius.

**134** Here the Maurists refused to print this piece even in their Appendix to St. Augustine because it was "conflated from Augustine's *Enarratio* on Ps. 50, with the addition of introduction and ending," but they failed to recognize, even from the numerous parallel expressions, that Caesarius, once again, is the "conflator."

**135** In this sermon on a verse of Ps. 75, much is drawn from St. Augustine's *Enarratio,* but Morin sees as Caesarian not only the opening and closing sections but the compiler's mode of selection.

**137** Here, as in Sermon 186, Caesarius has sought to cause his audience to profit from *Tractatus* 10 of those composed by Augustine on the first epistle of St. John. Here, however, Morin finds only a few Caesarian touches.

**138** Much borrowing here from Augustine's Sermon 37 and a characteristic Caesarian introduction. The absence of a conclusion is not surprising in what is less a complete homily than material assembled for presenting a homily (cf. above on Sermon 105).

**139** An extended conclusion marks this Caesarian adaptation of Augustine, Sermon 37.

**140** Largely derived from Augustine, Sermon 178, but intermixed and added elements bespeak the hand and workmanship of Caesarius.

**141** Characteristically marked as a Caesarian takeover—in this case of Augustine, Sermon 311. Caesarius's handling of his original shows his accustomed effort to adapt the Augustinian eloquence to the intelligence of his Gallic hearers.

**142** A fine Caesarian conclusion follows an assemblage of fragments of a lost sermon, probably one of Augustine's on Isa. 53.1.

**143** The adaptive hand of Caesarius is seen in both the opening and the conclusion of this little sermon, which appears to stem ultimately from the Eastern church, perhaps from Ephraem.

**144** Mostly, Morin believes, from an unknown author, but Caesarian elements are present.

**145** The Maurists saw here a mass of Augustinian material placed between a somewhat inappropriate introduction and conclusion but declined to propose that Caesarius, as Morin believes, was the author of the adaptation.

**147** Published by the Maurists as a genuine sermon of Augustine's (Sermon 59), without paying heed to the Caesarian conclusion and to other alterations indicative of Caesarian adaptation.

**148** The translation presents (in sect. 6, second sentence ff.) the longer ending published for the first time by Morin.

**153** Basically Augustine, Sermon 85.1-3, 6, ending with an altogether Caesarian conclusion.

**158A** The source of the second version is the widely dispersed collection (A) of 42 homilies called the "Book of St. Caesarius."

**159** Largely drawn from Augustine, Sermon 96. The workmanship of Caesarius is seen in the handling of the Augustinian material and in the conclusion.

**160B** The third recension is from the "Collectio Clichtovea"; the second (not translated) from the 12th-century Vatican Palatine MS lat. 430.

**161** A sermon first edited by Morin in 1906 *(Revue Bénédictine* 23.351-3) and shown to be Caesarius's, if only from the recapitulation and conclusion (sect. 2). Much of the central portion of the sermon comes from Augustine's *Quaest. evang.* 2.19.

**162** Mainly formed from the first part of Augustine's Sermon 254. The very title, however, the brief conclusion, and even the alterations made in Augustine's text reveal the hand of Caesarius.

**163** Clearly one of Caesarius's centos, as shown as well by the handling of the Augustinian texts used as by the characteristic recapitulation and conclusion.

**164** Another cento marked as Caesarian by the conclusion. Caesarius's source was a lost sermon of Augustine's.

**165** A second Caesarian cento on Dives and Lazarus, which apparently has suffered some truncation and alteration in the single known manuscript.

**167** Derived almost entirely from Sermon 3 of Eusebius "Gallicanus" but showing indications of adaptation by Caesarius.

**168** The first five of the six sections drawn from Eusebius "Gallicanus" (Sermon 5), but section 6 shows nothing from that source and presents individual words that reveal the Caesarian origin of the whole.

**170** The very end of this sermon shows it to be a Caesarian adaptation, viz. of a sermon of an unknown author not greatly dissimilar to the Latin Origen or St. Ambrose.

**172** The sermon is largely drawn, though with a free hand, from Augustine, Sermon 136. There is a characteristically Caesarian conclusion.

**173** Constructed apparently from a lost sermon of Augustine's; Caesarius's hand is seen in the conclusion.

**174** Sect. 1 from an unknown source; sect. 2 added by Caesarius, who gives in it an announcement of Sermon 160.

**175** Morin finds that Caesarius (whose work the conclusion certainly is) drew here upon Augustine, Sermon 247.2-3 and (in sect. 4) upon another African preacher, who opposed rebaptism.

**177** Largely drawn from Augustine, Sermon 151; Morin sees no possibility of doubt that Caesarius was the adapter.

**178** A Caesarian conclusion follows upon the initial three sections, drawn from a source (not Augustine) which Morin felt unable to identify.

**180** Passed over by the Maurists as being simply excerpts from Augustine's second *Enarratio* on Ps. 25; the compiler, surely Caesarius, has introduced, besides the conclusion, various elements characteristically Caesarian.

**181** The Caesarian authorship of this recension of Augustine, Sermon 167, Morin finds eminently clear, in spite of the Maurists' silence.

**183** A free adaptation by Caesarius of Augustine, Sermon 178.

**185** In this sermon Caesarius has excerpted Augustine's Sermon 211 almost entire and added a conclusion of his own.

# INDICES

# GENERAL INDEX*

Aaron, **2** 117, 126, 145, 147, 149-50
Abana River, **2** 230
abbots, **1** 22, 136
Abel, **1** 67; **2** 43, 113, 116, 276
abortion, **1** 13, 102, 220-21, 259, 261-62; **2** 343; **3** 61-62
Abraham, **1** 67, 106, 156, 252; **2** 3-22, 77, 113, 124, 136, 162, 178, 199, 276, 298, 332, 364, 390, 392, 395-96, 413-14, 416, 454, 476, 493; **3** 40, 103
abstinence, **2** 318; **3** 29, 33, 43, 53, 217
abyss, **2** 56, 154, 406; **3** 78, 81
Achab, **1** 313-15
Achan, **1** 210
actions, evil, **1** 75; **2** 4, 152, 197
Acts of the Apostles, **1** 335; **2** 35, 437; **3** 98, 127, 159
Adam, **1** 46, 66, 97, 292; **2** 19, 55, 113, 152, 163-64, 166 175, 194, 217, 231, 233, 242, 268, 323, 376, 378, 387, 389, 396, 447-48, 456, 459, 462-63; **3** 76
Adam, the new: *see* Christ
admonition, **1** 14, 24-25, 32-33, 38, 45, 79
adultery, adulterers (fornication, concubinage, etc.), **1**

12, 33-34, 61, 70, 75-76, 81, 88-89, 98, 107, 110-11, 158-59, 161-62, 205-19, 221, 232, 240, 265, 277, 279, 313-14, 317, 341, 351, 364-65; **2** 10, 25, 28, 54-55, 79, 88, 94-97, 123-24, 163, 173, 185, 215, 249, 251-54, 257, 259-61, 303, 305, 317, 325, 329, 337, 347, 356, 360, 399, 436, 443, 446, 450, 455, 471; **3** 9, 11, 13, 18-19, 37, 61, 149, 152, 165, 176, 188
adultery, spiritual, **1** 259
Advent: *see* seasons and feasts, sermons for
adversities, **1** 330
*Aeneid: see* Vergil
affections, evil, **1** 42
Agar, **2** 113,116
Agde, Council of, **1** xii-xiii, xv, 15
age of reason, **1** 309
*agios,* **1** 21
Agroetius (Agricius), Bp. of Antibes, **1** xvi
Alaric II, **1** viii, x
d'Alès, A., **1** xxvi, 3 n.
Alleluia, **3** 75, 78
alms, **1** 6, 8, 9-10, 16, 44, 50, 53, 61, 73-75, 81, 84, 86 99-

---

*Much of this index is the work of Sharon Kelly Heyob.—ED.

100, 102, 122, 128-30, 136-37, 141, 145-46, 148-49, and *passim*

almsgiving, **1** 9, 43-44, 52, 61, 71, 80, 93, 98-99, 129, 131, 142, 146, 149-50, 152-53, 158-61, 168, 170, 195, 197, 211, 223, 225, 242, 266, 273, 277, 280-81, 302-3, 309, 321, 366; **2** 29, 42, 64, 80, 106, 112, 134-35, 142, 174, 177, 226, 235, 238, 240, 245-46, 257, 277, 279, 281, 284, 308-11, 318, 327, 331-32, 337, 339, 349, 356, 359-61, 364, 373, 399, 407, 412, 446, 452-56, 477-78, 483, 493; **3** 8, 10, 13, 26, 47, 49, 53-54, 56-57, 68, 82, 88-90, 92, 120, 123, 127, 130, 143, 146, 149, 151, 155, 164-65, 168, 170-72, 175-77, 193, 200

altars, **1** 6, 13-14, 82, 89, 100-101, 197, 211, 216, 222, 224, 263-64, 269, 355, 367; **2** 20, 29, 135, 144-46, 160, 184, 204-5; **3** 57, 64, 68, 76, 130, 151, 155, 164-70, 175-78

Amalec, **2** 108, 111-12, 154, 157

ambition, **1** 113, 119, 227, 229, 246, 253, 272, 276, 335

Ambrose, St., **1** xix, 16; **2** 177, 276, 283; **3** 124 n., 230-31, 233

amendment of life, **1** 37, 61, 90, 92, 161, 220, 236, 242, 248, 277, 308, 323; **2** 42, 100, 138, 140-41, 221, 247, 249, 300, 343, 402, 405, 460, 483; **3** 208, 222

Amorrites, **2** 162

amulets, **3** 74

Ananias, **1** 203, 334-36; **2** 214, 221

Anathoth, **2** 148

angels, **1** 37, 46, 53, 80, 83, 88, 98, 120, 145, 151, 153-54, 156, 181, 183, 230, 241, 248, 282, 286, 288, 301; **2** 12, 30, 32-33, 37, 68-69, 78, 143, 146, 159-60, 177-78, 181, 200, 203-5, 237, 267-68, 294, 296, 299, 313-14, 321, 326, 328-32, 335-36, 363, 390, 395, 400-401, 412, 424, 447, 454, 457, 469-70, 490, 493; **3** 19, 37-38, 55, 60, 66, 69, 72, 79-80, 115, 117, 140, 150, 166, 176, 181, 211, 213, 227

angels, food of (banquet of), **3** 13

anger: *see* wrath

Anglo-Saxon, the language, **1** xxiii

animals, sacrifice of, **3** 169

Anna (mother of Samuel), **1** 122, 339

Anne, St., **1** 43-44

anniversary of consecration, **3** 184 n., 189 n.

anoint, **1** 56, 77; **2** 30, 33, 200, 220, 223, 482

Antichrist, **1** 57

antiphons, **1** 40

Apocalypse, **1** xvii

Apollos, **1** 7, 18; **2** 186

apoplexy, **1** 298

apostles, **1** xxii, 46-47, 58, 103,

157, 169-70, 180-81, 191, 246, 248, 268, 311, 334-36, 349; **2** 22, 30, 33, 41, 46, 69, 73, 111, 127, 130, 143, 153, 168, 170, 173, 182, 185, 190, 195, 205, 217-18, 230, 237, 240, 244, 253, 258, 265-66, 328-30, 338, 347, 358, 415, 418, 420, 439, 441, 443, 445-47, 450-51, 455, 463-64, 466-67, 473, 478-79, 492; **3** 40-41, 56, 72, 83, 105, 108, 110-11, 113, 115, 118, 128, 134, 137, 143, 153, 161-62, 180, 183, 189, 220, 222, 227

Apostles' Creed, **3** 229
Apostolic Fathers, **1** 135 n.
apostolic writings, **1** 342
Aquinas, St. Thomas, **1** 21 n.
archangel, **1** 246
Areuna, the Jebusite, **2** 203-4
Arians, **1** ix, xvi-xvii; **2** 73, 144, 207
  Arian heresy, **2** 206-7
Arigius, **3** 192
Arimathea, **2** 295
Arius, **2** 186
ark of the covenant, **1** 33
ark of the testament, **2** 20, 172
ark, Noah's, **2** 414
Arles, **1** vii-xii, xv, xvii, xxii, xxiv; **3** 82 n., 92 n., 111 n., 113 n., 230
  Council of, **1** xii-xiii
Arnold, C. F., **1** vi n., xvii n., xxvi
army of the devil, **2** 78
army of the Lord, **2** 74
Artemius, St., **3** 192 n.

artist, divine, **3** 169
ashes, **2** 12, 19, 89, 239, 298, 301, 338
  sprinkle head with, **1** 313
ass, **2** 16-18, 30, 123, 155, 159-60, 192, 195-96; **3** 154
assurance, false, **1** 83-84
Assyrians, the, **2** 298-99
astrologers, **1** 96, 291
Athanasius, St., **1** 26
Athanasian Creed: *see* Creed
athlete, **2** 166, 237-38
atonement, **1** 298, 303
augury, **1** 263; **2** 227
Augustine, St., **1** xvii-xix, xxi, xxiii-xxiv, 16, 90, 93, 98, 106, 118, 123, 189, 198, 275, 290, 305; **2** 85, 182, 198, 203, 206, 209, 241, 282-83, 304, 337, 379, 427, 437, 442, 467, 473; **3** 2, 15 n., 38 n., 75, 78, 93 n., 117, 124 n., 132 n., 134, 137, 139 n., 144 n., 156, 184, 186 n., 189, 225, 229-34
  Augustine Appendix, **3** 229, 232
  rule of, **1** xvi
authority, **3** 180
Auvergne, Council of, **1** xv
avarice, **1** 41, 52-53, 80, 93, 116, 119-20, 139, 141, 145, 154, 159, 164, 166, 169, 174, 197, 203-4, 216, 227, 249-50, 272, 276-77, 280, 289, 322, 325, 327, 334-36, 341, 366; **2** 3, 6, 24-25, 42, 64, 67, 70, 79, 95, 97, 106, 120, 123, 135, 164, 169, 175, 197, 224, 229, 239, 268, 270, 272, 275, 282,

291, 301, 303, 324-25, 331, 335, 340, 357, 366, 373, 401, 450, 468, 471, 476, 478-79, 490, 493; **3** 9, 11, 18, 37, 79, 93, 95, 110, 112, 114, 123, 143, 149-50, 152-53, 175

Baal, **2** 460
Babylon, Babylonians, **1** 247; **2** 408, 413, 490
Balaam, **2** 155-60
Balac, **2** 155, 157-58, 160
banquets, **2** 405; **3** 63, 124, 149, 183
  banquet, eternal and heavenly, **2** 493; **3** 165
  banquet, spiritual, **3** 85, 186
baptism, grace of, **1** 263; **2** 4, 6, 35, 63-64, 119, 175, 192, 203, 218-19, 231, 422
  robe of, **3** 71, 80
  sacrament of, **1** 69-71, 76, 78, 85, 87, 90, 101, 211, 216, 256, 260, 263, 266, 305, 308, 333, 336; **2** 116, 130, 155, 165, 167-68, 172, 184, 202, 210, 212, 224, 230-31, 234, 236, 314, 403, 405-7, 410, 414, 418-19, 421-23, 425, 433, 436, 440-41, 481; **3** 13, 16, 46, 58, 61-64, 72, 74, 92, 102, 152, 156, 173, 178, 227
  water of, **2** 35, 65; **3** 71
barbarians, **2** 162
Bardenhewer, O., **1** viii n., xxvi
Bardy, G., **1** ix n., xiii n., xv n., xviii n., xx n., xxvi

Bathuel, **2** 21
beasts, **2** 97-98, 122, 200, 222, 480; **3** 131
  spiritual, **2** 122-23, 265, 268
beatitudes, the, **1** 28, 131
Beck, H. G. J., **1** xiii-xiv n., xx n., xxvi; **3** 1 n., 31 n., 58 n., 82 n., 92 n., 111 n., 113 n., 117 n., 124 n., 152 n.
beggar, **2** 367, 394
Benedictines, Congregation of Saint-Maur (Maurists), **1** xxiii-xxiv; **3** 139 n., 184 n., 189 n., 225 n., 229-32, 234
benediction (blessing), **1** 358
benevolence, **1** 366
Benjamin, **2** 50; **3** 159
Berg, K., **1** xiv n.
Bethlehem, **3** 40, 139
Beuron, Abbey, and the Old Latin Bible, **1** xxv
birds, **2** 6-9, 268, 292
"birthday" (day of bishop's consecration or anniversary of that day), **3** 184 n., 189 n.
"birthday" (day of saint's death), **3** 35 n.
birthday festivals of the martyrs, **1** 271
birthday of the saints, **1** 272, 276
birthday, preparation for a, **3** 8
bishops, **1** 6-7, 11-15, 21-22, 44-45, 157, 212, 274, 300, 307; **2** xiii, 145, 357, 429, 473, 482; **3** 111-14, 122, 134, 154, 179-81, 190-91
Blanzac, monastery of, **3** 192

blasphemy, blasphemer, **1** 291; **2** 161, 166, 220, 237, 242, 287-89, 399, 462; **3** 158

blessing, **1** 188, 250, 329, 342, 344, 347, 352-53, 358, 360; **2** 119, 159, 216, 232; **3** 62, 88, 112, 143, 168, 172, 193, 223

blessing, nuptial, **1** 213, 217

blindness, **2** 188-89, 196-97, 294, 296, 424-27, 442; **3** 145, 159

blood, **2** 82, 84, 86, 92 n.-93, 133; **3** 111, 113, 159

body, the, **1** 37, 48, 80, 153-54 230

as temple, **2** 58; **3** 168-69, 171, 174; *see also* Holy Spirit, temple of, devil, temple of, Christ, temple of, God, temple of

Boniface II, Pope, **1** xii

Boniface, St., **1** xxiii

Bordeaux, **1** ix, 21 n.

Bouquillon, Thomas, **1** xxiv n.

Breviary, Roman, **3** 117 n., 144 n.

bracelets, **2** 21-22

brass, **2** 145, 241-42

bread, **1** 89; **2** 12, 27, 120, 178, 184-85, 313, 315, 461, 464-65, 476, 486; **3** 157-58, 186, 227-28

heavenly, **2** 58

bribes, **1** 13, 76, 132, 158; **2** 145; **3** 179

brothel, **2** 287

brother, love/hatred of, **2** 39, 45, 47, 52, 94, 258, 273, 306, 318, 331, 375, 424, 485-86, 489; **3** 10, 129-30, 137-38, 146, 165, 177, 213

brothers, harmony between, **2** 484, 486, 488

Brunck, E. F., **1** xiii n.,

buffoonery, **1** 19, 39, 49; **2** 67

"burdens of the world . . ." (favorite quotation of Caesarius), **3** 42 n., 230; cf. **1** 6, 8, 103, 171, 227, 348; **2** 87, 491; **3** 50, 181

Burgundy, Burgundians, **1** v, viii, xii; **3** 230

Cabillonum: *see* Chalon-sur-Saône

Caesar, **1** 159

Caesaria, sister of St. Caesarius of Arles, **1** xv

Caesarius,
    Latinity of, **1** xx
    life of, **1** v-xv
    works of
        *Breviarium fidei adversus hereticos,* **1** xvii
        *Expositio in Apocalypsim,* **1** xvii
        *De gratia,* **1** xvi
        *De mysterio sanctae Trinitatis,* **1** xvii
        *Rule for Virgins,* **1** xvi
        *Sermons,* **1** xxv; **3** 229-34; new sermon, **3** 225
        *Statuta Ecclesiae antiqua,* **1** xvii

Cain, **2** 43, 113, 116

Calends of January, **3** 26, 28,

30, 32-33; *see also* seasons and feasts, sermons for

calmness, **1** 32

calumny, calumniator, **1** 19, 49, 77, 207, 216, 260, 302, 308; **2** 80, 87, 426, 466, 474

Calvary, **2** 19, 187, 197, 222

camels, **2** 21, 30, 123

Cana of Galilee, **2** 402, 409-11

Canaanite woman, **3** 39

candles, **1** 75

Canon of the Mass: *see* Mass

canonical regulations, **1** 7, 15

canonical writings, **1** 365

canons, **1** 15

canticle of Isaiah, **1** 86

"Canticle of Blessings," **1** 325

Canticle of Canticles, **2** 66, 149

captives, to free, **1** 150, 195

Carmel, Mount, **1** 202; **2** 212

Carpentras, Council of, **1** xii, xiv-xvi

cataracts, **1** 240

catechumens, **2** 203, 236; **3** 58-63, 75, 156

Catholics, **1** 180; **2** 356

Catholic Church: *see* Church

Catholic mother, **2** 207

Catholic unity, **2** 273

cautery, **1** 36

Cayré, F., **1** ix n., xxvi

centurion, **1** 252

Cephas: *see* Peter, St.

chaff, **2** 27, 78, 177, 181, 184, 219, 243, 351-52, 366, 407, 459-60, 472; **3** 76-77, 81, 92

Chaillan, M., **1** vi n., xi, xiv n., xxvi

chains: *see* fetters

Chalon-sur-Saône, **1** v

Chanaan, Chanaanites, **2** 6, 126, 161-63, 175, 298

charity (love), **1** 4, 8, 15, 17, 24, 26, 28, 38, 43, 50, 89-90, 106, 108, 113-27, 139, 142, 144-47, 151, 173, 175-89, 193, 196-97, and *passim;* **2** 8, 14, 26, 29, 31, 40-43, 45-46, 48, 52-53, 57, 64, 70, 87, 91, 95-96, 101, 132, 142, 147, 151, 167-68, 174, 177, 182, 208, 217, 221, 223-26, 235, 252, 262, 270, 272-74, 288, 298, 306-8, 316-20, 327-28, 331-32, 340, 349, 352, 354, 365, 368, 372, 374-75, 387, 399, 412-13, 418, 428-33, 446, 448, 463, 467-70, 485, 487, 489-90; **3** 56-57, 64, 71, 73, 77, 97, 101, 110, 122, 129-30, 132, 135-36, 138, 145-46, 148-49, 152, 155, 168, 170-71, 175-77, 180, 190, 192-93, 196-202, 204-5, 207-8, 210-13, 215-16, 218, 222-23, 227-28

charmers, **1** 71, 77-78, 266

charms, **1** 13, 78, 82, 101, 254, 258, 262

chastity, **1** 12-14, 41, 43, 44, 80-81, 88-89, 100, 120, 154, 166-67, 173-74, 204-5, 207-9, 214, 216, 218-23, 225, 256, 260-61, 271, 275, 334, 363, 366; **2** 3, 8, 10, 25, 28-29, 34, 42-45, 54-59, 62-64, 67, 79, 91, 95, 98, 124, 135, 163, 177, 194, 197, 223, 235-36, 239, 258, 260, 277-78, 288, 298, 325,

329, 331, 346-47, 350, 372,
374, 385, 387, 404, 408, 412,
423, 437, 482; 3 8, 11-12, 25,
36-37, 42, 57, 61, 63-64, 68,
73, 76, 81, 83, 101, 120, 130,
145, 149, 151-53, 155, 166-
72, 175, 177-79, 218

Childebert, 1 ix

children, 1 222; 2 19, 25, 28,
33, 39, 61, 71, 90, 95, 140,
220-21, 227-29, 231, 236-37,
242, 252, 254, 281, 286, 290,
298-99, 302, 339-42, 396, 408,
416, 425, 436, 451-52, 462,
482; 3 61, 139, 145, 155-56,
166, 182-83

chrism, 1 56; 2 224, 377

Christ, 1 5, 27, 59, 61-62, 65,
98, 100, 102, 132, 139, 158,
167, 175, 181-82, 184-85, 207,
237, 254, 262, 265, 270, 277-
78, 281, 285, 289, 303-4, 321,
324, 341, 345, 349, 352, 354,
360, 366
  Ascension of, 1 27, 55, 58,
    60; 2 213; 3 11, 23, 93-94
  baptism of, 1 63; 2 165, 230
  beehive of, 3 84, 86
  birth of, 3 69, 118
  blood of, 1 96, 105, 155, 172,
    206, 211, 215, 272, 277,
    283, 345; 2 19, 23-24, 31,
    60, 72, 110, 127, 138, 205,
    223, 229, 239, 403, 414; 3
    40, 154, 190
  Body of as Holy Commun-
    ion, 1 xiii, 78, 89, 171,
    361; 2 211, 314; 3 7, 167,
    176

body of, 1 325; 2 127, 134,
  178, 190, 212, 217-18, 295
body of, the Church as, 1
  306; 2 130, 185, 190
Body and Blood of (Eu-
  charist), 1 77, 89, 100-101,
  167, 171, 211, 216, 224,
  254, 262, 321, 342, 347; 2
  29, 313, 377, 482; 3 7, 10-
  11, 57, 64, 66, 68, 151, 164,
  167, 176
  preparation for, 3 7-10,
    12, 21, 57, 64, 68, 151
  as spiritual remedy, 3 57,
    64, 151, 176
born of the Virgin Mary, 1
  55-56, 59-60
the Bridegroom, 1 103; 2
  22-23, 72, 143; 3 12, 71
charity of, 3 29-30
Circumcision of: see seasons
  and feasts, sermons for
conceived of the Holy
  Spirit, 1 55-56, 59
cross of, 1 43, 60, 62, 64-65,
  172, 202, 284
crowned with thorns, 1 60,
  65
crucifixion of, 1 55, 57, 59-
  60, 283; 2 18-19, 37, 39-40,
  134, 152-53, 187, 197-98,
  205, 211, 222, 229-30
death of, 1 55, 57, 59-60; 2
  13, 17, 39, 60, 152, 182,
  185, 188-90; 3 69-71
descended into hell, 1 27,
  55, 60, 283
and disciples, 1 141, 199; 2
  47, 49, 121, 127, 160, 188,

202, 228, 232, 265-66, 280, 296, 312, 338, 370, 401, 416-17, 424, 433-35, 437; **3** 67, 70, 108-9, 114, 119, 128

divinity of, **1** 27, 64; **2** 18

fasting of, **1** 64

as fountain, **1** 357; **3** 118

goodness of, **1** 231; **2** 38, 69, 111, 118, 327, 412; **3** 73

grace/mercy of, **1** 254; **2** 5, 17, 22, 41, 53, 63, 76, 134, 138, 140, 195, 203, 218, 228, 231-32, 238, 329, 415, 418, 423, 436, 448; **3** 76, 163, 191

the new Adam, **2** 164, 414

greatness of, **2** 207

as Head of His Body, the Church, **1** 18, 126-27, 141; **2** 31, 184

help of, **1** 32, 42, 52, 61, 66, 71, 73, 75, 87, 98, 102, 114, 121, 139, 204, 220, 360, 366; **2** 19, 45, 63, 67, 85, 92, 98, 108, 111, 118, 175-76, 203, 205, 409; **3** 24, 33, 37, 41, 67, 114, 181, 192, 205, 212

humanity of, **1** 27; **2** 18

humility of, **1** 47

husband of the Church, **1** 250

the Incarnate Word, **2** 217, 427

Incarnation of, **1** 27, 60, 62; **2** 151, 177, 199, 217, 239, 291, 377-78, 410; **3** 118

inspiration of, **1** 4; **2** 16, 74

instruments of, **3** 59

the Judge, **1** 25, 27, 58, 60, 83, 118, 132, 195, 265, 279, 286-87, 310, 320, 357; **2** 208, 235, 263, 295, 297, 300, 375; **3** 24, 129, 158-59

justice of, **2** 102

as King, **1** 46; **2** 62-63, 177; **3** 59, 70

the Lamb of God, **2** 388

as light of the world, **1** 254; **2** 47, 114

the living bread, **2** 120-21

Lord of the angels, **1** 301

love of, **1** 31, 90, 181; **2** 8, 252, 270, 358, 366; **3** 131, 200, 213

majesty of, **2** 177; **3** 69-70

meekness of, **1** 47

Passion of, **1** 47, 62, 66, 202; **2** 16-17, 18, 60-61, 68, 74, 127, 130, 133, 178, 182, 197, 205, 211, 213, 221-22, 229, 265, 281, 378, 414-16, 480; **3** 11, 68, 108

the Physician, **1** 312, 314, 319, 357; **2** 19, 85, 228-29, 235, 254-55, 293, 422, 483; **3** 9, 24, 84, 93, 137, 162, 208, 211

power of, **2** 189, 192, 201, 233

as power of God, **1** 57; **2** 217

the (one) Redeemer, **2** 23-24, 42, 60, 134, 187, 224, 228, 291, 297, 402, 417; **3** 13, 19, 23-25, 38, 69, 108, 163, 174, 190-91 as restorer of life, **3** 21-23

Resurrection of, **1** 27, 55, 57-58, 60, 141, 345; **2** 17, 37, 41, 61, 74, 155, 185, 188, 265-66, 280, 294-96, 368, 378, 396, 417; **3** 11, 23, 69-70, 72, 78, 94, 109, 125

sacraments of, **1** 89, 222, 260, 264

the Savior, **1** 28, 56, 64, 66, 126-27, 151, 153, 191-92, 199, 203, 251, 274, 278; **2** 28, 30-31, 33-34, 37, 39, 41, 56, 59-60, 63, 74, 85, 113-14, 122, 126, 129, 133, 146, 172, 181, 192, 205, 209, 211-13, 216-17, 221-23, 228-29, 231, 233, 273, 276, 291, 297, 353, 368, 378, 401, 414, 417, 422, 424, 426, 434; **3** 22, 52, 69-70, 73, 88, 93, 108, 117, 119, 128, 163, 181

second coming of, **2** 42, 146, 297

sitting at the right hand of God, **1** 27, 55, 58, 60

the Son of God, **1** 26-27, 55-56, 58-59, 140-41, 184, 326; **2** 158, 184, 190, 212

the Son of man, **1** 84, 91, 133, 286, 336; **2** 184, 212

suffering of, **1** 27, 55, 57, 59, 283; **2** 60, 133, 152, 184, 188-89, 291, 295, 387, 389, 417; **3** 160

sweetness of, **1** 52; **3** 84, 86

teachings of, **1** 250; **2** 218

temples of, **3** 173, 212

the true David, **2** 200-202, 205

the true Elijah (Elias), **2** 209, 213

the true Elisha (Eliseus), **2** 222

the true Gedeon, **2** 181

the true Isaac, **2** 415

the true Joseph, **2** 40-41

the true Joshua, **2** 167-68, 171

the true (high) priest, **2** 146-47, 149

the true Samson, **2** 198

the truth, **2** 86

truth of, **2** 84, 86

vine, **3** 162

the way, the truth, and the life, **2** 74, 93

will of, **2** 190

wisdom of, **2** 218

as wisdom of God, **1** 52; **2** 217

the word of God, **2** 33, 281, 293, 314, 321, 333; **3** 12, 66, 97

wounds of, **2** 280; **3** 70

Christians, **1** 13-14, 20, 30-32, 44-45, 48, 54, 56, 74-78, 83, 86-90, 93, 98, 100-101, 103-4, 118-19, 121-22, 124-25, 127, 155, 162, 169, 176, 191, 199, 204-5, 211, 217, 267, 365 and *passim*

Christian religion, **1** 68-69, 267

Christian times, **1** 216

Christian truth, **1** 27

Christmas, **1** xiii; **3** 8, 12, 14-15, 21, 23-24, 35, 41, 117-18, 186 n.; *see also* seasons and feasts, sermons for

church, **1** 4, 7-8, 10, 13-18, 23, 30, 40, 45-46, 61, 76-82, 88-89, 99-101, 104, 128-29, 140, 149, 174, 220, and *passim;* **2** 11, 19-20, 38, 42, 105, 107, 176, 183, 251-52, 264, 277, 283, 290, 310, 333, 351, 355, 383, 424, 429, 451, 473, 482; **3** 164, 168-70, 173, 175-78, 183

Church, the, **1** vi-vii, x, xii, 6, 10, 14, 18, 22, 30, 32, 43, 55, 58-60, 67, 86, 126, 139-41, 143, 160, 180, 199, 250, 262-63, 328, and *passim;* **2** 94

as the Body of Christ, **2** 266, 333, 439

members of the, **1** 126

circumcision, **2** 104, 148, 298, 439-40; **3** 25, 38; *see also* seasons and feasts, sermons for

Clement, St., apocryphal letter of, **1** 20

clergy, the, **1** 25, 34, 81, 241, 273-74, 277-78

clerics, **1** 15, 48, 136, 139, 237, 254, 274, 300, 347

junior, **1** 8

clothing, **2** 54-55, 59, 89, 95, 133, 238, 277, 279-80, 291, 331-32, 346, 357, 362, 369, 399, 440, 465, 469, 493; **3** 143-44, 148-50, 165, 167-68, 176, 224

coin, spiritual, **3** 183, 220

commandments of God, **1** 39, 60, 64, 71, 83, 86, 284; **2** 49, 81, 85-96, 101, 119, 122-23, 132, 145, 167, 243, 272, 297, 308, 313, 321, 337, 342, 358-59, 388, 399, 458, 461, 491; **3** 90-91, 96, 134, 146, 200, 224

Communion, Holy: *see* Christ, Body of (as Holy Communion) and Christ, Body and Blood of

communion with the Church, **1** 303-4, 321

communion of saints, **1** 55, 59-60

community of Christians, suspension from, **1** 217, 310, 321; **3** 18

compunction of heart, **1** 11, 23, 139, 152, 223, 256, 297, 315, 318, 321-22, 340, 342, 348, 350

conception of children, **1** 13, 221, 258-59

concubinage, concubines: *see* adultery

concupiscence, **1** 224, 287, 306, 322, 351; **2** 62, 69, 91, 124, 163, 169, 173

conduct, good, **3** 64

confession, **1** 34, 61, 105, 290-95, 304, 306, 310, 312, 316, 323; **2** 52, 150, 255, 280, 300, 314, 394, 449

confidence, **1** 96

Confraternity of Christian Doctrine translation, **3** 54 n., 91 n.

congregation, **1** 14, 319, 367

conscience, **1** 14, 16, 25, 33, 42, 71, 76, 89, 91, 100, 104, 108, 114-15, 118, 134, 143, 147, 149-50, 153, 160-62, 166, 168, 177-78, 181, 184, 186, 189, 194-95, 198, 211, 216, 222, 224, 230, 239, 243, 247, 259, 262, 272, 283, 286-87, 292, 297, 302-3, 317, 321, 324, 328, 337; **2** 29, 36, 43, 63, 70, 77, 79, 87, 91, 98, 107-8, 121, 135, 164, 191, 196, 204, 238, 240, 250, 262, 268, 270, 277-78, 282, 301, 350, 391, 399, 401, 460, 469, 485, **3** 7, 75, 95-96, 116, 126, 130, 134, 140, 147-49, 151, 155, 164, 167-69, 171, 194-95, 199-200

examination of, **1** 53, 69, 246, 280, 344; **2** 48, 123, 134, 176, 309, 335, 353, 370, 397, 401, 482, 493; **3** 8, 11, 14-15, 44-46, 55, 57, 59-60, 67, 79, 110, 147, 170, 194

consolation, **1** 35, 91

continence, **2** 26, 448

contrition, **1** 321, 356; **2** 215

Contumeliosus, Bp. of Riez, **1** xvi

conversation, **1** 19, 39, 52, 76, 79, 273, 338-39, 351, 358-59, 366

conversion (change of life), **1** 15, 94-98, 105, 267, 281, 308, 365; **2** 15, 78, 99-100, 138-41, 162, 176, 185, 251, 327, 375, 385, 406, 409, 430, 456-57, 472, 483; **3** 7, 80, 89, 92

converts, **3** 64, 74

Core, **2** 144

Cornelius, a centurion, **1** 252; **2** 437, 439-40

correction, duty of, **1** 349

Councils (Synods): *see* Agde, Arles, Auvergne, Carpentras, Orange, Orleans, Vaison, Marseilles

counsel, **1** 5, 186; **3** 32

covetousness, **1** 115, 118, 169, 197, 336; **2** 193, 197, 343, 357, 467; **3** 83, 143

Creed, **1** 14, 54-59, 75, 89, 100, 266; **2** 233, 236, 312; **3** 63, 229

cross, **1** 64; **2** 17-19, 30-31, 33, 38-39, 67-68, 72, 75-76, 81, 83, 85, 104-5, 110-11, 114, 127, 129, 133, 135, 147, 152-55, 177, 179, 181, 189-90, 192, 198, 200-202, 210-11, 213, 222, 227, 234; **3** 69, 73, 118, 121, 133, 222

cross, sign of the, **1** 74-75, 88, 98, 270, 298; **2** 155, 250, 390; **3** 177

crown, **1** 4, 268; **2** 42, 166, 235, 238, 262; **3** 20, 158, 161, 201

of martyrdom, **2** 351; **3** 111, 113, 127, 135, 140

of thorns, **2** 70

crow's "caw, caw," **3** 229

cruelty, **1** 302

cunning, **1** 335

curses, **2** 371

cursing, **1** 82, 89, 308

cynics, **2** 84
Cyprian, St., **1** v; **2** 276, 317; **3** 230

Dalila, **2** 194-95, 197-98
Daly, W. M., **3** 1 n.
Damascus, **2** 230
damnation, **1** 96, 169, 206, 311
dancing, **1** 14, 77-78, 89; **2** 387, 409; **3** 155
Daniel, **2** 363, 388, 415; **3** 17, 47
darkness, **2** 6, 9-10, 42, 47, 76, 83-84, 90, 95, 143, 173, 196, 205, 221, 226, 234, 264-65, 318, 323, 332, 347, 361, 363 n., 371, 373, 405-6, 436, 447, 449, 458, 485-86, 493; **3** 80, 97, 119, 125, 146, 163, 166, 171, 174-75, 177, 182, 223
darkness of soul, **2** 46
Dathan, **2** 144
David, **1** 177, 205, 252, 305, 313, 315; **2** 116-17, 180, 198-202, 204-5, 240, 250-56, 269-70, 413, 415; **3** 17, 46
David, the true: *see* Christ
daystar, **2** 294
deacons, **1** 13-16, 25, 101, 104, 274, 355, 357, 359; **2** 145; **3** 128
death,
    eternal, **1** 13, 66, 90, 133, 207, 279, 283, 287; **2** 23, 42, 46, 60, 94, 127, 141, 146, 149, 152, 188, 191, 211, 221, 228, 231-32, 234; **3** 141, 185-86, 193, 198, 201

law of, **2** 408, 445
physical, **1** 12, 63, 65-66, 69, 80, 85, 92, 94, 96-97, 99, 133, 167, 326; **2** 37, 39, 42, 78, 80, 82-83, 88, 90, 94-95, 136, 138, 140, 148, 151, 171, 185, 189-90, 193, 197-98, 214-15, 221, 227, 256, 270, 323, 332, 350, 383, 391, 395-96, 429, 431, 444, 447-48, 452; **3** 15, 18-19, 22-23, 25-26, 61, 66, 71-73, 80, 82, 94, 111, 113, 125, 128-29, 132-33, 139-41, 156, 163, 173, 181, 222
spiritual, **1** 20, 69, 96, 99, 326; **2** 4, 57, 89, 95, 124, 164, 176, 251, 254, 299, 304, 322, 327, 349, 352, 383, 422, 441-42; **3** 9-10, 21, 29, 45, 61-62, 71, 86-87, 92, 108, 122, 146-47, 154, 175, 177
debauchery, **1** 214, 235, 240, 273
deceit, **1** 42, 73, 84, 256, 277, 366
Deferrari, R. J., **1** xxiii n., xxvi
Dekkers, Dom E., **1** xv n.; **3** 1 n., 21 n., 225 n., 229, 231
demoniac, **1** 225, 363
demons, **1** 72, 75, 268, 363-64, 366; **2** 123-24, 156, 158-60, 292, 384, 386-87, 490; **3** 26-27, 30-32, 34, 59, 83, 101, 105
desert, **2** 66, 68, 74, 115, 117, 122, 136, 139-42, 151-52, 168,

172, 209

desires, evil, **1** 42, 154, 308

despair, **1** 91, 93, 95-97, 117-18, 300, 309-11, 365; **2** 77, 99, 102, 126, 135; **3** 9

detraction, detractor, **1** 61, 103, 287

devil, **1** 6, 12, 28, 40, 47, 52-53, 60, 62-66, 69-72, 81-82, 88-89, 91, 99-100, 104, 109-10, 113, 116-17, 132, 139, 158, 197, 254, 260-61, 284-85, 288, 291-93, 297, 306, 326, 349, 359, 364-65, 367-68; **2** 5, 7, 17, 23, 36, 46, 57, 62-65, 67-69, 76-79, 83, 88, 111, 122, 124-25, 146-47, 149, 152, 164, 174, 177, 181, 187, 190-91, 195, 197, 200-201, 203, 220, 224, 237-38, 242-43, 250, 265-68, 292, 320, 322-25, 329, 342, 351-52, 354-55, 357-58, 360-61, 371-73, 376-78, 385, 395, 400, 404, 406, 412, 423, 442, 444, 447-49, 459, 466, 478, 480-82; **3** 9, 16, 18-19, 23, 29-30, 37, 46, 55, 59-61, 74, 79-80, 83, 88, 115, 133, 164, 170-71, 174, 177, 193-94, 196, 198-99, 210, 215, 221

  cunning of, **1** 47, 134, 158, 169, 254, 262, 267-68, 311, 313, 315; **2** 78

  helpers of, **2** 79-80

  illusions of, **1** 267

  inventions of, **1** 266-67

  kingdom of, **2** 197-98

  malice of, **2** 218

  persuasion of, **1** 192, 209

  poison of, **1** 78, 82, 88, 237, 264, 351, 359; **2** 152-53, 236, 351; **3** 14, 28, 33, 86, 148, 206, 219

  seduction of, **1** 277

  the spiritual Goliath, **2** 200-203

  sword of, **1** 89

  temples of, **3** 173

  tyranny of, **1** 62

  vessels of, **2** 64, 353; **3** 58-59

  wickedness of, **1** 270

  works of, **1** 69-71; **2** 46, 110, 192; **3** 29, 63

  wounds of, **2** 352

devotion, **1** 25, 76, 79, 138, 266, 271, 273, 275, 302, 322, 344, 349, 352-53, 360; **2** 8, 18, 20, 44, 101, 107, 124, 246, 326, 333, 336, 352, 372, 374, 404, 408, 479; **3** 36, 38, 52, 64, 68, 73, 84-86, 94, 120, 161-62, 164, 173-74, 192-93, 200

diocese, **1** 3 n.

disciple, **1** 5; *see also* Christ and disciples

discipline, **1** 217; **2** 151, 181, 198, 216, 272, 302, 316, 407, 478; **3** 120, 195

disobedience, **2** 351-54, 420; **3** 23, 197, 201, 215, 217

dissipation, **1** 15, 35, 41, 53, 70, 80, 88, 93, 101, 154, 160, 166, 174, 216, 219, 222, 224-25, 227-30, 246, 260, 272, 276-77, 280, 284, 302, 325, 327, 341, 364, 366; **2** 6, 10,

42, 63- 64, 67, 109, 120, 135,
169, 175-76, 194-97, 233, 246,
288, 301, 316, 325, 331, 334,
345, 349, 385, 401, 404, 432,
446, 463, 471, 481, 483, 491,
493; 3 9-16, 29, 37, 43, 45,
63, 79, 87, 93, 95, 110, 115,
126, 149, 152, 154, 169, 171,
175, 217
distaff 2 278, 280-81
distractions (in prayer), 1 309
distress, 1 42
Dives, 1 155-56, 257; 2 389-95,
468; 3 233
doctors of the Church, 1 xx,
xxii; 2 33, 386; 3 122
doctrine, 1 9, 18-19, 23; 2 24,
33, 58, 121, 144-45, 148, 151,
153, 192-93, 198; 3 183
dogs, 2 4, 57, 78, 200-201, 262,
269, 285, 364, 390-91, 475;
3 175, 217
Donatists, 2 73
Donatus, 2 186
Dothain, 2 39
Douay Bible, 1 210 n.; 3 104
n., 105 n.
doves, 2 8, 123
    spiritual, 3 201
drachma, 1 300
dragon, 2 81
drunkenness, drunkards, 1 12,
15, 39, 61, 70, 76, 88, 100,
153, 209, 231-43, 271, 273,
277, 302, 306, 322-23; 2 10,
26, 28, 42, 79-80, 193, 197,
236, 258, 260, 301, 303, 317,
324, 331-32, 338, 349, 399,
405, 412, 423, 432, 450, 471,

482; 3 9, 11, 13, 18, 20, 29,
31, 37, 62, 64, 68, 76, 110,
126, 149, 152, 154-55, 165,
176
dryness, 1 330
dust, 2 76, 143, 191, 268
duty, neglect of, 3 31

ear-rings, 2 21-22
ears, pleasure of, 1 308
earth, 2 9, 20, 26, 31, 33, 36,
41, 51, 63, 69-70, 72, 81, 83,
89, 112, 119, 121-22, 124,
127, 132, 153, 155-56, 158,
162, 165, 178, 182, 185, 207,
212, 218, 239, 243, 266-70,
285-86, 291-92, 299, 312-13,
315, 325, 331, 337, 343, 362,
364, 398, 410, 415, 418, 420,
427, 431, 439-40, 447, 454,
468-71, 480, 486, 493; 3 54,
95, 102, 105, 141, 174, 213
Easter, 1 xiii, 14, 198-99, 222;
2 17, 28-29, 135; 3 44, 49,
59-60, 98 n.; see also seasons
and feasts, sermons for
Eastertide, 3 57
Easter, vigil of, 2 16
edification, 1 135
Edom, 2 157
Egypt, Egyptians, 1 199; 2
40-41, 43, 49-50, 53, 60-63,
67-69, 74-76, 78-79, 81-86,
88, 92-94, 98, 113, 126-27,
130, 135, 154, 156, 158, 161,
172, 227; 3 33, 140
Eleven, the (apostles), 1 58
Eli (Heli), 1 33, 36
Elijah (Elias), 1 199, 201-202,

Elijah, the true: *see* Christ
314, 356; **2** 167, 209-15, 223,
229, 460
Eligius, St.: *see* Eloi, St.
Elisabeth, **3** 117
Elisha (Eliseus), **1** 202-203,
356; **2** 154, 216-18, 220-24,
226-34
Elisha, the true: *see* Christ
Eloi, St., **1** xxiii
Emmaus, **2** 416
enchanters, **1** 13, 82, 102, 254
enemy, forgiveness of, **1** 71,
99, 149, 195, 197, 223, 309
love of, **1** 86, 105, 116, 144,
155, 171-97, 303; **2** 135,
273, 307-8, 327, 331, 375,
398, 432, 456; **3** 10, 57,
129-34, 145-47, 152, 200,
222
enmity, **1** 336
Enoch (Henoch), **1** 67
envy, **1** 12, 15, 88, 99, 124, 127,
183, 227, 287-88, 302, 308,
364-66; **2** 3, 10, 24-26, 28,
39-43, 46-48, 64, 79, 114,
123, 135, 164, 169, 175, 193,
197, 200, 335, 349, 351, 354,
375, 423, 450, 482; **3** 31,
61, 74, 79, 152-53, 165, 171,
222-23
Eonius, Bp., **1** vii
Ephraem (Ephraim), **2** 117;
**3** 232
Ephrem, **1** 338, 355
epileptics, **1** 225
Epiphany, **3** 38; *see also*
seasons and feasts, sermons
for

episcopacy, **3** 192
equality among men: *see* men
error, darkness of, **3** 111, 113
Esau, **2** 26, 28, 38, 113, 116
Ethiopians, **2** 66; **3** 35
Eucharist: *see* Christ, Body of
(as Holy Communion) and
Christ, Body and Blood of
Eusebius Gallicanus, **3** 2 n.,
15 n., 120 n., 139 n., 229,
233
evangelist, **2** 419
*excarpsum,* **3** 229
Eve, **1** 327; **2** 166, 186, 194,
231, 242, 414, 456
Eve (wife of Job), **2** 242
evening, **3** 159
exhortation, **1** 5
Exodus, **3** 230-31
Ezechiel, the prophet, **3** 185

fables, **2** 386
faith, **1** 27, 54-56, 58, 67-75,
77, 79, 87, 94, 105, 114, 122,
126, 147, and *passim;* **2** 5,
7, 14, 18, 23-24, 26-27, 40,
55, 58, 60, 76-77, 81, 89,
91, 93-96, 104, 107, 115, 117-
18, 121-22, 127, 129, 131,
133, 137, 140, 142, 144-45,
150, 152, 159, 165, 167-68,
179-80, 185-86, 197, 202, 208-
9, 222, 224, 237, 244, 246,
258, 262, 270, 280-81, 288,
294, 296, 302, 312, 333, 358,
371, 390-91, 395, 403, 406,
408-409, 416-17, 419, 422,
434, 436, 439-41, 448, 458-
59, 464, 467, 479-82, 490; **3**

83, 90-91, 94, 98-99, 104,
106, 108, 110-11, 113, 119,
121, 128-29, 135, 139, 153,
158, 161-63, 174, 177, 192,
227
59, 64, 66-67, 73-74, 77, 80,
faithful, the, **1** 10, 59, 74; **2**
xiii, 78, 124, 145; **3** 58, 62,
68, 77, 179
as branches, **3** 162
as the bride of Christ, **3** 12
familiarity, wicked, **1** 81, 204-
7, 214
famine, **2** 40, 50, 95
farm, farmer, **1** 40-42, 46, 163-
64, 225; **3** 188
Fastidius, Bp., **3** 229
fasting, **1** 6, 44, 52, 61, 122,
124, 137-38, 149, 223-24, 281,
288, 299, 302, 321-23; **2** 42,
112, 134-35, 148, 176, 257,
298-99, 302, 309, 311, 316,
318, 327, 335, 409, 451-52,
454, 483; **3** 15, 29, 32, 42-
45, 49-54, 56-57, 63, 68, 84,
88-89, 92-93, 127, 130, 155-
56, 164, 171, 178, 193, 200-
202, 205
Fatalis, **1** 103; **3** 229
fathers, holy ancient, **1** xx-
xxii, 16-18, 25, 179, 295; **2**
24, 71, 162-63, 206; **3** 29, 180
Faustinus, Bp., **3** 35
Faustus of Riez, **1** xix, 279,
285; **3** 35 n., 44, 48, 127 n.,
132 n., 229-30
fear, **1** 5, 7-8, 10-11, 15-19, 21,
23, 30, 33, 48, 72, 91, 98; **2**
5, 9, 52, 65, 134, 140-42, 165,

169, 172, 214, 219, 221, 238,
252-54, 264, 267, 271-72, 276,
285, 296, 319, 322, 324-25,
329, 344, 350, 355, 358, 368,
390, 405, 409, 411, 453, 468,
474, 480, 483, 489-91; **3** 26,
34, 77, 91, 110, 122, 131,
142, 174, 177, 181-82, 189,
191, 198, 204, 213, 219, 221
feasts, **1** 13-14, 77, 79, 89, 100,
160, 166-67, 171, 220, 222,
225, 237, 271-73, 275-77,
342, 344
sermons for: *see* seasons and
feasts
feet, washing of, **2** 13, 29, 310;
**3** 65-66, 74
Felix, St., **3** 113
fertility, **2** 381
fetters, **2** 50, 54, 56, 134, 160,
186, 201, 270, 479, 486, 492;
**3** 94, 125
fidelity, **1** 44, 70, 106, 214-15,
266, 337; **3** 32, 36-37
fire
eternal, **1** 28, 35, 42-43, 48,
76, 84, 91, 135, 139, 180,
216, 219, 265, 285, 297;
**2** 80, 118, 147, 286, 320,
324, 329, 342, 344, 355-57,
359-60, 363, 373, 390, 402,
406-7, 409, 453, 455, 468,
477-78; **3** 16, 18-19, 31,
45, 55, 80, 82, 88, 91, 143,
150-51, 166, 172
spiritual, **2** 52
Firminus, **1** v
firstborn, **2** 83-84, 90-91, 95,
115

firstfruits, 1 163-65; 3 35, 38, 41

Fischer, B., 3 42 n.

fishermen, 1 23; 2 240

flame, 2 392, 395, 407-8

flatterers, 1 294, 328

*flectamus genua,* 1 355

flesh, weakness of, 2 253

flock, 2 82
    the Lord's, 1 5-6, 16, 21-23, 25, 29; 2 25
        wayward members of, 2 xiii

Florianus, Abbot, 1 xix

font of baptism, 1 76, 336

food, 2 33, 47, 168, 183, 185, 190, 210-11, 225, 256, 264, 268-69, 273, 291, 332, 345, 362, 369, 378, 385-86, 397, 399, 408, 439, 451, 468, 470, 477, 493; 3 53, 62-63, 143-44, 146, 151, 153, 160, 172, 193, 200
    eternal, 3 66
    spiritual, 2 38, 106, 120, 167, 172, 174, 190, 213, 473; 3 181, 186

forgiveness, 1 55, 60-61, 95, 97, 101, 128-30, 148, 151, 166, 170, 178, 192, 196, 212, 268, 270, 285, 291, 293, 295-97, 311, 323, 338, 340-42, 357-58; 2 5, 19, 42, 48, 53, 99, 102-3, 135, 139, 191, 205, 235, 238, 250, 254-56, 262, 278, 301, 303, 309-10, 314, 322, 339, 446, 452-53, 482-88; 3 16, 20, 39, 45, 53, 56, 59-60, 63, 72, 74, 86-89, 100,

127, 129, 133-34, 147-48, 161, 164, 173, 178, 197-99, 201, 204-6, 209, 212, 214, 219

fornication, fornicators: *see* adultery

fortitude, 2 164, 238, 384

fortune tellers, 1 265; 3 74

forum, the, 1 216

Frank, R. M., 1 xxvi, 21 n.

Franks, Frankish, 1 viii-ix, xii; 3 230

frankincense, 3 36

freedom, 2 87, 94; 3 191

Friday, 3 92 n.

friendship, friend, 2 272-73, 286; 3 135-36, 149, 165
    love of, 1 107-9, 111-113

Fulgentius of Ruspe, 1 xvii, xix

future, inquiry into, 3 30

Gabriel, 2 158

Galileans, 1 333

Galilee: see Cana of Galilee

gall, 2 48, 185, 405; 3 198

garments
    for birthdays, weddings, etc., 2 143, 332, 405, 449, 493; 3 8, 11-12, 149, 165
    purple, 2 77, 146, 301, 332, 390-91, 393-95, 473, 476; 3 150
    white, 3 73

Gaul, 1 x, xii, xxii; 3 229

Gedeon, 2 177, 179-81

Gedeon, the true: *see* Christ

Gehenna: *see* hell

generosity, 2 45

Genesius, St., 3 152 n.

gentiles, **1** 143, 187, 212, 225, 264; **2** 22, 27, 30, 35-37, 40, 59, 66, 68, 115-17, 127, 129, 133, 136, 140, 147, 154, 160-61, 168, 178-79, 181, 185, 190, 192, 204-5, 209-213, 224, 227, 229-31, 298, 384, 387-89, 394, 439, 441, 446, 464; **3** 35, 38-41, 119, 140

Giezi, **2** 228-29

Glorie, Fr., **3** 2 n.

gluttony, **1** 61, 70, 88, 222, 242, 270, 273, 277, 308, 322, 324, 344; **2** 89, 316, 331, 349, 439, 449; **3** 63, 83, 217

God, **1** 35, 58, 140, 157, 164, 184, 251, 292, 313

    Author of the world, **1** 110

    as Charity, **1** 181

    the Creator, **1** 55, 110, 164, 291, 293, 300; **2** 76, 163, 369, 379, 410, 454

    dwelling of, the faithful as, **3** 110

    the Father, **1** 26-27, 49, 54-56, 58-60, 62, 71, 74, 79, 83, 90, 99, 102, 106, 123, 130-32, 144, 146, and *passim;* **2** 65, 158, 198-99, 206, 211-12

    fear of, **1** 87, 90, 212, 239, 275, 366; **2** 34, 100, 121-22, 198, 467, 480; **3** 31

    gifts of, **2** 42, 46, 369

    goodness, of, **1** 4, 36, 86, 92, 181, 235, 239, 242, 271, 275, 280, 290, 312-13, 320, 333, 338, 341, 362; **2** 76, 108, 129, 137, 141-42, 180,

216, 222-23, 239, 250, 255, 300, 318, 352, 366, 387, 389, 422, 455, 472; **3** 57, 63-64, 86, 108, 120, 148, 170, 180, 192-93, 202, 204

    grace/mercy of, **1** 31-32, 36-37, 40, 45, 71-72, 87, 91, 95, 111, 114, 124, 129, 170, 182, 190, 226, 235, 243, 250, 264-65, 269-70, 290, 298, 308, 311-14, 320, 340-41, 364, 366, and *passim;* **2** 15, 19, 36, 41, 50-51, 56, 66, 70, 85, 89, 100-101, 105, 108, 116, 118, 128-30, 140-42, 150, 154, 162-64, 182-83, 190-92, 194, 196-97, 202, 209-10, 212, 219, 224-26, 230, 235-36, 250-51, 255-56, 266, 269, 292, 297-98, 301, 309, 314, 320, 324, 327, 334, 336, 349, 351, 355-56, 359, 374, 377-79, 382, 388, 403, 410-13, 419, 421-23, 425-27, 437, 445, 455, 460, 466, 472, 483, 489, 491; **3** 7, 10-11, 20, 23, 28, 30, 34-35, 37, 40, 43, 45, 56, 59-61, 64, 72, 76-77, 84-85, 88-89, 93, 98, 100-101, 116, 120-21, 125, 129-30, 133-34, 145-6, 152-53, 156, 160-61, 164, 179, 191, 202, 208, 214, 217, 219

    (right) hand of, **2** 189, 234

    help of, **2** 4, 6, 15, 33, 46, 48, 57, 62, 64, 70, 77, 80, 108, 112, 119, 139, 150,

155, 162-65, 175, 193-94, 203, 216, 234-35, 243, 249, 257-58, 260, 262, 274, 299, 308, 318, 320, 322, 324, 327, 330-31, 336, 344, 349, 351, 354, 359-60, 363, 369-71, 412, 419, 422, 424, 427, 442, 449, 456, 480, 482, 484, 492; **3** 7, 9, 12, 28, 37, 43, 49, 56-57, 59-60, 63-64, 67, 83-84, 92, 94-95, 99, 110, 112, 127, 131-32, 145, 152, 166, 168, 170-71, 175-77, 183, 193, 201, 203, 207, 217-18, 220

the image of (the soul), **1** 37, 48, 51, 159, 177, 224-25, 230, 300, 315, 348

inspiration of, **1** 16, 266, 318, 341, 348; **2** 102, 158, 163, 210, 216, 260, 262, 281; **3** 57, 93, 155, 179, 193, 202

the (just) judge, **1** 83, 109, 211, 287, 320, 357; **2** 41, 81, 103, 118, 140, 143, 215, 235, 247, 307, 361-62, 389, 437, 446, 448; **3** 19, 45, 80, 112, 134, 138, 151, 165, 182-83, 201, 204, 212

just and good, **1** 173, 184, 308

justice of, **1** 308-9; **2** 15, 101, 138, 140-42, 161, 244, 256, 269, 287, 297, 300, 311, 353, 394, 455, 483; **3** 60

(just) judgment of, **1** 93, 142, 177, 203, 218, 235, 281, 285, 307; **2** 50, 86,

89-90, 101, 142, 161-63, 170, 187, 222, 240, 245, 267, 300, 323; **3** 28, 126

kindness of, **2** 147, 166, 323, 389; **3** 28, 34, 61, 88

our King, **1** 115, 279

knowledge of, **2** 148, 150; **3** 39

the living and true, **2** 20; **3** 34

love of, **1** 108, 175, 181-82, 199; **2** 3, 8, 93, 96, 132, 142, 168, 226, 270-71, 286, 309-10, 349-50, 369, 371, 403, 419, 470, 492; **3** 10, 18, 86, 91, 120, 146

majesty of, **1** 276

as mercy, **1** 38, 66, 94, 118, 127-30, 148, 196, 201, 220, 248, 309-10, 312-13, 320, 352-53; **2** 98

omnipotence of, **1** 312; **2** 206

patience of, **2** 101, 483

people of, **2** 112, 177

the Physician, **1** 172, 293, 357; **2** 326-27

power of, **1** 35; **2** 101, 234

precepts of, **1** 39, 41-42, 44-45, 47-48, 277, 283, 337

the primary agent, **1** xii-xiii

providence of, **1** 258-59, 268

our Redeemer, **3** 23

our Savior, **2** 193

sons of, **2** 48

temple of
    body of baptized person as, **2** 258; **3** 59, 175
    the faithful as, **1** 311; **2**

202, 235

will of, 1 307; 2 12, 76, 145, 163, 171

wisdom of, 2 148; 3 66

the word of, 1 xx-xxi, 4-5, 9-11, 16-17, 19-20, 23, 28-33, 40, 43, 48-49, 51, 56, and passim; 2 20, 41, 53, 78, 82, 105, 107, 110, 120-21, 124-25, 129, 182, 189-90, 204, 230

wrath of, 1 98, 337; 2 145, 204, 215, 467, 486

godliness, 1 169

gold, 2 23, 27, 51, 59-60, 109, 145, 153, 237, 243, 282-84, 287-89, 338, 361, 430-31, 448, 450, 455, 462, 491; 3 36, 142, 149-50, 226

Goliath, 2 198, 202-3

Goliath, the spiritual: see devil

Gomorrah (Gomorrha), 2 13-14, 162

good work: see works, good

goods, eternal, 2 366, 373

Gospels, the, 1 xx, xxii, 43, 57, 65, 91, 116, 127, 131, 141-42, 144, 146, 157, 186, 197, 199, 257, 268, 300, 342, 347, 357, 364; 2 127-29, 160-61, 164, 185, 293-94, 296, 300, 308-9, 312, 315, 319, 340, 348, 354, 359, 362-63, 370-71, 374, 376, 381-82, 384, 386, 389-90, 394, 401-2, 409, 413, 419, 422, 424, 428, 431-33, 435-36, 439-41, 449, 465, 479; 3 7, 21, 38, 47, 73, 91-92, 98, 109, 119, 121, 123, 125, 129, 139, 148, 165, 186-87, 225

gossip, 1 10, 39, 48, 51, 100, 103, 255, 271, 273, 277, 308-9, 323, 338, 342, 345, 353, 355, 359, 366-68 .

Goths, 3 230

grace: see God, grace/mercy of; Christ, grace/mercy of; Holy Spirit, graces of; mercy

grace, doctrine on, 3 35 n.

grain, 2 459; 3 76

grammarian, 2 284

granary, 1 138; 2 184, 279, 281

grapes, 2 70, 126-27, 129, 131-33, 135, 140, 471-72

grave: see tomb

greed: see avarice

Greek (the language), 1 21, 259; 2 12, 88, 128, 179, 181; 3 38

Gregory the Great, St., 1 xxiv

grief, 2 45, 47, 50, 52, 251

guilt, 2 53, 55, 83, 209, 236, 238, 243, 247, 255, 299-300, 302-3, 306, 319, 406, 427, 448, 478, 488; 3 186, 199, 202, 220

hail, 2 83-84, 94

haircloth, 1 105

hair shirt, 1 313-14, 319, 321; 2 301

handwriting, 1 25-26

harlot, 1 202, 206-7, 314-15; 2 167, 171, 173, 183-85, 187, 206-7; see also Venus, as harlot

harmony, **1** 75, 80, 89, 99, 197, 299, 309

harp, **2** 241

hatred, **1** 12, 14, 81, 88, 99, 113, 122, 150, 172, 176, 178, 183, 195, 197, 201, 220, 308, 323, 341, 351; **2** 42, 45-46, 94, 116, 135, 174, 272-73, 306-7, 317-18, 325, 352, 424, 428-30, 433, 444, 458, 467, 478, 485, 489; **3** 9-10, 13, 60, 64, 68, 74, 130, 135-37, 139-40, 144, 148-49, 153, 155, 165, 175, 177, 209, 213, 221-23

health, bodily, **1** 36-37, 77, 87, 90-91, 253

spiritual, **1** 37, 253; **3** 34

heathen, **1** 143, 210, 242

heaven, **1** 22, 37, 40-41, 43, 45-47, 49-50, 54, 59-60, 62-63, 71, 88, 91, 93-94, 98-99, 103-5, 114, 117, 125, 127-28, 132-33, 136, 138, 141-43, 145, 148, 153-55, 157, 161, 163, 166, 168, 174-75, 181, 186, 201, 208-9, 216, 221, 226, 230, 242-43, 246, 249-53, 255, 257, 265, 270, 273, 277, 285, 287-89, 303-5, 310, 315, 319, 334, 336, 362; **2** 8-10, 20, 26, 30-33, 36, 72, 77, 83-84, 89, 105, 112, 118-20, 154-55, 166, 173, 185, 188-91, 212-15, 227, 232, 239, 241, 268, 285, 299, 308, 312-13, 315, 319-20, 322, 325-26, 328-30, 332, 337, 355, 362-63, 368,

371, 386, 399, 435, 437-38, 441, 468-69, 484, 486; **3** 23, 36, 38, 41, 69, 72, 93, 102, 105, 123, 128, 141, 150, 158, 166, 174-75, 196, 210-11, 221

Hebrews, **1** 56; **2** 157, 408, 479

sons of, **2** 86

children of, **2** 82

Heli: *see* Eli

hell, **1** 13, 39, 69-70, 88, 91, 99, 114, 117, 133, 137, 139, 155-56, 166, 212, 218, 242, 247, 249-50, 257, 269, 272, 275-76, 278-79, 288, 367; **2** 9, 26, 40, 47, 56, 60, 77, 80, 154, 170, 174, 187-88, 190, 197, 200, 232, 234, 236, 239, 246, 285-86, 298, 320, 323-26, 329-30, 332, 343, 355, 361, 371, 391-92, 395, 423, 475-76, 490; **3** 23, 31, 33, 69-70, 78, 80, 87-88, 116, 123-24, 150, 166, 197

burning pit of, **3** 80

jaws of, **1** 60

prison of, **2** 57, 60, 396; **3** 71

Henoch: *see* Enoch

herald, **2** 295; **3** 182

herbs, **1** 78, 82; **2** 405

heresy, heretics, **1** 57-58, 140, 325; **2** 11, 73, 82, 84, 86, 93, 97, 132, 144-45, 185-87, 206-7, 281, 294, 344, 356, 433, 436, 439, 441, 457, 462, 478; **3** 92

*Hermas, Shepherd* of, **1** 135 n.

Herod, **1** 234; **3** 37, 122, 125-26, 139-40

Herodias, **3** 125

Hilary, St., **1** 16; **3** 111 n.

holiness, **1** 212, 225

holocaust, **2** 181, 205, 412, 414

Holy Innocents, **3** 139

Holy Orders, **1** xiii

Holy Spirit, **1** 26-27, 29, 32, 43, 47, 49, 54-60, 69, 74, 79, 83, 90, 106, 118, 123, and *passim;* **2** 6, 10-11, 14, 16, 19, 24, 27-29, 34, 38, 42, 49-51, 53, 58, 64, 66, 69-70, 74-76, 81, 84, 87, 100, and *passim*

  blessing of, **3** 60

  coming of, **3** 98, 108

  dispensation of, **2** 11

  divinity of, **3** 101-2, 106

  dwelling of, **2** 58

  as finger of God, **3** 105

  fire of (=charity), **2** 66, 70

  gifts of, **3** 99-100, 162

  graces of, **2** 84, 181, 205, 212, 218, 231, 266; **3** 99, 101

  in form of dove, **2** 231

  inspiration of, **2** 75, 216

  revelation of, **3** 124

  teaching of, **3** 108

  temple of, body of baptized person as, **3** 59, 109-10, 164

homiliary, **3** 173 n., 174 n., 230

honesty, **1** 166; **3** 16, 140, 146

honey, **2** 106, 108, 115, 130, 132, 140, 163, 189, 192-93; **3** 84, 86

  spiritual, **3** 218

Honoratus, St., **3** 111, 113

hope, **1** 95, 97; **2** 14, 26, 129, 133, 141, 168, 278, 329, 340, 343, 358, 392, 401, 417, 446, 483; **3** 34, 46, 94, 115, 157, 166, 177, 227-28

hospitality, **2** 241

human nature, weakness of, **2** 15, 39, 142, 301, 315-16, 383, 419-20, 422, 446, 457, 487; **3** 67, 92, 95, 156, 203

humiliation, **1** 62, 321; **3** 17

humility, **1** 4, 9, 10, 15, 24, 33-34, 37, 41, 60, 66, 168, 173, 183, 201, 227, 243, 246-50, 281, 291, 297, 302, 314-15, 321, 334, 343, 352, 355-57, 360, 366; **2** 3, 13, 17, 25-26, 28, 42, 67, 79-80, 101, 164, 197, 215, 221-22, 231, 235, 240, 243, 255, 263, 294, 300, 302, 309, 322, 331, 346, 349-52, 354, 368, 382, 415, 423, 433, 446, 452, 470, 482, 487; **3** 11, 15, 37, 39-40, 62-63, 65-66, 83, 87, 96, 100, 102, 110, 118, 121, 123-24, 145, 152, 163, 165, 177, 180, 192-202, 204-5, 207-12, 214-19, 225

husband, **1** 13, 15, 81, 165

hymn, **2** 97-98, 101

hypocrite, **3** 137

idols, **1** 101, 200, 201, 234, 263-64; **2** 36-37, 75, 93, 161, 173, 178, 185, 206, 210, 213-14; **3** 140

idolatry, idolators, **1** 240, 364; **2** 26, 93; **3** 27, 40

illness, spiritual, **3** 9, 16, 20,

24, 45, 101, 136
immodesty, 2 448
immorality, 1 204-5, 214; 2
    26, 32, 57
immortality, 2 376, 445, 447-
    48
    robe of, 2 387, 389; 3 168
imposition of hands, 3 59,
    155-56, 178
incantations, 1 260
incense, 2 144-46; 3 169
incontinence, 1 223
indignation, 1 113
infants, infancy, 2 50, 206, 231,
    298, 302, 339-40, 342, 413,
    434; 3 139-40, 178; see also
    children
infants, those just reborn in
    Christ as, 3 75-76
infidelity, 1 94, 203, 254, 330;
    2 7, 107, 116-17, 188
inheritance (from the Father),
    2 312
iniquity, 1 4-5, 12, 29, 33-35,
    48, 51, 82, 94-95, 118, 154,
    179, 190, 209, 223, 280, 282,
    296, 311, 335
injustice, 1 319, 335; 2 92, 98,
    101, 124, 163; 3 96, 99, 123-
    24, 126, 153
instruction, 1 8-9, 54
    spiritual, 1 21
instrument, musical, 2 96, 288
intemperance, 2 448; 3 63
intercession of the saints, 1
    106
intercourse, secret, 1 206
intimacy, shameful, 1 204
Isaac, 1 252; 2 16-23, 25, 29-

30, 33-34, 65, 113, 116, 198-
    99, 276, 414; 3 40
Isai: see Jesse
Isaiah, (Isaia, Isaias), 1 86; 2
    132, 178, 388; 3 104-5, 124
Ishmael, Ishmaelites, (Ismael,
    Ismaelites), 2 40, 43, 59
Israel, Israelites, 1 11, 163,
    252; 2 61, 74-75, 112, 126,
    128, 130-31, 133, 140, 157,
    159, 160-62, 164-65, 167, 179,
    199, 204, 265, 353, 377, 388,
    417, 420; 3 33
    children of, 2 61-63, 78-79,
    111, 131, 135, 155-56, 159,
    161, 163-64, 201; 3 185
    sons of, 2 74

Jacob, 1 176, 252; 2 21, 26-39,
    49-52, 65, 113-14, 116, 159,
    198-99, 276, 298, 419; 3 40
James, M. R., 3 42 n.
James, St., 1 20 n., 185; 2 482;
    3 134, 137 n.
January, calends of: see
    calends of January
Janus, 3 26-27
jealousy, 2 26, 47-48, 70, 114,
    303, 324, 467; 3 223
Jebusite, the: see Areuna
Jehu, 2 220
Jeremiah (Jeremia, Jeremias),
    2 148, 388
Jericho, 1 210; 2 155, 167-71,
    173-74, 376
Jerome, St., 1 23; 2 18, 144,
    155, 423 n.; 3 231
Jerusalem, 1 171, 180-81, 191,
    247, 314; 2 160, 203-4, 209,

222, 295, 299, 328-30, 376, 490, 492; **3** 115, 166
Jesse (Isai), **2** 198-99
Jesse, root of, **2** 150
Jethro, **2** 68
Jews, **1** 9, 60, 64, 76, 186, 199, 202, 223, 234, 344; **2** 11, 14, 17-18, 27, 30-31, 35-37, 39-40, 59, 65, 67-71, 100, 105, 113-19, 126-29, 131-34, 140-42, 147, 151, 153, 160-62, 168, 173, 179-81, 188-90, 192, 199-201, 203-5, 209-10, 214-15, 221-22, 228-30, 232, 265, 281, 293-96, 298, 344, 356, 384, 387, 389, 394, 396, 414-15, 425-26, 438-40, 457; **3** 35-36, 38-40, 69, 104, 125, 128, 132, 140
Jezabel, **1** 314; **2** 210
Joas, **2** 177
Job, **1** 44, 110, 177, 268; **2** 165, 237-38, 240-43, 399; **3** 96
John the Baptist, **1** 63, 162, 166, 234; **2** 72, 413, 415; **3** 117-26
   birthday of, **3** 117, 120-21
John the Evangelist, **1** 188; **2** 51, 150, 171, 242, 306, 318, 365, 402, 432, 489; **3** 104, 134, 137, 202
   Epistle of, **2** 306; **3** 232
   monastery of, **1** xi-xii
John II, Pope, **1** xv n.-xvi
Jonah, (Jona, Jonas), **2** 298-99
Jordan River, **2** 17, 30, 37-38, 115-17, 155, 161, 164, 167-

68, 172, 230, 233
Joseph (O.T.), **1** 176, 204, 252; **2** 38-41, 43, 45-46, 49-63, 65, 113-14, 117, 199, 419; **3** 222
Joseph, the true: *see* Christ
Joseph (N.T.), **3** 140
Joseph of Arimathea, **2** 295
Joshua (Josue), **2** 17, 71-72, 111 n., 116-17, 154, 161, 164-65, 167-68, 171-74
Joshua, the true; *see* Christ
Judah (Juda), **1** 326; **2** 40, 190, 415; **3** 139
Judas, **1** 64; **2** 21, 40, 228-29, 265, 371, 383
Judea, **2** 130, 179, 182, 210, 213, 220, 229; **3** 140
judgment, last, **1** 5, 10, 17, 19, 22, 44, 48, 54, 56, 70, 76, 80-81, 83-85, 93, 98, 102, 131-32, 139-40, 149, 162, 166, 193-94, 196, 205, 208, 211-12, 219-20, 237, 240-41, 255-56, 265, 274, 278-79, 281, 283, 285-86, 289, 306, 317, 353, 358-59; **2** xiii, 9-10, 13, 28, 34, 109, 142-43, 198, 232, 235, 246, 259, 297, 300, 342, 344, 347, 349, 353-54, 357-58, 363, 373, 397, 447-49, 451, 453-54, 466, 473-74; **3** 10, 12, 14, 17, 47, 55, 64, 91, 93, 112, 116, 126, 134, 141, 143, 147, 154, 158, 168, 174, 184, 203, 216
Jupiter (Jove), **1** 79, 101, 260; **3** 33-34
justice, **1** 28-29, 34, 43, 45, 62,

64, 66, 72, 88, 93, 105, 112,
143, 168-69, 186, 203, 205,
208-9, 216, 221, 239, 247,
256, 260, 271-72, 275-76,
333-35, 337, 363; 2 15, 42,
56, 59, 63, 67, 83, 91, 98,
101, 106, 109, 114, 120, 148,
150-51, 183, 191-92, 202,
208, 217, 234, 236-39, 242,
248, 258, 260, 262, 264, 270,
283, 285-86, 288-89, 316,
325, 352-53, 372, 374, 377-78,
380, 384-85, 394, 397-401,
408, 412, 422-23, 432, 437,
455, 457, 463, 472, 490; 3
11, 13, 31, 36-37, 48, 73, 76,
78, 80, 83, 122-24, 126-27,
133, 135, 138, 140, 143, 147,
153, 164, 168, 178-82, 198,
200, 206, 209
Juvenal, *Satires,* 1 8 n.; 3 143
n.

kindness, 1 64-65, 174, 183
kingdom, heavenly, 1 9, 12,
47, 54, 71, 75, 79, 81-82, 84,
87, 91, 100, 109, 139, 144,
146-47, 157, 209, 212, 215,
221, 242, 244, 251, 253, 257,
273, 277, 306; 2 23, 31, 41,
48, 51, 78, 80, 111, 118, 126-
27, 130, 147, 168, 185, 191,
223, 232; 3 23, 36, 40, 65,
71, 73, 91, 108, 112, 115,
144, 164, 168, 172, 203, 223
Kings, Book of, 2 203
knowledge, 2 276; 3 98
  divine, 2 106

Laban, 2 21, 34, 36-37
laity, 1 9, 13, 15, 25, 207, 241,
274, 278-79, 300, 311, 367;
2 98, 347, 357, 488
lamb, 2 23, 80, 133, 256, 294,
346, 377, 388
Lambot, C., 1 xii n., xiv n.,
xxvi, 21 n.; 3 225 n.
lamps, 2 344, 348, 350
  spiritual, 3 111, 113, 119
Latin (the language), 1 260; 2
14, 353 n.; 3 58 n.
Law, the 1 7, 12, 121-22, 187,
189, 196, 199, 274, 278, 320,
324, 329; 2 27, 53, 70, 73, 76,
78, 81-82, 85-86, 92-93, 96,
104-5, 108, 111, 120-21, 123-
24, 126, 128-30, 132-34, 148,
164, 167, 171, 175-76, 186,
188, 195, 227, 270, 272, 276-
77, 283-84, 295, 308, 319,
321, 353, 375, 377-78, 381,
384, 394, 396, 410-12, 416,
418, 426-27, 438, 444-46; 3
25, 39, 49, 57, 119, 125, 142,
155, 180, 190, 200
  Old, 1 9; 2 128
Lazarus, 1 141, 155-56, 280;
2 77, 136, 332, 364, 389-96;
3 88, 116, 123, 233
Leclercq, J., 3 117 n.
Lejay, P., 1 x n., xv n., xxv n.-
xxvi
Lent, 1 14, 222; 2 16, 19, 28,
155; 3 41-44, 48-49, 57, 63-
64, 68, 85, 93, 178, 220, 223;
*see also* seasons and feasts,
sermons for
lepers, leprosy, 1 225; 2 229,

231, 395

Lerins, 1 vi-vii; 3 111 n., 210 n.

Levi, Levites, 1 9; 2 145, 149, 377-78

Leviticus, 3 231

Leah (Lia), 2 35-37, 113-14, 116

liar: *see* lying

liberality, 1 335

licentiousness, 2 26

life

devout, 2 464

eternal, 1 22, 27, 44-45, 49-50, 53, 55, 59-61, 68, 83, 88, 91, 112-13, 128-29, 135-36, 138, 160, 176, 191, 197, 230, 250, 276, 292, 299, 317, 388; 2 30, 34, 36, 38, 45, 115-16, 118, 126, 129, 168, 172, 174, 185, 191, 204, 223, 226, 230, 236, 257, 267, 270, 289, 309-11, 315, 320, 325, 330, 345, 348-50, 359, 362, 365-66, 369, 373, 377-78, 380-82, 384, 401, 409-10, 413, 421, 423, 429-30, 443, 450, 453, 455, 462, 468-69, 472, 490, 492-93; 3 19, 23, 36-37, 43-44, 48-49, 59, 64, 73-74, 76, 87-88, 116, 129, 131, 139, 143, 148, 153, 174, 192, 198, 201-2, 214, 228

evil, 2 42, 247-49, 325, 329, 385, 457, 463, 474; 3 78, 90-92

future, 1 53, 88; 2 80, 106,

127, 148, 172, 250, 286, 399, 404, 452, 462; 3 65, 78, 86, 114, 116, 130, 153, 156, 172, 204, 206, 221, 228

holy, 2 194, 373, 413; 3 32, 62, 74, 100, 215

tree of, 2 109

uprightness of, 2 118, 249; 3 32, 76-78, 91, 99, 122-23, 133

virtuous, 3 32

light, 2 10, 41-42, 47, 63, 76-77, 173, 205, 221, 234, 308, 373, 421, 425, 436, 447, 457, 485; 3 69, 97, 119, 125, 141, 159, 163, 166, 174-75, 177, 196, 202

lightning, 2 83

lilies, 3 110

linen, 2 146, 199, 277, 281, 389-91, 393-95, 473, 476; 3 150

lion, 2 98, 122-23, 185, 189-92, 195, 200, 247, 264-65, 269, 335, 462

literate, 1 39, 49

liturgy, liturgical reforms at Council of Vaison, 1 xiv

locusts, 2 83-84, 90, 95

Lot, 1 234; 2 11-12, 259-60, 262

love: *see* charity

Lucian, St., 3 35

lust: *see* pleasures, bodily

luxury, 1 35, 105, 141, 153, 323

lying, liar, 1 12, 75, 82, 88, 365; 2 50, 90, 95, 236, 296, 298-99, 301, 311, 335, 349,

375, 424, 426, 456-57, 476;
**3** 10, 61, 130, 185, 203, 220

McCarthy, Sr. C., **3** 2 n.
Maccabees, the, **1** 111
Madian, Madianite, **2** 157, 161
magi, **2** 159; **3** 35-41
magicians, **1** 12-13, 101, 260, 267, 269, 331; **2** 69, 481; **3** 16, 46, 74, 177
majesty, divine, **1** 58, 64, 340, 359; **2** 336; **3** 103-4, 107, 109, 151, 164, 169, 171, 175
major orders (of clergy), **1** 34
malice, **1** 43, 63-64, 127, 227, 364; **2** 42, 47-48, 64, 83, 193
Malnory, A., **1** vi n., xxvi, and *passim*
Mamre, **2** 11, 14, 199
Manasses, King, **1** 314-15; **2** 117
maniac, **1** 89, 179
Manichaeans, **1** 291, 293; **2** 15, 73, 98, 100, 144, 161, 163, 214, 216, 220, 280, 457
Manichaeus, **2** 186
manna, **2** 103, 105-8
Mara, **2** 103-4, 154
marriage, **1** 15, 81, 107, 162, 208, 212-13, 215-17, 221-22; **2** 143, 236, 260-61, 347-48, 402, 409; **3** 149
    sexual act in, abstention from, **1** 13-14, 222-23; **2** 28; **3** 9, 13-14, 57, 61
Mars, **3** 33-34

Marseilles, Council of, **1** xii, xiv
Martin of Braga, **3** 34 n.
martyrs, martyrdom, **1** 46, 61, 199, 203, 205, 221, 239, 259-60, 271; **2** 27, 56, 59, 266, 281, 296, 317, 328-30, 429, 479-82, 484; **3** 35, 111-14, 117 n., 124-25, 128-29, 134-35, 139-40, 144-45, 148-49, 151-53, 155-57
Mary, the Virgin, **1** 27, 41, 43-44, 55, 57, 59, 122; **2** 18, 59, 132; **3** 12, 117, 121
Mass, **1** 273, 342-46, 348, 363; **3** 35
    Canon of the, **1** 343 n.
    Preface of the, **1** 117 n., 161 n., 343 n.; **2** 8 n., 269 n., 325 n.
Maurists: *see* Benedictines
Maximus of Turin, **3** 71 n., 127 n.
medicine, spiritual, **2** 29, 42, 85, 92, 102-3, 138, 141, 221, 300-301, 316, 327, 352-54, 382, 389, 396, 409, 421, 451, 461, 474, 483-84, 493; **3** 9, 11, 22, 24-26, 34, 42, 47, 50, 82-83, 85, 88-90, 93, 114, 122, 147-48
meekness, **1** 173, 246, 349
men, equality of, **3** 13
mercenaries, **1** 39, 44, 49
Mercury, **3** 33-34
mercy, **1** 41, 43, 62, 127-35, 140-44, 148, 153, 157, 174, 178, 208-9, 221, 227, 242, 247, 256, 271, 275, 363; **2** 62, 65,

67, 77, 79, 91, 98, 106, 150, 164, 221, 224, 231, 239, 247, 250, 258, 299, 331, 349-50, 356, 360-61, 363, 374, 377-78, 395-96, 432, 468, 472, 479, 484, 493; 3 11, 48, 83, 172, 198, 206; *see also* God, grace/mercy of; Christ, grace/mercy of

Mesopotamia, 2 21, 29-30, 34, 159, 198

Michael the Archangel, 2 158

Milan, 2 283

military service, 2 366

miracles, 2 173, 213, 221, 410, 424-25, 434-35; 3 194

miser, 2 239

Moab, 2 155, 157-58

moderation, 1 14; 2 438, 446

modesty, 2 26, 288, 448

monasteries, 1 207; 2 259, 264, 352; 3 111 n., 146, 192-93, 196, 200, 205, 207, 218

money, 2 106, 159, 229, 266, 270, 296, 361-62, 366-67, 383, 464-66, 478, 481, 483; 3 140, 143, 182, 186-87, 197

monks, 1 136, 139, 204, 257, 300; 2 346-47, 351, 353, 357; 3 192, 198-99, 204-5, 207, 209-10, 216-17, 220-21, 223

moon, 1 78; 2 10, 40-41, 239, 376, 419; 3 33, 141
eclipse of, 1 259

morals, good, 3 31

Morin, Germain, editor of Caesarius, 1 xxiv-xxv and *passim;* 2 xiii, 92 n., 363 n., 374 n., 423 n., 437 n.; 3 1-3,

15 n., 21 n., 30 n., 38 n., 44 n., 69 n., 71 n., 75 n., 78 n., 82 n., 93 n., 102 n., 113 n., 139 n., 144 n., 152 n., 156 n., 173 n., 174 n., 179 n., 189 n., 192 n., 225 n., 229-31, 233-34

mortifications, 1 269; 3 15, 45

Moses, 1 16, 177, 199-200, 326; 2 6, 34, 65-68, 70-75, 78, 81, 103-4, 109-11, 115-17, 119, 125-26, 135-36, 139, 144-45, 151, 154, 157, 159, 161, 164, 167-68, 171-72, 179, 215, 227, 381, 396, 417; 3 104

mountain, 2 167, 174, 188, 227, 270, 275, 277, 415; 3 125, 141, 203, 210

murder, murderers, 1 12-14, 61, 70, 98-99, 130, 158, 166, 176, 188, 198, 205, 221, 232, 240, 259, 313, 317; 2 43-44, 47, 52, 82, 89, 94, 251, 254-55, 258, 303; 306-7, 356, 360, 424, 450, 455, 458, 480, 485-86; 3 10, 16, 46, 61, 130, 137-38, 140, 146-47, 159, 178, 209

music, 2 387-88, 409

mustard seed, 2 292

Mutzenbecher, A., 3 2 n.

myrrh, 3 36

mystery, 2 16-18, 30, 34-35, 40, 59-60, 65-69, 75, 85, 102, 104, 110-11, 113-14, 117, 133-34, 136, 146, 148-49, 153-54, 161, 171-72, 177, 179-82, 184-85, 187, 189, 192, 197, 201, 210-11, 213, 217, 232,

234, 276, 298, 402, 410-11, 414, 418, 420-21, 425, 439-41; **3** 22, 35-36, 40, 66, 72, 86, 102-4, 118, 125, 127, 140

Naaman, **2** 229-32
Naboth of Jezreel, **1** 314
nails, **2** 17, 408; **3** 70, 82
Nathan, **2** 251, 254, 256
Nathanael, **2** 31
Nativity of the Lord: *see* Christmas
nature, divine, **3** 102-3, 109
Nazareth, **2** 416
Nazarite, the: *see* Samson
neighbors: *see* relatives and neighbors
Nepotian, **1** 23 n.
New American Bible, **3** 3, 17 n., 122 n.
New Testament, **1** xiii, xvii, xix, xxv, 252; **2** 3, 33, 110, 132, 216, 221, 411, 416
New Year's Day, **1** 78 n.
Nicodemus, **2** 131
Nîmes, **3** 21 n., 30 n.
Ninive, the Ninivites, **2** 247, 298-302
Noah (Noe), **1** 67; **2** 162, 276, 413-14
None (Nones), **2** 28; **3** 42
Numbers, **3** 231
Nun, **2** 171, 174

oaths, false, **2** 306, 349, 451; **3** 73
obedience, **1** 32, 34, 45, 104, 223; **2** 29, 133, 170, 228, 263, 351, 353, 355; **3** 17, 44, 47,

91, 93, 156, 192, 197-98, 200-202, 205, 208, 212-13, 215-18
offerings, **1** 13, 75, 82, 89, 101, 342
office, holy, **3** 42
oil, **1** 77, 101-2, 254, 262; **2** 33, 132, 211, 223-25, 273, 348-51, 377-78, 464, 471-72, 482; **3** 59, 155-56, 168, 178, 198, 202, 218
ointment, precious, **3** 97
old age, **2** 414, 429; **3** 90
Old Testament, **1** xiii, xix, xxv, 200, 203, 223, 252; **2** 3, 20, 33, 38, 41, 98, 111 n., 113, 116, 128, 132, 138, 161, 164, 183, 199, 205, 214-16, 220-21, 277, 353, 384, 387, 389, 411, 414, 416, 418; **3** 1, 102
olives, **2** 23, 467, 471-72; **3** 40
olive tree, **1** 85-86; **2** 23
Olivet, Mount, **2** 212
omens, **1** 13, 71, 260, 265-70; **2** 236; **3** 30, 46
oracle, **1** 77, 262
Orange, Council of, **1** xii; **3** 156 n.
oration (in the marriage ceremony), **1** 222 n.
ordination, age for, **1** 15
Orient, **2** 159
Oriental custom, **1** 15
Origen, **1** xix, 21 n.; **3** 230-31, 233
Orleans, Council of, **1** xv
orphans, **1** 244, 250-51; **2** 239, 448, 476
Ostrogoths, **1** viii-ix

Oudin, C., **3** 230
Owen (Ouen), St., **1** xxiii
ox, **2** 90, 192, 205, 335, 431; **3** 154

pagan customs, **1** 13, 78, 270; **3** 27, 29, 31-33
pagans, **1** 9, 77-78, 101, 187, 241-42, 254, 260, 263, 265, **2** 15, 27, 100, 117-18, 161, 206, 213, 356, 368, 437, 456-57, 462; **3** 26-27, 29, 32-33, 92
pain, **2** 310, 343, 368, 396; **3** 16, 142, 166, 188
palm
  martyr's, **3** 111, 113
  of victory, **2** 173
pantomime, **1** 14, 77, 89
parable, **1** 136; **2** 345, 376, 389
paradise, **1** 284; **2** 48, 109, 242, 267, 320-21, 323-24, 326, 328-29, 376, 423, 442, 463; **3** 73, 175, 200
paralytic, the, **1** 198
pardon: *see* forgiveness
parents, **1** 61, 82, 89, 167-68; **2** 21-22, 49, 66, 88, 91, 97, 189, 220-21, 328, 330, 424-25, 448, 463; **3** 74, 76, 156
parish, **1** 3, 13, 25, 74
Pasch, **1** 222; **2** 78, 222; **3** 57, 62-64, 68-69, 71-73, 75, 156
passions, **1** 95, 147, 161, 206, 209, 216, 227, 237; **2** 28, 47, 63, 70, 88, 106, 159, 164, 173, 196, 201, 252, 254, 270, 272, 334, 339, 383, 390-91, 407-8, 446, 478-79; **3** 37, 63,

82, 89, 110, 170-71; *see also* pleasures, bodily
Passover, **2** 222; **3** 68
pastor, **1** 25
patience, **1** 28, 32, 64-65, 124, 129, 144, 268, 271, 275; **2** 3, 25-26, 45, 79-80, 83, 90, 99, 140, 151, 163, 175, 177, 374; **3** 33, 66, 83, 131, 155, 157, 180-81, 197, 200-201, 207, 216-18, 222, 228
patients, **1** 282
patriarchs, **1** 44, 46, 248; **2** 34, 39, 168, 199, 216, 240, 328, 330, 381, 416, 419-20; **3** 111, 113, 115, 117-18
Paul, **1** 61, 122, 125-26, 137, 145, 189, 191-92, 204, 235; **2** 31, 120, 125, 147, 183, 186, 261, 270, 377-78, 411, 437 n.; **3** 104, 158, 162
  as herald of truth, **3** 104
  as a spiritual physician, **2** 467
peace, **1** 75, 80-81, 99, 180, 182-83, 197, 220-21, 299, 335, 363; **2** 26, 29, 35, 48, 72, 79, 121, 131, 151, 206-208, 298, 368, 374-76, 397, 399-401, 413, 432-33, 446, 458, 466-67, 469-70, 490; **3** 14, 37, 39, 54, 63, 73-74, 88, 93, 102, 106, 120, 136, 138, 143, 149, 153, 165, 177, 191, 209, 218
  kiss of, **2** 52
Pelagius, **1** xvii; **3** 230
penance, **1** 13, 36, 61, 72, 79, 90, 94, 102, 117, 179, 206, 211, 216, 235-36, 240, 252,

254, 256, 265-66, 270, 279, 281, 287, 295-96, 298-300, 304-10, 312-15, 321-22, 333; **2** 52, 138, 142, 162, 254, 286, 299-300, 303, 323, 330, 340, 406, 450, 452-53, 482-83; **3** 206, 229
  public, **1** 318-20; **2** 454
penitents, **1** 15, 297, 304, 319-22
Pentecost, **1** xiii; **2** 418; **3** 98 n.; *see also* seasons and feasts
perdition, **1** 15
perfumes, **2** 59
perjury, perjurers, **1** 61, 75, 82, 89, 260, 308; **2** 80, 236, 407; **3** 16, 176
persecution, persecutors, **1** 125, 192; **2** 8, 27-28, 31, 37, 61, 78-79, 92, 98, 108, 111, 174, 189, 197, 202, 209-10, 241, 254, 267, 292, 339, 368-69, 463-64, 470, 472, 476, 479, 481; **3** 129-30, 140, 145, 158-59, 213
Peter, the Apostle, **1** 11, 58, 61, 122, 159, 203; **2** 186, 214, 216, 221, 240, 266, 416, 437, 439-41, 447
Pharaoh (Pharao), **1** 234; **2** 51, 65-66, 74-78, 81, 98-102, 157
Pharisees, **1** 64, 255, 353, 356; **2** 126, 160, 248-49, 425; **3** 70-71
Pharphar, **2** 230
Philip, **2** 208; **3** 103
Philistia, **2** 157

Philistines, **2** 194, 197, 200-201
philosophers, **2** 84, 86
Phinees, **1** 34, 36, 201; **2** 215
Photinians, **2** 73, 280
  heresy of, **2** 280
Photinus, **2** 280
phylacteries, **1** 13, 77-78, 82, 101-2, 254-55, 259-60, 269
physician, **1** 36-37, 92, 206, 220, 282; **3** 83, 86
  spiritual, **1** 282, 295; **2** 143
piety, **1** 105, 263, 275, 335, 342, 363
Pirmin, St., **1** xxiii
Pius XI, Pope, **1** xxiv n.
plague, **2** 67, 81-95, 99-100, 102, 203-5, 238
pleasures
  bodily, **1** 70, 88, 154, 161, 203-8, 211-12, 214, 216, 219, 222-23, 225, 322, 324; **2** 5, 43-45, 55, 62, 123, 173, 176, 193-94, 253, 268, 272, 287, 299, 303, 322, 335, 349, 398, 430, 432, 443, 467, 481; **3** 19-20, 31, 43, 50-51, 56, 61, 82, 85, 97, 111, 114, 150
  worldly, **2** 93, 138, 173-74, 201, 269, 309-11, 319, 329, 333, 383, 405, 430, 432, 441; **3** 63, 86, 95, 97, 115, 150, 188, 192, 207
de Plinval, G., **1** viii n., xxvii, and *passim*
plunder, plunderer, **1** 42; **2** 239, 468, 479
poison, **2** 36, 135, 306, 352,

405; **3** 138, 213

pomegranates, **2** 126, 129

Pomerius, **1** vii

Pontius Pilate, **1** 55, 57, 59, 64; **2** 295-96

poor

  clothing of, **1** 50; **2** 112, 241, 279, 288, 339, 360-61, 373, 477; **3** 13

  feeding of, **1** 50, 89; **2** 112, 238, 279, 288, 339, 360-62, 373, 476; **3** 13, 50, 53-54, 56, 93, 124, 130, 186

  hand of, as treasury of Christ, **3** 56

  love of, **2** 240

  mercy to, **3** 47-48, 50

  offering to, **1** 80

  reception of equal to reception of Christ, **3** 55

Porcarius, Abbot, **1** vi-vii

Portuguese language, **3** 34 n.

potion, **1** 13, 36

poverty, **1** 141, 148, 167-68, 253, 280; **2** 107, 237-38, 322, 338, 349, 390, 424; **3** 142-43, 186

powers, special, **3** 99-101

prayers, **1** 6, 9, 21, 44, 49, 52, 54, 76-78, 81, 94, 102, 106, 122, 137-39, 171, 216-17, 272-73, 276, 280-81, 299, 302-3, 310, 319, 321, 323, 338-41, 350, 352, 355-60, 368; **2** 25, 29, 31, 42, 48, 70, 87-88, 101, 112, 124-25, 134-35, 156-58, 176, 207, 211-12, 220, 226, 250, 257, 278, 286, 289, 293, 298-300, 308, 310-11, 315, 322, 327-28, 333-34, 336, 350-51, 363, 373, 383, 396, 425, 446, 452, 455, 462, 472-73, 482-84, 486-87; **3** 16-17, 29, 37, 42-43, 46-47, 49, 57, 84-86, 88-89, 92, 100, 103, 106, 112, 127, 130, 133, 152, 164, 170-72, 177, 189, 191, 199-202, 204-5, 207, 209-12, 214, 223, 225

prayer, Lord's, **1** 14, 40, 75, 89, 100, 143, 149, 171, 195, 266, 298, 341-44; **2** 135, 311, 313, 315; **3** 10, 157, 178, 205

preacher, preaching, **1** 6-7, 14, 16, 23, 29-30, 32, 98, 145, 155, 204, 213, 249, 283; **2** 25, 32-33, 93, 134, 144, 153, 169-71, 182, 185, 212, 219, 221, 230, 235; **3** 122, 158-59, 172, 181, 183, 185, 187, 200, 204-5, 210 n., 212

Preface of the Mass: *see* Mass

prejudice, **2** 208

presbyters, **1** 12-14, 25, 77, 101; **2** 482

presumption, **1** 10, 24, 34, 204, 298

pride, **1** 12, 35, 41, 53, 60, 88, 142, 145, 154, 168, 183, 203, 227, 243, 246-50, 253, 280, 291, 295, 302, 351, 364-66; **2** 3, 10, 19, 24-26, 28, 42, 67, 77, 79-80, 83-86, 92, 100-102, 107, 120, 123, 135, 151, 164, 171, 175, 193, 197, 215, 221-23, 233-34, 239-40, 243, 254, 258, 260, 267-68, 289, 301-2, 316-17, 324, 335, 338,

343, 346, 349, 351-52, 354, 357, 371, 373, 391, 393-96, 399, 412, 423, 426, 433, 447, 450, 460, 463, 471, 482; **3** 9, 11, 30-31, 37, 61, 65, 74, 77, 83, 86, 88, 93-94, 96, 100, 122-24, 152-53, 158, 162-63, 171, 174, 180, 191, 193-98, 208, 215, 217-19, 221

priests, **1** 3-4, 7-10, 15-18, 20-22, 29-33, 36, 53, 70, 88, 101, 104, 161, 164, and *passim;* **2** 8, 18, 48, 59, 145-46, 148, 169-72, 213, 215, 269 n., 277, 304, 325, 334, 377-78, 408, 424, 473; **3** 11, 74, 80, 154, 159, 210

princes, **2** 168, 197

prison, **2** 45, 50-52, 56, 58, 60, 188, 195-96, 305, 307, 357, 448, 451, 453, 477, 479, 486, 493; **3** 125-26

procrastination, **1** 97, 105, 280

prodigal son, **2** 367, 384-87

Promised Land, **2** 161

prophecies, **1** 122, 266, 270, 342; **2** 20-21, 41, 136, 149, 159, 161, 183, 229, 414, 418, 420

prophets, **1** 12, 44, 46, 157, 167, 199, 202, 248, 296, 305, 320, 324, 365; **2** 10, 17, 27, 36, 56, 60, 65, 81, 96, 99-100, 103, 106, 108, 113, 122-23, 126, 128, 132-34, 141-42, 148, 159-60, 167, 171, 179-80, 182, 187, 195-96, 200, 204, 207, 210, 214-17, 220-21, 224, 230, 233-34, 256,

272, 295, 298-99, 319, 321, 328, 330, 377-78, 381, 388-90, 396, 416-18, 425, 427, 432, 460, 463; **3** 46, 57, 98, 104, 111-13, 115, 117-18, 126, 132, 137, 169, 183, 185, 197

proverb, **2** 465

providence, **2** 83

prudence, **2** 288, 309, 315, 325, 367, 404; **3** 11, 149

Prudentius, **3** 140 n.

Psalmist, the, **1** 171, 368

psalms, **1** 40, 180, 351-53; **2** 295

praying or chanting of, **1** 309, 338-39, 349-50, 352, 358; **2** 244, 250, 269, 334, 336, 350; **3** 14, 68, 85-86, 89, 224

Psalter, **3** 122 n.

psaltery, **2** 96

publican, **1** 143, 187, 210, 319, 353, 355-56; **2** 249, 425

punishment, **1** 7, 15, 34-35, 47, 68, 73-74, 90-91, 93, 218, 240-41, 243, 245-46, 257, 265, 269, 272, 276-77, 279-80, 282, 308, 318, 337; **2** 47, 52-53, 82-83, 114, 118, 136-38, 142, 187, 214-15, 221-22, 242-43, 245-47, 256, 285-86, 302, 307, 324-25, 344, 357, 359-60, 375, 382, 395, 402, 407-9, 442, 453, 475-76, 478, 480, 493; **3** 53, 65-66, 74, 78, 81-82, 84-85, 87, 126, 137, 140-42, 149, 159, 166, 175, 179, 184, 196-98, 206, 215

purgatory, **2** 452-53, 455; **3** 78

purity, **1** 220, 227, 231, 316;
**2** 54-56, 58-59, 254, 407-8;
**3** 82, 94-95, 110, 170-72, 176
of soul, **2** 235, 347-48, 351,
391, 405

quarrels, quarreling, **1** 52, 76,
89, 100, 174-75, 232, 235,
272-73
Quinquagesima Sunday, **3** 98
n.
Quodvultdeus, **3** 230-31

Rachel, **2** 34-35, 37, 113-14,
116; **3** 139
Rahab, **2**, 167, 171
Raphael (archangel), **2** 158
Raphidim, **2** 108-9
Ravenna, **1** ix-xi
reading, spiritual, **1** 5-6, 9, 19-
21, 31-32, 39, 46, 48-50, 54,
93, 106, 137, 139, 171; **2**
29, 42, 87-88, 350-51, 455
Rebecca, **2** 20-25, 28-29, 34,
382
rebirth, **2** 462
reconciliation, **1** 285, 306
redemption, **2** 60, 181, 189,
265, 298, 349, 360-61, 406,
454-56, 493; **3** 47-48, 69, 72,
154, 177, 190
Red Sea, **2** 74-77, 79, 103-4,
115-17, 154, 157, 168, 172
*Regula Magistri,* **3** 42 n.
relatives and neighbors, **1** 12,
49, 53, 61, 67, 76-77, 81-82,
89, 105-7, 119, 122, 151, 175,
177-79, 187, 189, 193, 195,
199-200; **2** 8, 48, 63, 89-91,

93, 95-98, 131-33, 142, 168,
223-24, 245, 256, 272, 301,
306, 308, 316-17, 321, 337,
340-42, 361, 375, 378, 381,
431-32, 451, 456-57, 474, 492;
**3** 14, 88, 135, 146, 154-55,
166, 200
relics, **2** 484
religion, the true, **1** 202
religious, **1** 13, 254, 257, 281,
311, 367
religious habit, **1** 281
remission of sins, **1** 4, 77, 148,
162, 193, 319, 356
reparation for sin, **1** 138
repentance, **1** 36-37, 43, 71, 80,
90, 92, 96, 98, 101, 117, 134,
154, 186, 191, 212, 217, 219,
236, 242, 245, 248, 280, 283,
285-86, 288, 295-98, 300, 303-
13, 315-20, 322-23, 333, 366;
**2** 42, 52, 62, 77, 99, 102,
138, 140-41, 176, 191, 193,
196, 239, 245, 295, 298-302,
343, 347, 357, 373, 380-82,
396, 402, 407, 415, 417, 449,
453, 455, 464, 483; **3** 9, 12-
13, 17-19, 21-22, 26, 33, 45-
46, 48, 56, 60-61, 65, 67, 81-
82, 87-90, 121, 123, 131, 138,
141, 149, 165-66, 170-71, 177,
207-8
resurrection of the dead, **1** 55,
59-60, 98; **2** 108, 148-50, 155,
232, 444-45, 454; **3** 72, 94
revelation, **2** 116
revenge, **1** 172
reverence, **1** 4
rewards, **2** 46, 117-119, 235,

278, 309, 325, 337, 344, 359, 432, 449-50, 452, 456, 472, 480; **3** 13, 30, 53, 56, 69, 74, 93, 125, 130, 140, 153, 156, 158, 161, 179, 190-91, 208, 224

eternal, **1** 24, 31-32, 36, 40, 42, 47, 52, 59, 68, 73-74, 76, 82, 88, 93, 102, 123, 148, 151-52, 157, 218, 220, 227, 231, 237, 243, 246, 248, 256, 311, 318; **2** 48, 118, 143, 185, 198, 226, 228, 263, 271, 339, 344, 351, 361, 437, 455, 467, 479, 483; **3** 10, 13, 15, 32, 34, 36, 44, 48, 59, 63-64, 73, 77, 86, 144, 179, 197, 215, 219, 223

rivers, **2** 65-66, 82, 86, 110, 115, 154, 165, 192, 217, 230-31, 233-34; **3** 203

Riviere, J., **1** xviii n., xxvii

robbers, robbery, **1** 61, 70, 73, 75-76, 80-81, 88-89, 98, 102, 158, 210, 216, 257, 296, 302, 306, 319; **2** 10, 67, 89-91, 95-98, 175, 186, 229, 239, 248-49, 258, 282, 285, 305, 317, 324, 337, 342, 360, 376, 378, 399, 417, 424, 450, 459, 464, 468-69, 475-79, 481, 491; **3** 60-61, 96, 149, 152, 176

rod: *see* staff

Rogation Days, **3** 82, 84-85, 87, 89, 92; *see also* seasons and feasts, sermons for

Rogationtide, **3** 82 n.

Roman customs, **1** 15

Roman empire, **3** 79

Rome, **1** x, xxii, 213; **2** 222

Rufinus, **3** 230

Ruricius, Bp. of Limoges, **1** xv

sabbath (Jewish), **1** 76, 266

Sabbath, the, **1** 344-45; **2** 87, 93, 104-6

sacrament, **2** 69, 110, 184, 235, 279; **3** 72, 75, 77, 152, 176

Sacrament of the altar, **2** 313

sacrifice, **1** 66, 131, 192, 197; **2** 16-18, 74, 148, 177-78, 190, 212

sacrilege, **1** 82; **2** 450, 455; **3** 70

saints, **1** 3, 15, 36, 47, 60, 67, 77, 109, 176, 179, 184, 199, 241, 247, 252, 255, 276-77, 302, 316, 366; **2** 50, 75, 127, 163, 185, 200, 258, 261, 310, 313, 327, 345, 356, 408, 438-39, 441, 444-46, 451, 455, 457, 467, 480, 482, 494; **3** 65-66, 72, 117, 120, 126, 133, 144, 148, 150, 155, 166, 175

salvation, **1** 4, 15, 17, 27, 31-36, 38-39, 42, 44, 49, 55, 59, 62, 76, 79-80, 88, 90, 98, and *passim;* **2** 6, 39, 48, 58, 78, 117, 125, 127, 133, 135, 141, 143, 146, 152, 169, 182, 185, 190, 199-200, 214-15, 221, 232, 234, 246, 254, 263, 265, 268, 297, 305, 322, 327, 343, 352, 380-81, 388-89, 394-95, 403-4, 409-10, 421, 435, 441, 460, 472, 491; **3** 10, 16, 29,

32-35, 38-41, 43-45, 58, 64, 69-71, 73, 82-83, 85, 93, 98, 100, 108, 121, 155, 160, 163, 173, 182, 189-91, 199, 208

Salvian, St., **1** 152

Samaria, **2** 419-20

Samaritans, **1** 199; **2** 377-78, 419-20

Samson (the Nazarite), **2** 182-98, 194

Samson, the true: *see* Christ

Samuel, **2** 116, 200

sanctuary, **3** 141

Saphira (Sapphira), **1** 203; **2** 214, 221

Sarah (Sara), **1** 44; **2** 12, 14, 113, 116

Sarephta, **2** 210, 213

Satan: *see* devil

Saturn, **3** 33

Saul: *see* Paul

Saul, King, **2** 116-17, 200, 254

scandals, **1** 76, 174-75, 323; **2** 7, 78-79, 133; **3** 155

scars from spiritual wounds, **3** 9

schisms, **1** 140, 325

scholars, **2** 25

scribes, **2** 126, 160

Scriptures, **1** xv, xix, 10-12, 16, 18, 19, 22, 31, 38-40, 44-47, 49-52, 54, 58, 63, 67, 76, 96-97, 100, 106, 114-15, 122, 157, 164, 169, 176, 178, 180, 184, 188, 191, 198, 215, 226, 229, 235, 241, 243-51, 267, 271, 273, 275, 277, 290, 292, 302, 309, 314, 324, 338, 342-44, 347-48, 351, 354, 359,

364-67; **2** 14, 16, 19, 24, 26-27, 32, 35, 51, 55, 57, 60, 63, 89, 99, 102, 109, 113, 119, 127, 129-32, 141-42, 144, 148, 150, 156, 158-60, 171, 184, 186-87, 190, 198, 215-16, 225-27, 240, 248, 274, 277, 282, 301, 304, 306, 314, 317-18, 324, 339-40, 344, 358-59, 378-79, 383, 408, 411, 415-19, 471-84; **3** 1, 26, 31, 39, 42, 50-51, 57, 64, 86-87, 96, 102, 106-7, 128, 138, 140-41, 147, 154, 181, 194, 203, 206-7, 220, 225 n.-26

reading of, **2** 3, 11, 17, 20, 25, 74, 98, 103, 116, 125, 131, 135, 139, 144, 151, 155, 161, 171, 182, 189, 193, 206, 209, 214, 216, 220, 227, 233, 315, 319, 355, 359, 416, 427, 456, 463; **3** 42-43, 49-52, 85, 98, 141, 159, 181, 183, 200-202, 214, 220-21, 223

sea, **2** 63, 76, 104, 154, 172, 212, 239, 267, 285, 434; **3** 205

seasons and feasts, sermons for

Advent, **3** 7, 11, 15

Ascension, **3** 93

calends of January, **3** 26, 30

Christmas, **3** 7, 11, 15, 21

Circumcision of Christ, **3** 25

Easter, **3** 69, 71, 75

Epiphany, **3** 35, 38

Lent, **3** 41, 44, 48, 220

Nativity of St. John the

Baptist, **3** 117, 120

Pentecost, **3** 98

Rogation Days, **2** 354; **3** 82, 87, 89

Sedatus, Bp. of Nîmes, **3** 21 n., 30

seducers, **1** 107

seers, **1** 13, 71, 77-78, 101-2, 254, 260, 262, 265, 267, 269, 331; **2** 156, 158-59; **3** 16

self-discipline, **1** 204; **3** 45

Sem: *see* Shem

Sephora, **2** 34, 68

Sepphor, **2** 155, 158

Septuagint, **1** 67 n., 198 n.

seraphim, **3** 104

sermons, **1** 4, 15-17, 25, 44; **2** 25

Serpent, the: *see* devil

serpents, **1** 107, 324, 326; **2** 68-69, 81, 122, 130, 151-53, 186, 191, 330, 336; **3** 153

servant

of Christ, **2** 191

the unprofitable, **1** 11

Sext, **2** 28; **3** 42

sheep, **2** 34-35, 39, 66, 90, 94, 146, 179, 199-200, 237, 256, 275, 285, 293-94, 354, 426; **3** 91, 181, 183, 190-91, 219

sheepfold, **2** 200, 277, 282, 285

Shem (Sem), **2** 162

*Shepherd of Hermas*, **1** 135 n.

shepherds, **1** 23, 84, 91; **2** 35, 240, 275, 285, 400; **3** 38-40, 112, 159, 181, 191

priests as, **1** 21-22

ship, **2** 267, 459; **3** 205

Sichar, **2** 419

Sichem, **2** 39

Sidonians, **2** 210

Sidonius Apollinaris, **3** 122 n.

Siloe, the Pool of, **2** 422, 426

silver, **2** 23, 40, 59-60, 145, 153, 205, 237, 288, 341, 361, 430, 448, 450, 455, 462, 481; **3** 142, 226

Simeon, **2** 50

Sinai, Mount, **1** 223; **2** 16

Sin, desert of, **2** 109

singing: *see* song

sins, **1** 4, 6, 8, 17-18, 24, 29, 33-37, 42, 51, 59, 61, 64, 66, 73, 75-78, 81-82, 89, 92-96, 99, 130, 144, 148-50, 159-62, 188, 194-195, 210, 224, 271, 275, 279-80, 284, 286, 296-300, 303, 306, 308-11, 313, 315, 317-18, 324, 335, 365; **2** 4, 6-7, 39, 42-43, 51-52, 54, 65-66, 99-100, 102-3, 136-37, 141-42, 146, 152, 162, 169, 176, 179, 181, 191-92, 194-95, 200-202, 205, 209, 211, 214-215, 223-27, 229, 231, 234-35

actual, **1** 47; **2** 75, 164, 227, 231

capital, **1** 98, 311, 315; **2** 50

filth of, **3** 167

mortal, **1** 70

occasion of, **1** 367

original, **1** 47, 66, 185; **2** 66, 75, 85, 164, 217, 227, 231

serious, **1** 6, 30, 35, 78-79, 98, 100, 150, 159-60, 168, 215, 235, 237, 240, 279, 295-

96, 298-99, 303-10, 312, 315-17, 356, 365

slavery of, **2** 58

slight, **1** 65, 224, 240, 296, 300-301, 310, 338

sword of, **3** 47

sinners, **1** 34, 36, 64, 66, 73-74, 91-92, 94, 117, 119, 126, 150, 159-61, 181, 189, 191-93, 200, 210, 212, 243-45, and *passim*

Sion, **1** 255; **2** 160; **3** 197

Sirach (Ecclesiasticus), **2** 437 n.

slander, slanderer, **1** 13, 82, 181, 260, 321; **2** 48, 83, 199, 244, 341, 349, 353, 371, 375, 399, 423, 450, 465-66; **3** 30, 50, 203, 208-9, 213

slave, slavery, **2** 43, 54, 58, 79, 102, 194

sloth, slothful, **1** 4, 337; **2** 4, 151, 164-66, 257, 260, 277, 337, 474; **3** 191, 216, 220

sobriety, **1** 39, 236, 239-41, 243, 256; **2** 91, 98, 236

Sodom, **2** 11-12, 14-15, 162, 259, 262

sodomites, **1** 209, 240; **2** 463

soldier, **2** 169, 214, 238

of Christ, **2** 125

of God, **2** 108; **3** 181

solicitude, **1** 5-6, 25, 37, 48, 54, 79, 98; **2** 134, 143, 176, 319, 437, 489; **3** 26, 41, 43

Solomon, **1** 206; **2** 104, 120, 206-7, 253, 274; **3** 169-70, 203, 212, 221 n.

songs, **1** 14, 40, 77-78, 89, 100, 167; **2** 236, 241, 345; **3** 73,

75-76, 78-79, 85-86, 88-89, 120, 155, 221, 223

soothsayers, **1** 71, 77, 253-54, 262, 265, 269, 331; **2** 156, 481; **3** 16, 46, 177

sorcerers, sorcery, **1** 71, 77-78, 101-2, 265, 331; **3** 177

Spain, **1** x, xxii

speech

evil, **1** 321

measured use of, **3** 14

spindle, **2** 278-79, 281

sponsor (at baptism), **1** 336

spouse, heavenly, **2** 346-47, 436, 452

staff, **2** 30, 38, 67-69, 109-10, 147, 149-51, 154, 177-78, 181, 200-202, 227

stars, **2** 10, 40-41, 159, 239, 419; **3** 35-36, 38, 69, 141

Stephen, St. (martyr), **1** 61, 185, 191; **2** 322; **3** 127-29, 132-33, 135

cathedral of at Arles, **1** xxi

sterility, **2** 462; **3** 117, 121

steward, chief, **2** 411

stones, **3** 40, 129, 132-33, 168-69, 173-74, 227

precious, **2** 275-76, 286, 450, 455; **3** 149

suffering, **2** 148, 237, 242, 286, 293, 341, 366, 480; **3** 113, 118, 128, 142, 144, 157-58, 163, 174, 176-77, 181; *see also* Christ, suffering of

suicide, **1** 259

sun, **2** 6, 9, 11, 40-41, 61, 101, 239, 264-66, 299, 419, 458-59, 461; **3** 33, 95, 119, 141,

145, 159, 226

Sunam, **2** 226

Sunday, **1** 10, 76, 79, 101, 182, 220, 225, 334, 342, 344, 363; **2** 105, 433; **3** 53, 98 n., 183

superstition, **2** 97; **3** 30-31

supper of the Lord, **3** 65

supplications, **2** 157

Susanna, **1** 43-44, 122; **2** 55, 59

suspicion, **2** 214, 304, 317, 485

swearing, **1** 12, 82, 308

sword, **1** 92; **2** 8, 71, 137, 156-57, 201-2, 222, 269, 463, 479-80; **3** 46, 138, 185
 spiritual, **2** 124-25, 244
 two-edged, **2** 125

Sylvester, Bp., **1** vi

Symmachus, Pope, **1** x, xv-xvi; **3** 122 n.

synagogue, **2** 17, 23-24, 30, 37, 56, 60, 66, 68, 113-15, 117, 126, 128, 133, 157, 182, 187, 197, 209, 213

Syria, **2** 21, 29

tabernacle of our body, **1** 286

tales, idle, **1** 181, 360

tares, **1** 10; **2** 472

Tarragona, **1** xxii

tassels (on phylacteries), **1** 255

taxes, **1** 169

teaching, teacher, **1** 4-5, 9, 20, 23; **2** 87, 105, 119, 124, 127, 130, 150, 157, 173, 185, 190, 236, 240, 255, 304, 318, 390, 433, 479, 484; **3** 181, 183, 187, 191, 205, 209

tears, **2** 46, 52, 138, 200

teeth, gnashing of, **1** 30, 33; **2**

47, 143, 332

temperance, **2** 384, 448; **3** 8, 37, 62-63, 83, 120, 151, 177-79

temple, **2** 20, 224, 425

temptation, **1** 64, 122, 169, 246, 288, 292, 327, 329; **2** 43, 109, 176, 195, 314, 340, 370, 383, 446, 468, 480-81, 484; **3** 79, 135

Terce: *see* Tierce

Terebinth, valley of, **2** 200

testimony, false, **2** 84, 360, 407, 450, 481; **3** 16, 46, 60, 177, 220

thanksgiving, **3** 38

theater, **2** 471

Theodoric, **1** viii-xi

theriaca, **1** 283

Thomas, **3** 70

thoughts,
 evil, **1** 222, 226, 228, 230, 308; **2** 77, 137, 219, 334-36, 349, 372, 440; **3** 75
 good, **3** 79
 impure, **2** 76

threshing floor, **2** 180-82, 203-5, 219, 459
 Catholic Church as, **2** 184, 351; **3** 91-92

throne, **2** 117, 172
 of God, **3** 104

Thursday, **1** 78-79, 101, 260

Tierce (Terce), **2** 28; **3** 42

tithes, **1** 14, 61, 76, 81, 88, 100, 149, 157, 162-69, 296, 336; **3** 175

Titus, **2** 222

Tixeront, J., **1** xiii n., xxvii

tomb, **2** 295-96, 434; **3** 70, 150-51

tongue, **1** 207; **2** 31, 69, 112, 137, 157, 170, 249-50, 257, 288, 298, 335, 351, 392, 395, 478; **3** 75, 78, 153, 196, 198, 213, 215, 220-22

traitor, **2** 465

transgressions, **1** 283

treachery, **2** 306

treasure, spiritual, **2** 237, 352-53, 370, 374, 433; **3** 36, 48, 186-87

tribulations, **1** 22, 35, 42, 126, 330, 333

tribunal
of Christ, **1** 8, 13, 17, 23-25, 30, 32, 46, 98, 132, 135, 150, 158, 166, 170, 173, 183, 219-21, 226, 231, 237, 258, 279-80, 282, 285, 287, 290, 311, 323, 345, 362; **2** 42, 69, 235, 245-46, 358, 484; **3** 26, 47, 219
heavenly, **2** 81, 103, 118, 143, 235, 361-62, 389, 437; **3** 17, 134, 138, 151, 165, 182-83

Trinity, the Holy, **1** 24, 26-27, 56-58; **2** 7, 13-14, 16, 167-68, 185, 199, 211-12, 402, 409-410, 418, 440-41; **3** 12, 36, 40, 90, 102-5, 108-9
mystery of, **2** 7, 12-14, 16, 167-68, 185, 199, 211
unity of, **1** 26-27; **3** 103-6

trumpet, **2** 169-72, 176, 241
archangel's, **2** 10
of the Lord, **2** 243

truth (s), **1** 5, 14, 17, 19-20, 28, 32, 35, 49-50, 68, 94, 160, 168, 205, 239, 333, 366; **2** 8, 18, 32-33, 38, 51, 59, 62, 67, 85, 92-93, 98, 102, 116-17, 127, 130, 132, 140-41, 143-44, 149, 184, 186, 200, 213, 218, 226, 234, 236, 254, 260, 283, 294, 296-97, 301-2, 304-5, 311, 320, 326, 332, 334, 344, 347, 357-58, 361, 375, 289-90, 393, 396, 411, 424, 440, 446-47, 456-57, 460, 467-68, 471, 473, 476, 487; **3** 16, 21, 26, 35, 41, 43-44, 46, 55, 57, 74, 77, 98, 104, 107, 119-20, 122-23, 126-30, 135, 153, 155, 163, 188, 198, 200, 202, 204, 218-19, 222, 226
herald of, **2** 235
light of, **3** 111, 113, 215

Tuesday, **2** 25, 161

tunic, **1** 79, 104, 224

turtledove, **2** 6-10

tyrant, **2** 402

ulcers, **1** 124; **2** 82-84, 89, 389-90, 475

unbelievers, **1** 74, 192

unity, **2** 208

Vaison, Council of, **1** xii, xiv

vanity, **1** 154, 230; **2** 240, 246-47, 251, 296, 309-11, 332, 385-86, 423; **3** 100, 149-50, 159, 213

Venus as harlot, **3** 33

Vergil, *Aeneid* of, **1** 255 n.; **2**

335 n.; **3** 83 n.
Vespasian, **2** 222
Vespers, **2** 193, 206
vessels, the faithful as, **2** 353; **3** 118; *see also* devil, vessels of
vestments of priests, **1** 7
Vetus Latina, **1** xxv
vice (s), **1** 15, 19, 41-42, 71, 75, 95, 119, 154, 159-60, 174, 204-5, 210-11, 213, 216, 229-30, 232, 235, 245, 249, 280, 289, 300, 302, 306, 310, 318, 324, 337, 340-41, 351, 364
fetters of, **2** 8
Vichi, A.M.G., **3** 225 n.
Vigilius, Pope, **1** xvi
vigils, **1** 120, 122, 124, 137-38, 149, 195, 299, 353, 363; **2** 19, 28, 135, 257, 299, 318, 350-51, 453, 483; **3** 14-15, 41-43, 45, 52, 57, 84, 92, 101, 127, 146, 156, 161, 171, 178, 193, 200-202, 205, 217, 223-24
vine, heavenly, **2** 177
vineyard, **1** 6; **2** 128, 180, 186
violence, **2** 282, 306; **3** 167
vipers, **2** 7, 46
Virgin, the (Mary): *see* Mary
virginity, virgins, **1** 14, 38, 43-44, 48, 81, 121-22, 124, 162, 180, 183, 186, 199, 204, 212-213, 215, 217, 221, 251, 324, 327-28, 333; **2** 59, 72, 124, 127, 130, 132, 173, 186, 258-61, 294, 328, 330, 344-51, 387, 412, 434, 443, 475; **3** 16, 46, 70-71, 73, 110, 201-2,

216-18
virtues, **1** 12, 41, 62, 67, 73-74, 85, 87, 105-6, 121, 124, 145-46, 170, 173, 177, 205, 213, 221, 289, 340, 364, 366
Visigoths, **1** viii-ix, xxii
*Visio Pauli*, **3** 42 n.
Viventius, **1** v
vocation, **2** 263
de Vogüé, A., **3** 42 n.
vows, **1** 13, 71, 78, 82, 263, 269, 276; **2** 257-59, 261
Vulgate, **1** 72 n.; **2** 112 n., 353 n., 474 n.

wages of sin (= death), **1** 276
wantonness, **2** 253-54; **3** 83, 110, 126, 141
warfare, **2** 97, 111, 123, 155-56, 175, 366, 375, 433, 445
warrior, **2** 237
watchman, **3** 185
water, **2** 21-22, 34, 65, 75-76, 82, 84, 86, 92 n.-93, 101, 103-5, 109-10, 115-17, 154-55, 172, 180, 212, 217-18, 233, 320, 324, 329, 391-92, 403, 405, 409-11, 413-14, 416-17, 419, 421, 472; **3** 54, 88, 102, 124, 145, 176, 205, 211, 227
divine, **3** 102
water-jars, **2** 21, 403, 405, 409-11, 413-16, 418
wealth as measure of amount of almsgiving, **2** 29, 325, 361, 424; **3** 13, 68
weapons, spiritual, **3** 83
wedding feast, **1** 212, 217; **3** 165

heavenly, **2** 281
Wednesday, **3** 92 n.
weeping, **1** 30, 33; **3** 17, 21, 29, 46-47, 49-50
welfare, spiritual, **2** xiii
wheat, **2** 27, 50, 61, 177, 180, 184, 219, 366, 472; **3** 92
wickedness, **1** 52
widows, **1** 38, 43-44, 244, 250-52; **2** 59, 71, 73, 209-11, 213, 223-27, 239, 253, 258-59, 357, 362, 365, 469-70, 476
wife, **1** 13, 81, 97, 100, 165-66, 212, 214-20, 223, 225
will, **3** 157, 180
  divine, **3** 101, 108
  free, **1** 63; **2** 159, 231; **3** 161-63
  good, **1** 151, 193; **2** 207, 397, 467, 469-70; **3** 47-48, 54, 80, 123
wine, **2** 32, 127, 133, 318, 377-78, 404-6, 409-12, 414, 416-19, 464, 471-72; **3** 146
  spiritual, **2** 29
wisdom, **1** 267; **2** 32, 53, 68-69, 81, 86, 104, 177, 190, 196, 217, 238, 266, 309, 384, 403, 411, 438; **3** 98, 220
witch, **1** 262
witness, false, **1** 12, 61, 75, 81, 88-89, 99; **2** 90, 96-97, 236, 337, 423
wolf, **2** 282, 285, 335; **3** 159, 219
womb, **1** 284; **2** 25, 28, 46, 165, 294, 364, 424-25, 434, 436; **3** 118, 139, 169
works, good, **1** 32, 40, 49, 53-55, 67-68, 72-75, 77, 80, 85-88, 90, 93-94, 105, 114-15, 121-22, 140, 154, 175, 182, 189, 193, 196, 198-99, 230, 232, 246-47, 252, 256, 258, 265, 269-70, 272, 281, 295-96, 298-99, 301, 308-9, 315, 321, 324, 335, 337, 361-62; **2** 3, 22, 34, 48-50, 64, 70, 76, 78-79, 88-89, 91, 95, 106-7, 118, 134, 136, 142-43, 146, 172, 175-76, 186, 197, 203, 210, 217-19, 223-24, 226, 234; **3** 7, 10-11, 14, 17, 24-25, 37, 43, 47-48, 56, 59, 62, 71, 79-80, 91-92, 98, 101, 111-16, 121-22, 130, 141, 143, 148, 150-51, 161, 164, 170-72, 175, 179, 201, 212, 216, 219, 226
pearls of, **3** 12, 71, 201, 212
world, end of the, **1** 7; **2** 23
worldly goods, **3** 42, 50
worms, **2** 106-8, 242, 338, 412, 431, 454; **3** 151, 166
wounds of sin, **1** 176, 182, 194, 281, 284, 290, 366; **2** 85, 102-3, 138, 143, 327, 474; **3** 9, 22, 25, 34, 42, 67, 82, 85, 88-90, 92-93, 134, 147-48, 163, 165-66, 194
wrath, **1** 14, 81, 113, 130, 145, 178-79, 183, 197, 202-4, 213, 229, 235, 271, 275, 287, 302, 308, 341; **2** 24, 26-28, 42, 83-84, 89, 94, 97, 99, 107, 123, 135-36, 163, 173, 175, 193, 221, 230-31, 245, 255, 304, 316-18, 323, 352, 357, 369, 399, 407, 415, 433, 450, 457-

59, 482, 485; **3** 9-11, 13, 32, 60, 74, 79, 88, 131-32, 136-37, 148-49, 152-53, 165, 167, 171, 173, 196-97, 200, 207, 209, 213, 215, 217-18

yoke

   of Christ, **1** 120, 166, 324, 334; **2** 134, 196, 292, 365,

386; **3** 37, 200, 214

   of the devil, **2** 134; **3** 208

   of God, **2** 400

Zachaeus, **1** 252; **2** 469-70; **3** 61

zeal, **1** 4, 16-17, 21, 28, 34, 36, 124, 201, 203

# INDEX OF HOLY SCRIPTURE

## (Books of the Old Testament)

Genesis
1.1: **3** 102
1.2: **3** 102
1.5: **1** 266
1.26: **3** 102
1.27: **3** 103
1.28: **3** 103
1.31: **1** 266
2.21-22: **2** 414
3.1: **2** 122
3.6: **2** 443
3.7: **2** 443
3.10: **2** 55
3.14: **2** 268
3.18: **2** 69
3.19: **2** 191, 268
12.1: **2** 3, 4 (bis), 5
15.9-12: **2** 7
15.16: **2** 162
15.17, 12, 17: **2** 9
15.17: **2** 7
17.5: **2** 7
18.1-2: **2** 11
18.1: **2** 14
18.2: **2** 12
18.3: **2** 13
18.4: **2** 13 (bis)
18.6: **2** 12
18.7: **2** 12 (ter), 13
18.20-21: **2** 14
19.3: **2** 12

21.32: **2** 23
22.2-4: **2** 16
22.5: **2** 18
24.2-3: **2** 20
24.10-58: **2** 21
24.62: **2** 23
24.63: **2** 23
24.67: **2** 23, 24
25.22: **2** 25
25.23: **2** 25, 26, 28
27.27: **2** 6
32.10: **2** 30, 38
32.27: **2** 37 (bis)
32.29: **2** 37
37.4: **2** 40, 43
37.10: **2** 40
39.7: **2** 54 (bis)
40.14: **2** 51
42.21: **2** 52
48.18: **2** 115
48.19: **2** 115
49.9: **2** 190
49.11: **2** 133
49.27: **3** 159

Exodus
1.6-7: **2** 61
1.8: **2** 61
3.2: **2** 69
3.3: **2** 66
3.5: **2** 66, 71, 72, 73

3.10: **2** 67
4.2-3: **2** 67
4.10: **2** 67
4.12: **2** 67
4.21: **2** 100, 101
5.3: **2** 74
8.27: **2** 16
9.27: **2** 102
12.13: **1** 66
14.14: **2** 157
14.15: **2** 75
14.16: **2** 154
15.4: **2** 77
15.14-15: **2** 157
16.15: **2** 105
16.20: **2** 106
16.24: **2** 106
17.3: **2** 109
17.5-6: **2** 109
17.9: **2** 111
17.10-11: **2** 111
19.15: **1** 223; **2** 17
20.3: **2** 86, 93
20.7: **2** 86, 93
20.8: **2** 87, 93
20.12: **2** 88, 94, 96 *(bis)*
20.13: **2** 89, 94, 96, 97
20.14: **2** 88, 94, 96, 97 *(bis)*
20.15: **2** 89, 94, 96, 97
20.16: **2** 90, 95, 96, 97
20.17: **2** 90 *(bis)*, 95 *(bis)*, 96 *(bis)*, 97 *(ter)*
21.24: **2** 214
22.20: **1** 264
22.29: **1** 163
23.5: **1** 177; **3** 154
23.15: **3** 36
30.12: **1** 164 *(bis)*
32.6: **1** 234

32.32: **1** 177, 201
32.34: **2** 159
33.14: **3** 104
34.12: **2** 6

Leviticus
7.20: **1** 223
11.44: **1** 20
16.29: **3** 15, 45
19.18: **1** 177
26.3: **2** 119
26.5: **2** 120 *(bis)*, 121
26.6: **2** 121 *(bis)*, 122, 123
26.7: **2** 123
26.8: **2** 124 *(bis)*
26.9: **2** 125
26.12: **2** 67; **3** 124, 169

Numbers
11.4: **2** 178
11.29: **1** 16
12.3: **1** 200; **2** 215
13.3: **2** 126
13.24: **2** 126 *(bis)*
13.33-34: **2** 126
14.1-2: **2** 126
14.8: **2** 136
14.12: **2** 136
14.29-30, 23, 31: **2** 139
14.30, 23, 32: **2** 141
14.33: **2** 136
14.34: **2** 136
16.37-38: **2** 144
16.46: **2** 145
17.5: **2** 149
17.8: **2** 147, 149 *(bis)*
20.11: **2** 110
22.1-2: **2** 155
22.4: **2** 112, 157

22.5: **2** 156
22.6: **2** 156
22.9-12: **2** 158
24.17: **2** 159
25.11: **1** 34, 201

Deuteronomy
13.3: **1** 267
16.19: **1** 76
18.18-19: **2** 417
22.4: **3** 154
23.10: **1** 223
27.9: **2** 353
30.19: **2** 320, 324, 330
32.1-2: **2** 119
32.2: **1** 18, 354, 358; **2** 179
32.4: **2** 101
32.13: **2** 132
32.14: **2** 133
32.22: **3** 141

Josue
1.11: **2** 167, 168, 172
5.12: **2** 173
5.14: **2** 71

Judges
2.21-22: **2** 204
6.36-38: **2** 179
13.25: **2** 183
14.14: **2** 183, 185, 190
14.18: **2** 185
14.19-20: **2** 185
16.2-3: **2** 187
16.3: **2** 187
16.25: **2** 189
16.30: **2** 189, 193

1 Kings (1 Samuel)
1.10, 13: **1** 339

2.24-25: **1** 33
2.25: **1** 24
15.22: **2** 353
17.17-18: **2** 199
17.28: **2** 199

2 Kings (2 Samuel)
12.1ff.: **2** 256
12.13: **1** 305
24.16: **2** 204
24.18: **2** 204
24.24: **2** 205

3 Kings (1 Kings)
3.26: **2** 206, 207
6.20: **3** 169
8.64: **3** 169
10.6-7: **3** 213
17.9: **2** 210
17.12: **2** 211
18.42: **2** 212
18.43: **2** 212 *(ter)*
18.44-45: **2** 212
19.10, 15, 18: **2** 460
21.29: **1** 314
22.21-22: **1** 365

4 Kings (2 Kings)
1.9-14: **1** 201
1.9: **2** 215
2.19: **2** 217
2.20-21: **2** 217
2.23: **1** 202; **2** 220 *(bis)*, 222
2.24: **2** 220
4.1: **2** 223
4.2: **2** 223
4.3-4, 6-7: **2** 223
4.3-4: **2** 224

4.6: **2** 225
4.9-10: **2** 226
4.29: **2** 227
5.10: **2** 230, 231
5.12: **2** 230
5.14: **2** 231
6.5: **2** 233
9.11: **2** 220

Tobias
4.11: **2** 361

Job
1.9: **1** 110
1.21: **1** 267, 268; **2** 166, 237, 240, 242, 364, 399; **3** 96
2.9: **2** 242
2.10: **2** 166, 243
7.1: **2** 480
14.4: **2** 51, 396
31.20: **2** 237
31.29: **1** 177
31.32: **2** 237

Psalms (the principal enumeration is that of the Septuagint and Vulgate; the alternative enumeration is given in parenthesis)
1.2: **1** 46, 171, 351; **2** 175; **3** 49
1.3: **2** 155 (bis), 210
1.4: **2** 243
2.3: **2** 134, 492; **3** 94
2.11: **2** 253
4.1: **2** 270
4.3: **3** 95
4.5: **1** 287, 294
5.4: **3** 52

5.7: **1** 120, 365; **3** 61
5.11: **1** 323
6.6: **1** 323; **3** 48
6.7: **1** 313; **3** 17, 46
6.8: **2** 317
7.5-6: **1** 178, 351
7.15: **2** 342
8.4: **3** 105
9.18: **1** 244, 251
9 (10).3: **1** 294; **2** 272; **3** 122
9 (10).14: **1** 244
9 (10).15: **1** 244
10 (11).4: **1** 65
10 (11).6 (5): **1** 209; **2** 306, 429, 432; **3** 167
10 (11).7: **1** 248
12 (13).4: **2** 272
13 (14).1: **1** 218
14 (15).5: **3** 179
16 (17).4: **2** 365; **3** 197
17 (18).12: **2** 83
17 (18).28: **1** 245, 252; **2** 346
18 (19).2: **3** 38
18 (19).5: **2** 41, 153, 312, 415
18 (19).6: **2** 72, 294, 410; **3** 12
18 (19).7: **2** 101
18 (19).11: **1** 350; **2** 106
18 (19).13: **3** 203
20 (21).12: **2** 297
21 (22).7: **2** 108
21 (22).21-22: **2** 200
21 (22).21: **3** 17, 47
21 (22).23: **2** 199
22 (23).5: **2** 403, 411, 419; **3** 52
23 (24).1: **1** 163
24 (25).1: **2** 471
24 (25).15: **1** 208; **3** 29

25 (26).5: **3** 222
26 (27).1: **2** 122
26 (27).3: **2** 122
26 (27).13: **2** 4
30 (31).19: **2** 426
31 (32).1: **1** 190
31 (32).5: **1** 290
31 (32).9: **2** 88, 196
31 (32).11: **2** 107
33 (34).2: **1** 368; **2** 400
33 (34).3: **2** 271
33 (34).7: **1** 244, 250
33 (34).3: **1** 115, 147; **2** 121, 403, 491
33 (34).15: **1** 83, 324; **3** 37
33 (34).17: **1** 218
35 (36).6: **1** 127, 132
35 (36).10: **2** 421
36 (37).8: **2** 107
36 (37).20: **1** 244, 251
37 (38).9: **1** 339; **3** 17, 46
37 (38).14: **2** 353
38 (39).2: **3** 222
38 (39).13: **2** 493
40 (41)5: **1** 34, 293; **2** 383
41 (42).3: **2** 109
41 (42).6: **1** 172
43 (44).8: **2** 36
43 (44).13: **1** 332
44 (45).3: **2** 24
44 (45).11: **2** 5, 65
44 (45).17: **2** 168
45 (46).11: **2** 87, 93
46 (47).7: **1** 367
48 (49).13, 21: **2** 88, 94, 103, 196
48 (49).13: **3** 51
49 (50).3: **2** 245
49 (50).16: **2** 248

49 (50).18: **1** 210
49 (50).20: **2** 244
49 (50).21: **1** 287; **2** 245 (quater), 246, 247
49 (50).22: **2** 247 (bis)
49 (50).23: **2** 249
50 (51).3: **2** 255 (ter)
50 (51).5: **1** 34; **2** 103, 247, 256
50 (51).7: **1** 223; **2** 209
50 (51).9: **2** 209
50 (51).13: **3** 103
50 (51).14: **3** 98
50 (51).19: **2** 107, 483
51 (52).10: **1** 86
54 (55).7: **1** 171; **2** 8; **3** 201
55 (56).11: **2** 271
56 (57).8: **3** 157
57 (58).5-6: **1** 348
59 (60).5: **2** 404, 419
60 (61).3: **2** 66
61 (62).2, 6: **3** 157
65 (66).12: **2** 472
67 (68).11: **2** 129
67 (68).19: **2** 36, 57
68 (69).3: **2** 233
68 (69).5: **2** 152, 195
68 (69).10: **2** 316
68 (69).15-16: **1** 236
68 (69).16: **2** 406; **3** 81
68 (69).24: **1** 251; **2** 39, 127, 133
68 (69).30: **3** 209
68 (69).34: **1** 244
71 (72).6: **2** 180
72 (73).5-7: **1** 35; **2** 100
72 (73).17: **3** 141
72 (73).20: **1** 135
72 (73).26: **2** 404

72 (73).27-28: **1** 111
72 (73).27: **1** 351
72 (73).28: **1** 110; **2** 270, 432
73 (74).19: **2** 123
74 (75).9: **1** 244
74 (75).11: **1** 244
75 (76).2: **2** 61, 415
75 (76).12: **2** 257, 259, 261
76 (77).3: **3** 226
77 (78).25: **3** 66
77 (78).60: **1** 333
79 (80).6: **2** 138
79 (80).14: **2** 222
81 (82).8: **2** 415 *(bis)*
83 (84).3: **2** 404
83 (84).4: **2** 8, 274
83 (84).5: **2** 314; **3** 224
83 (84).8, 5: **1** 255
84 (85).12: **2** 132; **3** 12
85 (86).13: **2** 323
87 (88).5-6: **2** 56
87 (88).5: **1** 65
87 (88).7: **2** 56
90 (91).2-3: **2** 474
90 (91).3: **1** 205
90 (91).5: **2** 122
90 (91).13: **1** 92
93 (94).2: **1** 246
93 (94).18: **2** 166
93 (94).21: **1** 65
94 (95).6: **2** 382; **3** 49
95 (96).5: **1** 264
96 (97).7: **1** 264
97 (98).4: **2** 241
97 (98).5: **2** 241
97 (98).6: **2** 241 *(bis)*
100 (101).7: **3** 221
101 (102).10: **1** 313; **3** 17, 46
102 (103).3: **2** 107

102 (103).8: **2** 323
102 (103).10: **3** 159
102 (103).12: **3** 159
102 (103).17-18: **1** 45
103 (104).15: **3** 158
103 (104).19-20: **2** 264
103 (104).20-21: **2** 264
103 (104).20: **2** 265, 268
103 (104).21: **2** 268
103 (104).22: **2** 265 *(bis)*
103 (104).23: **2** 266
103 (104).24: **2** 266 *(ter)*
103 (104).25-26: **2** 267
103 (104).25: **2** 267
103 (104).26: **2** 267
105 (106).3: **1** 45, 120
105 (106).30-31: **1** 34
108 (109).7: **2** 383
108 (109).18: **1** 217
109 (110).3: **2** 294
111 (112).5, 7: **1** 131
111 (112).5: **2** 362
111 (112).7: **1** 289; **2** 355
111 (112).9: **1** 246; **2** 291, 356
111 (112).10: **3** 126
112 (113).3: **2** 61
112 (113).7: **2** 107
113B (115).8: **2** 416
114 (116).3-4: **2** 254
115 (116).12: **3** 128, 160, 190
115 (116).13: **3** 160
115 (116).15: **3** 128
115 (116).16-17: **2** 257, 492; **3** 94
117 (118).1: **1** 290
117 (118).8: **2** 51
117 (118).10: **1** 325
117 (118).22: **2** 202
117 (118).24: **3** 72

118 (119).2, 11: **1** 46
118 (119).28: **2** 121
118 (119).37: **1** 208; **2** 427;
  **3** 30
118 (119).51: **1** 245
118 (119).62: **3** 52
118 (119).73: **3** 169
118 (119).78: **1** 245, 252, 351
118 (119).81: **2** 404
118 (119).85: **2** 272
118 (119).96: **2** 269
118 (119).103: **1** 51, 350; **2**
  108, 130, 182, 193; **3** 84
118 (119).105: **1** 18, 354
118 (119).137: **1** 173; **2** 243
120 (121).1: **2** 174
120 (121).4: **2** 377
122 (123).1: **3** 29
123 (124).7-8: **2** 269
124 (125).4: **1** 247
124 (125).5: **1** 255
125 (126).5: **2** 380, 384; **3** 87,
  114, 188
125 (126).6: **1** 54; **2** 384
126 (127).1: **3** 161
128 (129).4: **1** 248
131 (132).15: **1** 244, 250, 252
135 (136).25: **2** 268
137 (138).6: **3** 94
138 (139).7: **3** 104
140 (141).3-4: **3** 222
140 (141).4: **1** 8, 238
140 (141).5: **1** 293; **2** 273; **3**
  198
141 (142).8: **2** 60
143 (144).1: **2** 97
145  (146).9: **1** 250
147.12, 14: **1** 180
147.13: **1** 180

148.3: **2** 41
149.5: **2** 155 *(bis)*

Proverbs
  2.11: **1** 226, 227
  3.9-10: **1** 163
  3.10: **1** 164
  3.12: **2** 100
  3.18: **2** 104
  3.24-25: **2** 122
  3.34: **1** 245; **3** 61
  4.23: **1** 208; **2** 77; **3** 207
  5.3-4: **2** 405; **3** 188, 198
  6.27-28, 26: **1** 206
  6.26: **3** 19
  7.23: **2** 196
  8.17: **1** 184, 186
  8.35: **3** 157
  9.2: **2** 411
  9.8: **3** 155
  9.9: **3** 204
  10.6: **1** 249
  10.7: **3** 126
  11.18: **2** 197
  11.28: **1** 247
  12.28: **1** 177, 198; **3** 147
  13.8: **1** 142
  13.25: **2** 120
  14.13: **3** 87
  16.5: **1** 247, 364
  17.5: **1** 178
  18.3: **1** 300, 309; **2** 99, 102
  18.17: **1** 310
  18.19: **1** 320, 349
  18.21: **2** 395
  19.5: **1** 12, 81, 99
  19.9: **2** 424
  19.17: **2** 362

20.13 (20): **1** 13, 82, 101; **2** 353, 423; **3** 209
21.17: **1** 235
21.20: **1** 329; **2** 213, 438
22.2: **1** 50
22.20-21: **2** 148
23.14: **3** 206
23.29-30: **1** 233
23.31-33: **1** 235
23.31-32: **3** 20
24.16: **2** 51; **3** 203
24.17-18: **1** 178
25.21-22: **1** 179
26.11: **1** 73, 150, 160; **3** 207, 217
27.1: **1** 117, 191; **2** 141; **3** 89
27.6: **3** 198
28.1: **2** 122
28.9: **1** 7, 48
28.27: **1** 152
30.27: **2** 83
31.4-5: **1** 235
31.10: **2** 275 *(bis)*, 276
31.13: **2** 277
31.19: **2** 278
31.20: **2** 278, 279
31.21: **2** 279, 280
31.22: **2** 280, 281

Ecclesiastes
1.5: **2** 461
3.4: **3** 114
5.3-4: **1** 72
5.4: **3** 198
7.10: **2** 352
7.16: **2** 379
7.19: **1** 54

Canticle of Canticles
1.4: **2** 66, 209

1.13: **2** 129
2.15: **2** 186
4.8: **1** 67

Wisdom
1.4: **1** 289
1.11: **1** 12, 82, 120, 365; **2** 424; **3** 61, 203
2.24-25: **1** 365; **2** 46; **3** 61
2.24: **1** 12, 99; **2** 40
5.6: **2** 264
5.7: **2** 321
8.16: **2** 45
9.15: **1** 11

Sirach (Ecclesiasticus)
2.1: **2** 471
2.14: **1** 74
3.33 (29): **1** 61, 129, 152, 155, 223; **2** 339; **3** 170, 176
5.6-7: **1** 318
5.8-9: **1** 97
5.8: **1** 281, 298, 299, 303, 311, 317, 365; **2** 141, 461, 483; **3** 89
5.13: **2** 87
7.40 (36): **3** 26
9.5: **1** 204
10.7: **1** 246
10.14 (12): **1** 365; **3** 194
10.21: **1** 246
11.4: **3** 150
11.7: **2** 319
12.2: **1** 53
13.19 (14): **3** 152
14.2: **1** 311
14.12: **1** 279, 318; **3** 26
15.9: **2** 248
15.17-18: **2** 329

15.17: **2** 320, 330
15.18: **2** 320
18.26: **3** 89
19.1: **1** 235; **3** 203
19.2: **1** 214, 234; **3** 20
19.7: **2** 367
19.10 (9): **3** 136
21.1: **1** 160
23.12 (11): **1** 12, 82, 120; **3** 62
24.29: **1** 28, 52; **2** 404
27.6: **2** 51, 165
28.3-5: **1** 130, 178
28.6: **1** 279; **3** 26
28.22: **2** 137
29.15: **1** 129; **2** 339
30.8: **2** 99
30.12: **2** 99
30.24: **2** 142
31.8: **1** 246; **2** 282, 287
31.9: **2** 287
31.10: **2** 282, 287
31.32: **1** 235
31.35-40: **1** 235
34.25: **2** 437
34.30: **1** 150, 159; **2** 219

Isaiah
1.3: **1** 163; **2** 192
3.12: **1** 294
5.2: **1** 86
5.4: **2** 70
5.6: **2** 180
5.7: **2** 128
5.13: **1** 7, 47
5.20: **1** 272
6.1-3: **3** 104
6.5: **3** 104
6.8-9: **3** 104

6.10: **2** 105
7.14: **2** 132
7.15: **3** 220
8.18: **1** 23; **3** 112, 183
9.5-6: **2** 17
13.9: **2** 10
26.10-11, 9: **1** 28
26.9: **3** 52
26.18: **2** 343
29.13: **2** 248
30.6: **2** 123
30.15: **1** 296, 299; **2** 139, 327, 483; **3** 85
35.10: **1** 330
40.3-4: **3** 125
40.3: **3** 121, 123
40.4: **3** 123
40.6-8: **2** 459
40.12: **3** 105
43.2: **2** 363
46.8: **1** 183
50.1: **2** 224
50.4: **3** 220
52.5: **2** 118
52.7: **3** 136
53.1: **2** 386
53.2-3: **2** 293
53.2: **2** 291 *(bis)*, 292, 293
53.3: **2** 293 *(ter)*
53.4-6: **2** 293
53.4, 11: **2** 377
53.6-8: **2** 294
53.7-8: **2** 294
53.7: **1** 65; **2** 353
53.8: **2** 294, 295 *(ter)*
53.9: **2** 295 *(bis)*, 296
55.6-7: **1** 95
55.6: **2** 461
56.10: **1** 7

58.1: **1** 4, 29, 33, 282, 367; **2** 169, 473; **3** 180
58.6-7: **3** 54
58.7: **1** 128, 167; **2** 362; **3** 53, 54, 55, 96
58.9: **1** 155; **2** 363
63.17: **2** 100
65.1: **2** 420
65.20: **2** 124
66.2: **1** 246; **2** 87; **3** 97
66.24: **2** 106

Jeremiah
  1.5: **3** 169
  2.27: **2** 134
  2.30: **1** 203; **2** 221
  6.7-8: **3** 197
  9.1: **1** 332
  9.21: **1** 207, 327
  17.5: **2** 367
  18.7-8: **2** 141
  24.1-2: **2** 128
  31.15: **3** 139
  48.10: **1** 355
  50.23: **1** 206; **2** 243

Lamentations
  5.3: **2** 448

Baruch
  3.38: **2** 155

Ezechiel
  3.17: **1** 11
  3.18: **1** 5, 17, 29, 32, 282; **2** 304, 473; **3** 122, 154
  3.19, 18: **1** 4
  3.19: **3** 180

18.4, 20: **2** 376
18.6: **1** 225
18.20: **1** 162, 215, 221, 317
18.21-22: **1** 94, 280, 317; **3** 90
18.21: **1** 296, 311
18.32: **1** 96; **2** 251, 327
24.11: **2** 407; **3** 82
33.2-7: **3** 185
33.7-9: **3** 186
33.11-12: **1** 312
33.11: **2** 78, 99, 327
33.12: **1** 365
34.4: **1** 22
34.10: **1** 22
37.27: **3** 124

Daniel
  2.34: **2** 415
  4.24: **1** 155; **2** 363; **3** 17, 47
  7.10: **2** 407; **3** 81
  12.3: **1** 49

Hosea (Osee)
  4.12: **1** 365
  6.3: **2** 74
  7.4: **1** 215; **3** 19
  9.10: **2** 128

Joel
  2.12: **3** 49

Amos
  4.7: **1** 17
  8.11: **1** 16, 32

Jonah
  3.4,6: **2** 301
  3.4: **2** 247
  4.5: **2** 299

Micah (Michea)
  5.4-5: **2** 207

Habakkuk
  1.16: **2** 444
  3.2, LXX: **2** 131, 142

Haggai (Aggeus)
  2.9: **1** 174

Zechariah
  1.3: **3** 85

7.9: **2** 315, 318
9.9: **2** 160

Malachi
  1.2-3: **2** 113
  2.7: **1** 8, 53
  3.8-12: **1** 165
  3.10: **1** 163
  4.2: **2** 114, 264

(BOOKS OF THE NEW TESTAMENT)

St. Matthew
 1.2: **2** 21
 2.12: **3** 37
 2.18: **3** 139
 3.7-9: **2** 416
 3.7: **2** 5
 3.10: **1** 83, 186; **3** 80, 91
 3.12: **1** 43; **2** 407; **3** 81, 92 *(bis)*
 3.15: **1** 64
 3.17: **2** 39
 4.4: **1** 16, 19, 51
 4.17: **2** 300
 5.3: **1** 244, 251, 253
 5.5 (4): **1** 36, 282, 324; **2** 380; **3** 50, 87, 188
 5.6: **1** 28; **2** 109, 148
 5.7: **1** 127, 131, 170; **2** 356, 361; **3** 153, 172
 5.8: **1** 255; **3** 95
 5.9: **2** 374
 5.13: **1** 23; **2** 218
 5.14-15: **1** 18
 5.14: **2** 41, 275
 5.16: **2** 118, 308; **3** 7, 196
 5.17: **2** 416; **3** 25
 5.22: **1** 70
 5.23-24: **1** 197; **3** 130
 5.24: **3** 165
 5.25-26: **2** 305, 448
 5.25: **2** 304, 305
 5.26: **2** 407
 5.28: **1** 207
 5.34, 37: **1** 82
 5.40: **2** 465
 5.43: **1** 178

5.44-45: **1** 86, 186; **3** 131, 145, 146
5.44: **1** 189, 197; **2** 375
5.45: **2** 119
5.46-47: **1** 187
5.48: **3** 145
6.1: **2** 308
6.3-4: **2** 308
6.3: **2** 308, 309
6.5-6: **2** 310
6.9, 12: **1** 186
6.9: **2** 312 *(bis)*, 486 *(bis)*
6.10: **1** 259; **2** 313 *(bis)*, 486 *(bis)*
6.11: **2** 313, 486; **3** 157
6.12-13: **1** 343
6.12, 14-15: **1** 195
6.12: **1** 99, 144, 149, 171, 189, 194, 305, 351; **2** 53, 135, 314, 446, 484, 486; **3** 10, 60 *(bis)*, 68, 178, 205
6.13: **2** 314
6.14-15: **1** 130, 188; **3** 129, 147
6.14: **1** 144, 149, 194; **3** 88, 134, 206
6.15: **1** 194, 297
6.17-18: **2** 309
6.19, 21: **1** 168
6.20: **1** 80; **2** 493
6.24: **1** 9, 74, 269
6.26: **2** 268
6.33: **1** 9; **2** 311
7.1-2: **2** 315
7.1: **2** 315, 317, 318
7.2: **1** 255, 274

7.3, 5: **3** 137
7.3: **2** 307, 317, 485
7.5: **1** 3
7.7: **3** 99 *(bis)*, 225
7.8: **2** 166; **3** 99
7.9-11: **3** 227
7.12: **1** 196, 214, 221, 320, 324; **2** 283, 319; **3** 57
7.13-14: **2** 319, 324
7.14, 13: **2** 327; **3** 87
7.13: **2** 77, 330
7.14: **3** 43, 197
7.15: **1** 319; **3** 219
7.16: **1** 298
7.17-19: **1** 116
7.17, 19: **1** 136
7.19: **2** 357
7.21: **1** 71
7.23: **2** 15, 147
8.5-9: **3** 39
8.10: **1** 252
8.11: **3** 40
8.12: **1** 279; **2** 9; **3** 141
8.13: **2** 107
9.5: **2** 321
9.17: **3** 59
10.8: **2** 232
10.14-15: **2** 13
10.16: **2** 68, 81
10.22: **1** 70, 256, 350; **2** 203, 354; **3** 10, 68, 92, 193, 201
10.28: **1** 69
11.11: **3** 117, 121
11.28-29: **1** 302
11.29: **1** 60, 173, 185, 247; **2** 240, 322, 386; **3** 61, 145, 194
11.30: **1** 334; **2** 134, 365; **3** 214

12.7: **1** 131
12.28: **3** 105
12.29: **2** 164, 201
12.33: **1** 73
12.34: **1** 368 *(bis)*; **3** 195
12.35: **1** 150
12.36: **1** 359; **2** 353
12.43-45: **2** 4, 203, 219
13.7: **1** 11
13.43: **1** 288; **2** 41
13.55: **2** 292
14.8: **3** 125
15.24: **2** 179, 199, 426
15.27: **2** 57; **3** 39
15.28: **3** 39
16.13: **2** 212
16.16: **2** 416
16.24: **2** 127
16.26: **1** 142; **2** 428; **3** 42
16.27: **1** 279, 286; **2** 297, 358, 483
17.5: **1** 56
18.15-17: **1** 210
18.15: **1** 142
18.16-18: **1** 143
18.19: **1** 320
18.20: **2** 333 *(bis)*
18.32-35: **1** 187, 196
19.12: **1** 186
19.17: **2** 337
19.18-19: **2** 337
19.21: **1** 61; **2** 337
19.22: **2** 338
19.23: **2** 338
19.25: **2** 338
20.28: **2** 180
21.43: **2** 394
22.12-13: **1** 230, 361
22.12: **2** 143, 281, 332, 405,

449, 493; **3** 11, 149, 165
22.13: **2** 143, 332, 347, 449, 493; **3** 12, 149, 165, 166
22.21: **1** 159
22.30: **1** 288
22.37, 39: **1** 12; **2** 132
22.37: **2** 272, 321, 378; **3** 146
22.39-40: **2** 321
22.39: **1** 107; **2** 272, 306, 378; **3** 146
22.40: **1** 12, 199; **2** 96, 132, 272, 378
23.3: **1** 274, 278
23.5: **1** 255
23.9: **1** 251
23.12: **3** 165, 194
23.27: **1** 323
24.12: **1** 179, 335; **2** 274, 340
24.13: **2** 354; **3** 10, 68, 92, 193, 201
24.19: **2** 339, 340, 342
24.29: **2** 10; **3** 141
25.1: **2** 344
25.4-7: **2** 348
25.4: **1** 327
25.5: **2** 348
25.7: **2** 348
25.8: **2** 350
25.9-11: **2** 348
25.9: **1** 328 *(bis);* **2** 350 *(ter)*
25.11: **2** 347
25.12, 41: **2** 118
25.12: **1** 48, 180; **2** 347
25.21, 23: **2** 81; **3** 14
25.21: **1** 118, 139, 289, 361; **2** 28, 223, 331, 332, 347, 454, 493; **3** 151, 168, 183
25.23: **1** 315
25.25: **1** 11

25.26-27: **3** 182
25.26, 30: **1** 30
25.30: **1** 10; **3** 182
25.31-35, 41-42: **1** 84, 91
25.34-35: **1** 130, 132, 139, 146, 257; **2** 360, 468; **3** 14, 172
25.34-36: **1** 99; **2** 373; **3** 144
25.34-35, 37, 40: **1** 157
25.34: **1** 87, 102, 144, 288; **2** 48, 80, 118, 147, 232, 247, 282, 336, 354 *(bis),* 355, 359, 365, 393, 402, 449, 477, 494; **3** 62, 112, 168, 223
25.35: **1** 81; **2** 14, 241, 356, 477; **3** 55
25.35-36: **1** 133
25.37: **2** 477
25.40, 42: **1** 128
25.40: **1** 100, 134, 138, 233; **2** 238, 350, 362, 365, 477; **3** 47, 55, 172
25.41, 34: **1** 135
25.41-43: **2** 477
25.41-42: **1** 139, 297; **2** 342, 356, 360
25.41: **1** 219, 285; **2** 80, 147, 355 *(bis),* 359, 361, 363, 373, 402, 406, 453, 477; **3** 14, 55, 80, 91, 143, 151, 172
25.42: **1** 142; **3** 55, 91
25.43-45: **1** 125
25.43: **2** 56; **3** 55
25.45: **3** 55
25.46: **1** 91
26.33: **3** 67
26.34: **3** 67

26.35: **3** 67
26.41: **1** 355; **2** 176; **3** 52, 67
27.23: **1** 202
27.25: **2** 229
27.62-65: **2** 296
28.5: **2** 296
28.10: **2** 73
28.12: **2** 296
28.13: **2** 296
28.18: **2** 36
28.19: **2** 230, 418; **3** 109
28.10: **1** 133

St. Mark
8.34: **2** 365 *(bis)*, 368, 369
9.22: **1** 67
9.47, 43, 45: **3** 166
10.21: **2** 337
10.23: **2** 338
12.43-44: **2** 470

St. Luke
1.35: **1** 57
2.10-11: **2** 401
2.10: **2** 400
2.14: **1** 151, 183; **2** 207, 397,
    413, 469, 470; **3** 38, 54
2.34: **2** 464
3.4: **3** 123
3.5: **1** 50, 358; **3** 123
6.25: **1** 36, 282; **3** 50, 87, 116
6.31: **1** 13
6.37-38: **1** 193
6.38, 37: **1** 149, 194, 195,
    297; **2** 489; **3** 60, 133, 173
6.37: **1** 294
6.38: **1** 128
6.45: **1** 368; **2** 67, 370 *(bis)*,
    371, 373, 374

6.46: **1** 71, 74, 84, 86, 197;
    **2** 358, 437
8.23: **2** 458
8.24: **2** 458
9.23: **1** 60
9.48: **2** 47
10.2: **2** 180
10.16: **1** 346
10.27: **2** 431, 492
10.30: **2** 376 *(ter)*
10.33: **2** 377
10.34: **2** 377 *(ter)*
10.35: **2** 378
11.9: **3** 225
11.11-13: **3** 227
11.20: **2** 395; **3** 105
11.24-26: **1** 160; **2** 64; **3** 217
11.24, 26: **1** 114
11.41: **1** 86, 129, 146, 152,
    170; **2** 339; **3** 176
12.13: **2** 208
12.14: **2** 208
12.16-20: **1** 141
12.16: **2** 474
12.19: **2** 474
12.20: **2** 475
12.32: **2** 436
12.33: **1** 129
12.35-37: **1** 337
12.46: **2** 382
12.49: **2** 70, 83, 178, 181, 287,
    418; **3** 170, 207
13.2-3: **1** 333
13.6: **2** 128
13.7: **2** 381
13.8-9: **2** 381
13.25: **2** 347, 348
13.27: **1** 48
13.29: **3** 40 *(bis)*

14.11: **1** 358 *(bis);* **3** 123
14.12-14: **3** 13
15.7: **2** 330; **3** 112
15.13: **2** 385
15.15: **2** 385
15.17-18: **2** 385
15.17: **2** 367, 385
15.18-19: **2** 386
15.20: **2** 386 *(ter)*
15.22: **2** 387
15.23: **2** 387
15.25-26: **2** 387
15.16: **2** 388
15.27-28: **2** 388 *(bis)*
15.29: **2** 388
15.31: **2** 389
16.16: **2** 171
16.19: **2** 390, 393 *(bis),* 394, 476 *(bis);* **3** 116, 150
16.21: **2** 476
16.22-23: **2** 476
16.22: **2** 390
16.24: **1** 156; **2** 364, 392
16.25: **2** 364, 392, 395
16.26: **2** 396
16.28: **2** 391
16.29, 31: **2** 396
16.29: **2** 81, 171
17.6: **1** 67
17.19: **1** 67
17.21: **1** 106; **2** 397, 413
17.32: **2** 259, 262
18.1: **1** 355
18.8: **1** 336
18.11: **2** 248
18.13: **2** 249, 412
18.14: **1** 356; **2** 249
18.25: **2** 435
18.27: **2** 435

19.8: **2** 469; **3** 47
19.10: **1** 133
19.21: **3** 187
19.22-23: **1** 3, 10
19.22: **3** 187
19.23, 30: **1** 33
19.23: **1** 30; **3** 187
21.3-4: **2** 362, 470
21.18: **3** 156
21.19: **3** 157
23.21: **2** 222
23.34: **1** 172, 185; **2** 293, 322; **3** 133
23.42: **2** 417; **3** 73
24.11: **2** 265
24.17: **2** 416
24.19: **2** 416
24.21: **2** 265, 417 *(bis)*
24.25: **2** 47
24.26, 46-47, 27: **2** 417
24.32: **2** 418 *(bis)*
24.44 **2** 295
24.46: **2** 295
24.47: **2** 295

St. John
1.1-2: **2** 281
1.1: **2** 33, 293, 321; **3** 66, 97
1.3: **2** 294
1.5: **3** 97
1.9: **2** 114
1.11: **2** 133
1.14: **2** 33, 281, 321; **3** 66, 97
1.16: **3** 118
1.17: **2** 396
1.23: **3** 119
1.27: **2** 72
1.47: **2** 32, 131
1.51: **2** 32

2.1: **2** 402, 409
2.3: **2** 410
2.6: **2** 410, 418
2.10: **2** 411, 412
3.4: **2** 436
3.5: **3** 71
3.13: **2** 31
3.14: **2** 152
3.16: **1** 184; **2** 13
3.18: **2** 357
3.20: **1** 134
3.27: **3** 162
3.29: **2** 72 *(bis)*
3.30: **3** 118, 121
4.5-6: **2** 419, 420
4.7: **2** 420 *(bis)*
4.10: **2** 421
4.11: **2** 421
4.13-14: **2** 116, 421
4.14: **1** 347
4.34: **2** 426
5.8: **1** 199; **2** 422, 423
5.14: **1** 160; **2** 5, 436
5.22: **2** 136
6.27: **1** 53; **2** 38
6.41: **2** 185; **3** 158
6.44: **3** 162
6.51: **2** 58, 120, 121
6.54 (53): **3** 7
6.59: **2** 120
7.24: **2** 283, 315, 476
7.37-38: **1** 357; **2** 115
7.38: **1** 367; **2** 110, 192; **3** 211
8.12: **2** 48, 114
8.34: **1** 364; **3** 216
8.44: **2** 5, 65, 447
8.48: **2** 292
8.56: **2** 14, 179

9.2: **2** 424
9.3: **2** 425
9.6: **2** 426
9.31: **2** 425
9.35-37: **2** 426
10.16: **2** 35
10.30: **2** 418
12.6: **2** 229
12.24-25: **2** 61
12.25: **1** 112; **2** 427, 429
12.31: **1** 113
12.35: **3** 48, 90
12.39-41: **3** 104
12.43: **2** 126
13.2: **2** 266, 371
13.4-5: **3** 65
13.8: **3** 65
13.35: **1** 187, 197; **2** 49
14.6: **2** 74, 86, 93, 320
14.9: **2** 208 *(bis)*; **3** 104
14.15: **1** 86
14.20: **2** 202
14.21: **1** 71, 84, 197; **2** 358; **3** 91
14.23: **1** 301; **2** 67, 358; **3** 91, 95, 172
14.26: **3** 108
14.27: **1** 197; **2** 121, 207, 432
14.30: **1** 64; **2** 36, 152
15.5, 4: **3** 162
15.5: **3** 67, 162
15.12: **1** 187; **2** 49
15.13: **1** 113
15.14: **3** 91
15.16: **2** 111
15.18: **2** 174; **3** 144
15.22: **2** 107
15.26: **3** 107, 108 *(bis)*
16.13: **3** 98

16.20: **2** 340; **3** 114
16.22: **2** 401
16.24: **1** 320
16.33: **2** 164, 340; **3** 114
18.4: **1** 65
18.31: **2** 188
19.6: **2** 295
19.10-11: **1** 326
19.10: **2** 480
19.11: **2** 480
19.15: **2** 229
19.34: **2** 414
20.22: **2** 228; **3** 107
20.27: **2** 27
21.17: **1** 6, 11; **3** 181, 190

Acts of the Apostles
2.3: **2** 69
2.4: **3** 98
2.13: **2** 127
4.26: **1** 64
4.32: **2** 8, 261, 388, 389
5.1-11: **1** 203
5.4: **1** 336
5.11: **2** 214
7.48: **3** 173
7.51-52: **3** 132
7.56: **3** 127
7.59: **3** 133
7.60: **1** 185; **3** 128, 133
9.1ff.: **3** 159
9.4: **1** 125; **2** 31
10.9-15: **2** 438
10.11-12: **3** 41
10.13: **2** 439, 441
10.15: **2** 440
10.28: **2** 440
10.34: **1** 211
13.46: **2** 30, 129, 204, 230

14.21 (22): **2** 51, 111, 339, 379, 471; **3** 115, 197
20.26-27: **1** 5
20.26: **1** 5
20.31: **1** 5, 29; **3** 183

Romans
1.17: **3** 135
1.21-22: **2** 86
1.21: **2** 93
1.32: **1** 210, 262
2.4-5: **1** 312; **2** 99
2.5: **2** 245
2.21: **1** 3
3.5: **1** 330
5.5: **1** 200
5.6: **1** 185
5.16: **2** 163
6.9: **1** 326
6.12: **2** 253
6.13: **2** 202
6.19: **2** 202
7.15: **2** 443, 444
7.23: **2** 210, 442, 444, 445
7.24-25: **2** 210
7.24: **2** 445
7.25: **2** 445 *(bis)*
8.3: **1** 64
8.7: **2** 62
8.9: **2** 228; **3** 107, 109
8.14: **3** 216
8.15: **2** 75
8.18: **2** 165
8.23: **2** 387
8.24-25: **3** 228
8.24: **1** 331
8.26: **1** 259, 341; **2** 75
8.27: **2** 75
8.32: **1** 333; **2** 387

8.35, 38-39: **1** 181
8.35: **1** 267; **2** 8
8.39: **2** 8
9.14: **2** 101
9.16: **3** 161
9.22-23: **3** 173
10.3: **2** 394
10.4: **2** 270
10.10: **2** 395
10.14: **2** 312
11.1: **3** 159
11.17: **2** 23; **3** 40
11.18: **2** 128
11.25-26: **2** 388
12.11: **2** 274
12.14: **1** 244 *(bis)*
12.17, 14, 21: **1** 188
12.18: **3** 145
13.10: **2** 270
13.12: **2** 447
14.2: **2** 106
14.7: **3** 74, 197, 214
14.17: **2** 397
15.4: **2** 63
16.20: **2** 76

1 Corinthians
1.10: **2** 387
1.11-12: **2** 186
1.23: **2** 68
1.24: **1** 57; **2** 217
2.6-7: **2** 32
2.6: **3** 160
2.9: **2** 412
2.12: **3** 162 *(ter)*
2.13: **2** 171
3.2: **1** 31; **3** 160
3.3: **3** 223
3.6, 9: **1** 7

3.6: **1** 18; **3** 191
3.9: **3** 191, 196
3.11-15: **2** 450
3.11: **3** 193
3.12: **2** 455
3.13, 15: **2** 452
3.13: **2** 9, 455
3.15: **2** 449, 453, 456; **3** 81
3.17: **2** 204; **3** 59, 164, 169,
    174 *(bis)*
4.3: **1** 328
4.7: **3** 157, 163
4.9: **2** 237, 335
4.11: **2** 120
4.15: **2** 73
4.20: **1** 75; **3** 91
4.21: **2** 147
5.6: **1** 269
5.11: **1** 210, 217; **3** 153
6.9-10: **1** 81, 209, 212, 240
6.9: **1** 215, 221
6.10: **1** 12, 82, 100, 120, 236,
    242, 244, 273, 277; **2** 423,
    451; **3** 20, 203
6.16: **3** 19
6.18: **1** 81, 204, 214; **2** 32,
    57; **3** 19
6.19: **3** 59, 109, 164
6.20: **2** 60, 134
7.9: **1** 161
7.24: **2** 263
7.27: **2** 263
7.29: **1** 212
7.29, 5: **1** 216
7.29, 32: **1** 258
7.32: **1** 21
7.38: **2** 263
7.40: **2** 259
9.11: **1** 53

9.22: **1** 23
9.24: **2** 377, 492
9.26: **2** 492; **3** 146
9.27: **2** 194, 195
10.1, 4: **2** 110
10.2: **2** 104
10.4: **2** 132, 178, 181
10.9: **3** 208
10.10: **2** 353
10.11: **2** 3, 11, 20, 25, 32, 38, 62, 163, 216
10.20-21 (21): **1** 262, 269, 270; **3** 30
10.31: **3** 52
11.3: **2** 30
11.15: **2** 188
11.19: **2** 145
11.27-28: **3** 68
11.27: **1** 224
11.29: **3** 7, 130
11.32: **2** 165
12.4: **3** 100
12.8-9, 11: **3** 99
12.11: **3** 100
12.26: **1** 124
13.1, 3-4: **1** 145
13.3: **1** 122, 188, 197, 316; **2** 470; **3** 130
14.15: **2** 334
14.37-38: **1** 7; **2** 15
14.38: **1** 47
15.5-6: **1** 58
15.10: **3** 161, 190
15.19: **1** 88
15.22: **2** 163, 231, 376
15.34: **2** 33
15.54: **2** 445
15.55-56: **2** 444
15.55: **2** 444 *(bis)*; **3** 23

2 Corinthians
1.7: **2** 480; **3** 144
2.2: **2** 380
2.11: **1** 255
3.6: **2** 11, 38, 104, 105, 209
3.15: **2** 171
4.18: **2** 226, 310
5.3: **1** 46; **2** 281
5.6: **2** 492; **3** 115
5.10: **1** 286, 323; **2** 358, 448, 484
5.17: **2** 411
6.1: **2** 219; **3** 76, 191
6.2: **3** 44
6.16: **2** 67, 177; **3** 9, 124, 175
7.5: **2** 464
7.10: **2** 380, 383
8.9: **2** 240; **3** 186
8.13: **1** 148
8.14: **1** 138
8.15: **1** 50
9.6: **1** 138
9.7: **1** 152; **2** 29; **3** 155
10.4-5: **2** 170
11.2-3: **1** 327
11.2: **1** 251; **2** 72, 173, 186, 347, 387
11.3: **2** 186
11.24-25: **2** 464
11.26: **2** 464
11.27: **2** 120
11.28: **2** 378
12.21: **2** 464

Galatians
3.27: **2** 202, 279 *(bis)*
4.4: **2** 130
4.6: **2** 75
4.10,11: **1** 268

5.6: **2** 96, 490
5.9: **3** 28
5.14: **1** 122, 187, 189, 196; **2** 308
5.15: **2** 84, 90, 95
5.16: **2** 443
5.17: **2** 175, 398, 444
5.19-21: **2** 26
5.22-23: **2** 26
6.1: **1** 349
6.2: **1** 200; **2** 53; **3** 155, 190
6.3: **3** 162
6.7: **3** 90
6.8: **1** 54; **2** 106, 244
6.10: **1** 138, 323; **2** 244
6.14: **2** 153
6.16: **2** 131

Ephesians
1.4: **2** 118; **3** 25
2.8-9: **3** 163
2.14: **2** 35, 401; **3** 39
3.16-17: **2** 202, 371; **3** 174
3.17: **1** 115, 122, 146
4.5: **2** 436
4.8: **2** 57
4.25-26: **2** 457
4.25: **2** 456 *(bis)*
4.26-27: **2** 459
4.26: **2** 457; **3** 137
4.28: **2** 459
4.32: **2** 488
5.1: **1** 173; **3** 145
5.2: **1** 66, 185
5.8: **2** 76, 173
5.14: **2** 176, 234
5.15-16: **2** 461
5.16: **2** 461
5.18: **1** 214, 235, 240, 273; **2**
32
5.25: **1** 251
5.27: **1** 160; **2** 232, 452
5.29: **2** 428, 430
6.12: **2** 122; **3** 201
6.16, 14, 17: **3** 83
6.16: **2** 76, 137
6.17-18: **2** 125

Philippians
1.17: **2** 386
1.18: **1** 16
1.29, 6: **3** 163
2.6: **2** 293
2.7-8: **1** 60
2.7: **2** 15
2.8-9: **2** 17
2.8: **2** 228
2.12: **3** 199
2.13: **3** 163
3.13-14: **2** 261
3.20: **1** 117, 208; **2** 8, 191, 268, 325, 441
4.1: **1** 90
4.5-6: **1** 21
4.7: **2** 121
4.11: **3** 143
4.17: **2** 279

Colossians
1.10: **3** 25
1.20: **2** 72
2.17: **2** 438
3.1-2: **1** 21; **2** 234, 343
3.2: **2** 33
3.3: **2** 441
3.4: **1** 208
3.5: **1** 61; **2** 193
4.2: **1** 355; **2** 112, 334

4.6: **2** 217

1 Thessalonians
2.9: **1** 227
4.4-5: **1** 225
4.4-5, 12: **1** 212; **2** 446
4.6: **1** 100
4.12: **2** 349
4.17: **2** 10
5.14: **1** 349; **3** 191
5.17-18: **1** 355
5.17: **2** 87

2 Thessalonians
3.1: **3** 191
3.10: **1** 227

1 Timothy
1.5: **1** 114, 147; **2** 270
1.9: **3** 180
1.13: **2** 255; **3** 159, 160
2.8: **2** 112
3.1: **3** 179
4.13: **1** 6; **2** 87; **3** 181, 183
5.6: **1** 323; **2** 332
5.12: **2** 259
5.14: **2** 258
5.23: **1** 321
6.4: **3** 221
6.8-11: **1** 169
6.8: **2** 291, 369
6.9: **1** 246; **2** 370, 376
6.10-11: **2** 467
6.10: **1** 115, 118, 197, 336;
    **2** 32, 197, 467; **3** 18
6.17-19: **2** 107
6.17: **1** 252; **2** 338 *(ter)*
6.18-19: **1** 252; **2** 338
6.18: **1** 335; **2** 468

2 Timothy
2.4: **1** 6; **2** 109; **3** 181
2.5: **2** 336
2.19: **2** 15
3.1-4: **1** 337
3.2: **2** 367 *(bis)*
3.12: **2** 108, 111, 339, 463; **3**
    115
4.1-2: **1** 5, 29
4.2: **2** 304, 318; **3** 181
4.5: **1** 6
4.7-8: **2** 263; **3** 158
4.7: **2** 492

Titus
2.12: **3** 145

Hebrews
2.14: **2** 146
4.12: **2** 125
4.13: **1** 132
6.6: **1** 134
7.19: **2** 164, 227
10.31: **2** 406
11.4-40: **1** 67
11.6: **1** 67
11.13: **3** 143
11.36-37: **2** 479
11.38: **2** 479
12.6: **1** 35; **2** 51, 100, 165; **3**
    197
13.4: **1** 212, 215, 221; **3** 19
13.15: **1** 368
13.17: **2** 353, 473

James
1.17: **3** 162
1.20: **2** 353; **3** 209
1.26: **3** 198

2.10: **1** 121, 187; **2** 96
2.13: **1** 131, 157; **2** 297, 356
2.14-17: **1** 94
2.14: **3** 90
2.17: **3** 90
2.19: **1** 72; **2** 358
2.20: **2** 358, 490
2.26: **1** 69, 72, 75, 87
4.4: **1** 110
4.6: **1** 12, 82, 251, 357; **2** 352; **3** 18, 96, 221
4.7: **1** 359
4.11: **2** 353
4.15: **1** 112
5.1-3, 5: **3** 56
5.1-3: **1** 175
5.14-15: **1** 77, 101; **2** 482
5.16: **1** 290, 320
5.20: **1** 349; **3** 29

1 Peter
1.18-19: **2** 23, 60
1.18: **1** 345
2.9: **1** 20; **2** 173
2.21: **1** 172, 185; **3** 145
2.22: **1** 357
3.4: **2** 90
3.9: **1** 188
4.8: **1** 151; **2** 308; **3** 18
4.18: **2** 9
5.5: **3** 96
5.6: **2** 303, 352
5.8-9: **1** 359
5.8: **1** 327; **2** 122, 265; **3** 221

2 Peter
2.16: **2** 160
2.19: **1** 219, 364; **3** 216
2.20-22: **3** 217

2.20, 22: **1** 159
2.20: **2** 436
2.21: **1** 264; **3** 207
2.22: **1** 264; **2** 262; **3** 207
3.8: **2** 453
3.12: **2** 9; **3** 141

1 John
1.8: **2** 51, 242, 302, 487; **3** 202
2.1-2: **2** 139
2.6: **1** 185; **2** 322, 368
2.8: **2** 485
2.9, 11: **1** 188, 198; **2** 47
2.9: **2** 485, 486
2.11: **1** 12, 14, 130; **2** 318, 458; **3** 10, 137, 146
2.14, 13: **2** 150
2.15: **2** 291; **3** 42
2.16-17: **2** 171
2.17: **3** 43
3.2: **2** 286
3.14: **3** 10, 130, 137, 146
3.15: **1** 12, 14, 99, 130, 188, 198; **2** 47, 306, 424, 458, 485; **3** 10, 130, 137, 146, 178, 209
4.8: **1** 115, 121, 147, 181
4.20: **1** 188; **3** 10
5.1: **2** 489, 490

Revelation (Apocalypse)
2.7: **2** 109
3.15-16: **3** 206, 215
3.19: **1** 35; **2** 52, 100, 165; **3** 197
3.20: **1** 301, 364; **2** 372; **3** 9, 172

5.5: **1** 326
14.4: **2** 346
14.5: **2** 346
14.11: **2** 10; **3** 141

17.15: **2** 218
20.9: **3** 141
20.14, 15: **3** 141
22.11: **1** 35, 331; **3** 204

# THE FATHERS OF THE CHURCH SERIES

*(A series of approximately 100 volumes when completed)*

VOL. 1: THE APOSTOLIC FATHERS (1947)
> LETTER OF ST. CLEMENT OF ROME TO THE CORINTHIANS (trans. by Glimm)
> THE SO-CALLED SECOND LETTER (trans. by Glimm)
> LETTERS OF ST. IGNATIUS OF ANTIOCH (trans. by Walsh)
> LETTER OF ST. POLYCARP TO THE PHILIPPIANS (trans. by Glimm)
> MARTYRDOM OF ST. POLYCARP (trans. by Glimm)
> DIDACHE (trans. by Glimm)
> LETTER OF BARNABAS (trans. by Glimm)
> SHEPHERD OF HERMAS (1st printing only; trans. by Marique)
> LETTER TO DIOGNETUS (trans. by Walsh)
> FRAGMENTS OF PAPIAS (1st printing only; trans. by Marique)

VOL. 2: ST. AUGUSTINE (1947)
> CHRISTIAN INSTRUCTION (trans. by Gavigan)
> ADMONITION AND GRACE (trans. by Murray)
> THE CHRISTIAN COMBAT (trans. by Russell)
> FAITH, HOPE, AND CHARITY (trans. by Peebles)

VOL. 3: SALVIAN, THE PRESBYTER (1947)
> GOVERNANCE OF GOD (trans. by O'Sullivan)
> LETTERS (trans. by O'Sullivan)
> FOUR BOOKS OF TIMOTHY TO THE CHURCH (trans. by O'Sullivan)

VOL. 4: ST. AUGUSTINE (1947)
> IMMORTALITY OF THE SOUL (trans. by Schopp)
> MAGNITUDE OF THE SOUL (trans. by McMahon)
> ON MUSIC (trans. by Taliaferro)

ADVANTAGE OF BELIEVING (trans. by Sr. Luanne
Meagher)
ON FAITH IN THINGS UNSEEN (trans. by Deferrari
and Sr. Mary Francis McDonald)

VOL. 5: ST. AUGUSTINE (1948)
THE HAPPY LIFE (trans. by Schopp)
ANSWER TO SKEPTICS (trans. by Kavanagh)
DIVINE PROVIDENCE AND THE PROBLEM OF EVIL
(trans. by Russell)
SOLILOQUIES (trans. by Gilligan)

VOL. 6: ST. JUSTIN MARTYR (1948)
FIRST AND SECOND APOLOGY (trans. by Falls)
DIALOGUE WITH TRYPHO (trans. by Falls)
EXHORTATION AND DISCOURSE TO THE GREEKS
(trans. by Falls)
THE MONARCHY (trans. by Falls)

VOL. 7: NICETA OF REMESIANA (1949)
WRITINGS (trans. by Walsh and Monohan)
SULPICIUS SEVERUS
WRITINGS (trans. by Peebles)
VINCENT OF LERINS
COMMONITORIES (trans. by Morris)
PROSPER OF AQUITANE
GRACE AND FREE WILL (trans. by O'Donnell)

VOL. 8: ST. AUGUSTINE (1950)
CITY OF GOD, Bks. I-VII (trans. by Walsh, Zema;
introduction by Gilson)

VOL. 9: ST. BASIL (1950)
ASCETICAL WORKS (trans. by Sr. M. Monica
Wagner)

VOL. 10: TERTULLIAN (1950)
APOLOGETICAL WORKS (vol. 1), (trans. by Arbes-
mann, Sr. Emily Joseph Daly, Quain)
MINUCIUS FELIX
OCTAVIUS (trans. by Arbesmann)

VOL. 11: ST. AUGUSTINE (1951)
COMMENTARY ON THE LORD'S SERMON ON THE
MOUNT WITH SEVENTEEN RELATED SERMONS
(trans. by Kavanagh)

VOL. 12: ST. AUGUSTINE (1951)
    LETTERS 1-82 (vol. 1), (trans. by Sr. Wilfrid Parsons)

VOL. 13: ST. BASIL (1951)
    LETTERS 1-185 (vol. 1), (trans. by Deferrari and Sr. Agnes Clare Way)

VOL. 14: ST. AUGUSTINE (1952)
    CITY OF GOD, Bks. VIII-XVI (trans. by Walsh and Mother Grace Monahan)

VOL. 15: EARLY CHRISTIAN BIOGRAPHIES (1952)
    LIFE OF ST. CYPRIAN BY PONTIUS (trans. by Deferrari and Sr. Mary Magdeleine Mueller)
    LIFE OF ST. AMBROSE, BISHOP OF MILAN, BY PAULINUS (trans. by Lacy)
    LIFE OF ST. AUGUSTINE BY POSSIDIUS (trans. by Deferrari and Sr. Mary Magdeleine Mueller)
    LIFE OF ST. ANTHONY BY ST. ATHANASIUS (trans. by Sr. Mary Emily Keenan)
    LIFE OF ST. PAUL, THE FIRST HERMIT; LIFE OF ST. HILARION; LIFE OF MALCHUS, THE CAPTIVE MONK (trans. by Sr. Marie Liguori Ewald)
    LIFE OF EPIPHANIUS BY ENNODIUS (trans. by Sr. Genevieve Marie Cook)
    A SERMON ON THE LIFE OF ST. HONORATUS BY ST. HILARY (trans. by Deferrari)

VOL. 16: ST. AUGUSTINE (1952)—Treatises on Various Subjects:
    THE CHRISTIAN LIFE, LYING, THE WORK OF MONKS, THE USEFULNESS OF FASTING (trans. by Sr. M. Sarah Muldowney)
    AGAINST LYING (trans. by Jaffee)
    CONTINENCE (trans. by Sr. Mary Francis McDonald)
    PATIENCE (trans. by Sr. Luanne Meagher)
    THE EXCELLENCE OF WIDOWHOOD (trans. by Sr. M. Clement Eagan)
    THE EIGHT QUESTIONS OF DULCITIUS (trans. by Mary DeFerrari)

VOL. 17: ST. PETER CHRYSOLOGUS (1953)
    SELECTED SERMONS (trans. by Ganss)
ST. VALERIAN
    HOMILIES (trans. by Ganss)

VOL. 18: ST. AUGUSTINE (1953)
    LETTERS 83-130 (vol. 2), (trans. by Sr. Wilfrid
    Parsons)

VOL. 19: EUSEBIUS PAMPHILI (1953)
    ECCLESIASTICAL HISTORY, Bks. 1-5 (trans. by
    Deferrari)

VOL. 20: ST. AUGUSTINE (1953)
    LETTERS 131-164 (vol. 3), (trans. by Sr. Wilfrid
    Parsons)

VOL. 21: ST. AUGUSTINE (1953)
    CONFESSIONS (trans. by Bourke)

VOL. 22: ST. GREGORY OF NAZIANZEN and
    ST. AMBROSE (1953)
    FUNERAL ORATIONS (trans. by McCauley, Sullivan,
    McGuire, Deferrari)

VOL. 23: CLEMENT OF ALEXANDRIA (1954)
    CHRIST, THE EDUCATOR (trans. by Wood)

VOL. 24: ST. AUGUSTINE (1954)
    CITY OF GOD, Bks. XVII-XXII (trans. by Walsh
    and Honan)

VOL. 25: ST. HILARY OF POITIERS (1954)
    THE TRINITY (trans. by McKenna)

VOL. 26: ST. AMBROSE (1954)
    LETTERS 1-91 (trans. by Sr. M. Melchior Beyenka)

VOL. 27: ST. AUGUSTINE (1955)—Treatises on Marriage
    and Other Subjects:
    THE GOOD OF MARRIAGE (trans. by Wilcox)
    ADULTEROUS MARRIAGES (trans. by Huegelmeyer)
    HOLY VIRGINITY (trans. by McQuade)
    FAITH AND WORKS, THE CREED, IN ANSWER TO THE
    JEWS (trans. by Sr. Marie Liguori Ewald)
    FAITH AND THE CREED (trans. by Russell)
    THE CARE TO BE TAKEN FOR THE DEAD (trans. by
    Lacy)
    THE DIVINATION OF DEMONS (trans. by Brown)

VOL. 28: ST. BASIL (1955)
    LETTERS 186-368 (vol. 2), (trans. by Sr. Agnes
    Clare Way)

VOL. 29: EUSEBIUS PAMPHILI (1955)
ECCLESIASTICAL HISTORY, Bks. 6-10 (trans. by Deferrari)

VOL. 30: ST. AUGUSTINE (1955)
LETTERS 165-203 (vol. 4), (trans. by Sr. Wilfrid Parsons)

VOL. 31: ST. CAESARIUS OF ARLES (1956)
SERMONS 1-80 (vol. 1), (trans. by Sr. Mary Magdeleine Mueller)

VOL. 32: ST. AUGUSTINE (1956)
LETTERS 204-270 (vol. 5), (trans. by Sr. Wilfrid Parsons)

VOL. 33: ST. JOHN CHRYSOSTOM (1957)
HOMILIES 1-47 (vol. 1), (trans. by Sr. Thomas Aquinas Goggin)

VOL. 34: ST. LEO THE GREAT (1957)
LETTERS (trans. by Hunt)

VOL. 35: ST. AUGUSTINE (1957)
AGAINST JULIAN (trans. by Schumacher)

VOL. 36: ST. CYPRIAN (1958)
TREATISES (trans. by Deferrari, Sr. Angela Elizabeth Keenan, Mahoney, Sr. George Edward Conway)

VOL. 37: ST. JOHN OF DAMASCUS (1958)
FOUNT OF KNOWLEDGE, ON HERESIES, THE ORTHODOX FAITH (trans. by Chase)

VOL. 38: ST. AUGUSTINE (1959)
SERMONS ON THE LITURGICAL SEASONS (trans. by Sr. M. Sarah Muldowney)

VOL. 39: ST. GREGORY THE GREAT (1959)
DIALOGUES (trans. by Zimmerman)

VOL. 40: TERTULLIAN (1959)
DISCIPLINARY, MORAL, AND ASCETICAL WORKS (trans. by Arbesmann, Quain, Sr. Emily Joseph Daly)

VOL. 41: ST. JOHN CHRYSOSTOM (1960)
HOMILIES 48-88 (vol. 2), (trans. by Sr. Thomas Aquinas Goggin)

VOL. 42: ST. AMBROSE (1961)
  HEXAMERON, PARADISE, AND CAIN AND ABEL (trans. by Savage)

VOL. 43: PRUDENTIUS (1962)
  POEMS (vol. 1), (trans. by Sr. M. Clement Eagan)

VOL. 44: ST. AMBROSE (1963)
  THEOLOGICAL AND DOGMATIC WORKS (trans. by Deferrari)

VOL. 45: ST. AUGUSTINE (1963)
  THE TRINITY (trans. by McKenna)

VOL. 46: ST. BASIL (1963)
  EXEGETIC HOMILIES (trans. by Sr. Agnes Clare Way)

VOL. 47: ST. CAESARIUS OF ARLES (1964)
  SERMONS 81-186 (vol. 2), (trans. by Sr. Mary Magdeleine Mueller)

VOL. 48: ST. JEROME (1964)
  HOMILIES 1-59 (vol. 1), (trans. by Sr. Marie Liguori Ewald)

VOL. 49: LACTANTIUS (1964)
  THE DIVINE INSTITUTES, Bks. I-VII (trans. by Sr. Mary Francis McDonald)

VOL. 50: OROSIUS (1964)
  SEVEN BOOKS AGAINST THE PAGANS (trans. by Deferrari)

VOL. 51: ST. CYPRIAN (1965)
  LETTERS (trans. by Sr. Rose Bernard Donna)

VOL. 52: PRUDENTIUS (1965)
  POEMS (vol. 2), (trans. by Sr. M. Clement Eagan)

VOL. 53: ST. JEROME (1965)
  DOGMATIC AND POLEMICAL WORKS (trans. by John N. Hritzu)

VOL. 54: LACTANTIUS (1965)
  THE MINOR WORKS (trans. by Sr. Mary Francis McDonald)

VOL. 55: EUGIPPIUS (1965)
    LIFE OF ST. SEVERIN (trans. by Bieler)

VOL. 56: ST. AUGUSTINE (1966)
    THE CATHOLIC AND MANICHAEAN WAYS OF LIFE
    (trans. by Donald A. and Idella J. Gallagher)

VOL. 57: ST. JEROME (1966)
    HOMILIES 60-96 (vol. 2), (trans. by Sr. Marie
    Liguori Ewald)

VOL. 58: ST. GREGORY OF NYSSA (1966)
    ASCETICAL WORKS (trans. by Virginia Woods
    Callahan)

VOL. 59: ST. AUGUSTINE (1968)
    THE TEACHER, THE FREE CHOICE OF THE WILL,
    GRACE AND FREE WILL (trans. by Russell)

VOL. 60: ST. AUGUSTINE (1968)
    THE RETRACTATIONS (trans. by Sr. Mary Inez
    Bogan)

VOL. 61: ST. CYRIL OF JERUSALEM, VOL. 1 (1969)
    INTRODUCTORY LECTURE (trans. by Stephenson)
    LENTEN LECTURES 1-12 (trans. by McCauley)

VOL. 62: IBERIAN FATHERS, VOL. 1 (1969)
    MARTIN OF BRAGA, PASCHASIUS OF DUMIUM,
    LEANDER OF SEVILLE (trans. by Barlow)

VOL. 63: IBERIAN FATHERS, VOL. 2 (1969)
    BRAULIO OF SARAGOSSA, FRUCTUOSUS OF BRAGA
    (trans. by Barlow)

VOL. 64: ST. CYRIL OF JERUSALEM, VOL. 2 (1970)
    LENTEN LECTURES 13-18 (trans. by McCauley)
    MYSTAGOGICAL LECTURES (trans. by Stephenson)
    SERMON ON THE PARALYTIC (trans. by Stephenson)
    LETTER TO CONSTANTIUS (trans. by Stephenson)

VOL. 65: ST. AMBROSE: SEVEN EXEGETICAL WORKS (1972)

ISAAC, OR THE SOUL, DEATH AS A GOOD, JACOB AND THE HAPPY LIFE, JOSEPH, THE PATRIARCHS, FLIGHT FROM THE WORLD, THE PRAYER OF JOB AND DAVID (trans. by McHugh)

VOL. 66: ST. CAESARIUS OF ARLES, VOL. 3 (1973)

SERMONS 187-238 (trans. by Sr. Magdeleine Mueller)